D0562626

THE IMMACULATE CONCEPTION

A DOGMA OF THE CATHOLIC CHURCH

THE IMMACULATE CONCEPTION

A DOGMA OF THE CATHOLIC CHURCH

BY J. D. BRYANT, M. D.

"Thou art all fair, O my love, and there is no spot in Thee."
—Canticles of Solomon, Chapter IV

"O Mary, conceived without sin, pray for us sinners,
who have recourse to thee."
—Miraculous Medal Inscription

— AMERICA NEEDS FATIMA —

If you'd like to order more copies of this book, please contact:

America Needs Fatima
(888) 317-5571
P.O. Box 341, Hanover, PA 17331
ANF@ANF.org · www.ANF.org

Design copyright © 2021 The American Society for the Defense of Tradition, Family and Property® — TFP®
1358 Jefferson Road
Spring Grove, Penn. 17362
Tel.: (888) 317-5571
TFP@TFP.org

All rights reserved. No part of this publication may be reproduced, stored in a retrieval system, or transmitted, in any form or by any means, electronic or mechanical, including photocopying, recording or any information storage and retrieval system, without prior written permission from The American Society for the Defense of Tradition, Family and Property® — TFP®.

The American Society for the Defense of Tradition, Family and Property®, TFP® and America Needs Fatima® are registered names of The Foundation for a Christian Civilization, Inc., a 501(c)(3) tax-exempt organization.

ISBN: 978-1-877905-63-6
Library of Congress Control Number: 2021940087

Printed in the United States of America

B108

"If you desire to be consoled in every affliction, have recourse to Mary, invoke Mary, honor Mary, recommend yourselves to Mary. Rejoice with Mary, weep with Mary, pray with Mary, walk with Mary, and with Mary seek Jesus: in a word, with Jesus and Mary desire to live and to die."

THOMAS À KEMPIS

TO THEE,

Mary

MOST VENERABLE MOTHER OF MY REDEEMER;

TO THEE,
IMMACULATE MAID;

TO THEE,
FAVORITE DAUGHTER OF GOD THE FATHER,
MOTHER OF GOD THE SON,
SPOUSE OF GOD THE HOLY GHOST;

TO THEE,
MOST SWEET AND PERFECT MODEL OF HUMILITY,
    CHASTITY, MODESTY, AND OF EVERY GRACE,
IS THIS HUMBLE OFFERING
MOST AFFECTIONATELY, MOST FONDLY, AND
MOST LOVINGLY INSCRIBED,

BY THE UNWORTHY
AUTHOR.

Contents

Episcopal Approbation ix
Dedication... xi
Preface.. xiii
Introduction xvii

CHAPTER I
*Preliminary Observations — The Statement of the Doctrine —
And the Nature of the Proof which Sustains It*....................................1

CHAPTER II
Definition of the Doctrine — Its Reasonableness — Objections Answered 7

CHAPTER III
The Doctrine Considered in the Light of the Sacred Scriptures 11

CHAPTER IV
*The Ancient Liturgies and Menologies Prove the Doctrine —
The Abstract Value of the Terms Do Not Impair their Force*.......................17

CHAPTER V
*Remarkable Document — The Testimony of St. Andrew and
St. James, Apostles — St. Mark, the Evangelist — The Fathers
of the First Five Centuries*.. 23

CHAPTER VI
*"She shall crush thy head." — "Thou hast upheld me by reason
of my innocence." — "Hail, full of grace!"*.....................................31

CHAPTER VII
Festivals Instituted in Honor of the Immaculate Conception 37

CHAPTER VIII
*Testimony of the Saints and Eminent Writers Subsequent to the
Fifth Century, and During the Medieval Times* 47

CHAPTER IX
St. Bernard 55

CHAPTER X
St. Thomas Aquinas 61

CHAPTER XI
"Behold a Virgin shall conceive and bear a Son whose name
shall be called Emmanuel, God with us." 65

CHAPTER XII
The Religious Orders, Academies, Universities, and Theologians
Adopt the Doctrine of the Immaculate Conception 69

CHAPTER XIII
Various Councils Favor the Belief of the Immaculate Conception 77

CHAPTER XIV
The Declaration of the Council of Trent 83

CHAPTER XV
The Sovereign Pontiffs Favor the Doctrine of the
Immaculate Conception 87

CHAPTER XVI
Pius IX, the Illustrious Friend of Mary 95

CHAPTER XVII
"He that heareth the Church, heareth Me." 111

CHAPTER XVIII
The Festival of the Immaculate Conception of the Most Blessed
Virgin Mary, and the Ceremonies Incident to the Publication of
the Dogmatic Decree — Given at Rome, December 8th, 1854 117

CHAPTER XIX
Letters Apostolic of Our Most Holy Lord Pius IX, by Divine Providence
Pope, Concerning the Dogmatic Definition of the Immaculate
Conception of the Virgin Mother of God 127

CHAPTER XX
The Immaculate Conception: a Dogma for the Errors of our Times 139

CHAPTER XXI
Conclusion — Motives for Venerating the Most Blessed and
Immaculate Virgin Mary — And Certain Duties and Obligations
Arising Out of the Recent Dogmatic Decree 145

THE APPROBATION

OF THE

RIGHT REV. BISHOPS OF PHILADELPHIA AND BOSTON.

The following treatise on the Immaculate Conception of the Most
Blessed Virgin Mary, having been duly examined, is cordially recommended
to the perusal of the Catholic community.

JOHN N. NEUMANN
Bishop of Philadelphia.

Also, published by permission of
JOHN B. FITZPATRICK,
Bishop of Boston.

1855

Oil on canvas by Giovanni Battista Tiepolo (1696-1770). The painting "The Immaculate Conception" is from 1769, and was part of a series of canvases commissioned from Tiepolo to decorate the altars of the church of the Franciscan convent of San Pascual.

To the Blessed Virgin

MOST BLESSED MOTHER OF GOD:——

WILT THOU DEIGN TO SMILE UPON and accept my humble gift? It is most unworthily laid upon Thy shrine — unworthy in itself, unworthy on the part of the giver. My infant lips were never taught to lisp Thy Blessed name; my youthful feet were never led to Thy thronged Court; and too late, I fear, has my manly heart learned to throb in love and devotion at the mention of Thy holy name — too late have my lips been attuned to Thy praise. But, with Saint Bernard, I piously believe that it has never been heard of that any who have had recourse to Thy protection, implored Thy aid, and sought the suffrage of Thy prayers, have ever been forsaken. Thy loving Redeemer and mine, when on the cross, gave Thee, in the person of the beloved disciple, to be the Mother of His Church. I am, therefore, Thy child; dedicated and pledged to Thee. Thou cannot cast me off. Turn, then, Most Gracious Queen, Thine eyes of mercy on me. I give my soul in charge to Thee. See to it, my Mother, that it be not lost. Thy Divine Son refuses nothing to Thy prayers. He will not refuse, at Thy request, the boon of my salvation. Ah! I see Thy loving, smiling, gracious face, beaming with approving joy in view of what I ask.

But alas! How dare I hope — presumptuous sinner that I am; a sin-polluted soul; a friendless wanderer in this vale of tears; a ship-wrecked mariner, tossed upon the stormy billows of the sea of life? But did not Jesus die for such? Did not He shed His sacred blood to cleanse and purify? Did He not become Thy Son to sympathize with me? Thou know that He did. And Thou, fair Morning Star, hast Thou not, in virtue of being Mother of God, become the Guide, the Protectress of just such helpless, tempest-tossed, and sinful souls? Thou know that Thou hast. In Him, Thou art the Health of the weak, the Refuge of sinners, the Consolation of the afflicted, and the Help of Christians. Queen of Angels, Saints, and Martyrs, be each of these to me. None needs them more, and none will repay Thee with a richer, freer, or more gushing tide of gratitude and ardent love.

It is in veneration of Thee, Most Clement Virgin, and to vindicate thy Immaculate and spotless worth, that I have aspired, with devout and generous zeal, to lay this gift, together with my heart, at Thy sacred feet. Would that the offering were more acceptable; but one favoring glance from Thy radiant eye will make them all I wish. It is for Thee, Immaculate, and for the honor of the Lord, I write. Procure for me, by Thy powerful prayers, most Potent Virgin, fresh stores of love for Him. Absorb me in this boundless ocean of everlasting bliss. Let this heavenly flame burn within, and consume me with its ravishing delights. Let this be the heavenly fire which shall try all my works. Say to Thy Divine Son for me, "Jesus, I love Thee with all the power of my soul, and mind, and heart. I love Thee with a sovereign love; so that, whatever I possess of health, strength, mind, talent, credit, or goods, is humbly consecrated to Thee, and employed for the honor and glory of Thy Most Holy Name."

Finally, O Queen of my heart, and perfect Symbol of purity and love, I ask to be enrolled by Thee among even Thy least favored children. So that, when Thou make up Thy jewels, and set Thy starry crown of saved souls, I may be one of those proclaimed by Thee Thine own.

Sweet Mother, this is the sum of what is asked by Thy unworthy, but most loving, son.

December 8th, 1854.

Preface

THERE HAS EXISTED IN THE CHURCH from its commencement, a dogma, which, fondly and lovingly cherished in the Catholic heart, foreshadowed in Sacred Scripture, spoken of by Apostles, Evangelists, Saints and Martyrs, has, from various causes, remained until now without that solemn definition, which renders it essential to Faith. That dogma is the Immaculate Conception of the Most Blessed Virgin Mary, Mother of God.

Though many volumes, replete with learned research, have been published upon this subject, yet, so far as the author is aware, none have been put within the reach of the mere English reader. The present volume is, however, presented to the public not without some diffidence, arising from the consciousness, that there are many eminent writers, more competent than himself, to illustrate this sublime theme. But the present momentous interest which the subject possesses, and the immediate urgent demand for such a work, will extenuate, if not wholly excuse, the presumption of the undertaking.

Our Holy Father, Pius IX, impressed with zeal and the piety of his own heart, and urged by the Prelates in every part of the Catholic world, and also by the Christian people of his entire flock, has just solemnly defined the doctrine of the Immaculate Conception; and it cannot but be of great and general interest both to faithful Christians, and others, to have set forth the grounds upon which the definition has been made. It is true that to the devout Christian the authority of the Church is sufficient ground for belief in whatever it may solemnly teach as of Faith. "I would not receive even the Gospels," says St. Augustine; "unless the authority of the Catholic Church moved me thereto." *(Contr. Epist. Fund. cap. 5.)* Nay, with the great Apostle to the Gentiles, "Even if an angel from heaven should bring us a gospel besides that which the Church teaches, we would not receive it." *(Gal 1:8)* Nevertheless, in the language of the Chief of the Apostolic College, it is well to be "ready always to satisfy every one that asketh you a reason of that hope which is in you." *(1 Peter 3:15)* May the evidence given below satisfy many, who are not yet walking in the way of salvation, of the solidity and truth of what the Catholic Church now more solemnly teaches upon so interesting a subject as that at present before us.

The truth or falsehood of any doctrine depends upon evidence, and is established or refuted according to the credibility of the witness testifying. If the witness be as the Church, infallible, the doctrine is established beyond all controversy. The Church teaches that the Most Blessed Virgin was conceived without sin. This is enough for every sincere Catholic; it is true; "The Church is the pillar and ground of truth;" it cannot err. But this does not suffice for all men. Faith grows cold, as the course of time recedes from the original standpoint of primitive Christian revelation. Hence the Redeemer himself prophetically has asked: "The Son of Man when He cometh, shall He find, think you, faith on the earth?" (*St. Luke, chap. xviii, 8.*) The further we recede from that point, the greater the necessity for an infallible guide, and also for concurrent testimony. The voice of the first, we have heard — Mary is Immaculate in her Conception. That of the second is presented in the following pages. It consists, first, in the evidence of the Sacred Scriptures; then of writers in the Apostolic times; next of the Liturgies and public festivals of the Church; afterwards the unanimous testimony of the Fathers, Doctors and Theologians of every age, from first to last; and finally, the record of the fact of the authoritative teaching of the inerrant Church, which has now affixed its seal to no new doctrine, but that which has ever been believed and taught.

There are many who deny the truth of a thing, because they are ignorant of its history. Such are they, who with a triumphant pertness exclaim; "I thought your Church never changed, never taught anything new." Heretofore, the ignorance of such persons has been so far excusable as the works, in which the truth of the Immaculate Conception is attested, have been beyond their reach, and concealed from their view in languages with which they are not at all, or but little acquainted. Henceforth this plea will not avail; and whether or not they receive the evidence, the doctrine, at least, will have been vindicated from the charge of being a novelty, since it is clearly proved to have been taught in every age from the very commencement of Christianity.

There be some, who absurdly affirm of any given doctrine, that it did not exist before such and such a period, the date at which it was solemnly defined. The fallacy of such an assertion is sufficiently exposed by the following. The Canon of the Sacred Scriptures was not defined until the time of the Council of Hippo in the fourth century. Therefore, according to these men, the Sacred Scriptures did not until then exist. Apply this rule to the doctrine of the Immaculate Conception, and to every other, and words need not be multiplied or wasted in vindicating the Church in every case.

As to the facilities which have been offered to the author for executing such a task, it may be proper to remark, that he has had free access to several valuable and extensive libraries; and among them, that of the Diocesan Theological Seminary. Aside from his own private resources, he has made ample use of their invaluable treasures; and he has, without stint or remorse, taken full advantage of the research and learned labors of those who have preceded him in this field of exposition. Of course, after this acknowledgment, the author will feel greatly mortified, when it shall have been discovered and published to the world, that this work, like "The Faith of Catholics," is less an original than a compilation. It is precisely this, which constitutes its claim to public confidence, as a correct and genuine history of the Immaculate Conception; the task before him being, to collect and cull — not invent. There is also a certain amount of matter resting upon the bosom of literature, like uninhabited and beautiful islands upon the surface of the ocean, or oases in the desert. Wherever found, they have been seized as common property, and appropriated to some use. It is not, however, to be inferred from these avowals, that the author presumes to have exhausted the subject. For, though he has adduced testimony in favor of the doctrine from every age of the Christian era, he has but sketched the outlines of the picture, leaving the filling up of its majestic and faultless proportions to some master hand, which may even now be engaged upon the superior task.

The author takes great pleasure in making his acknowledgments to an eminent theologian, without whose valuable suggestions, some portions of the work may not have appeared as accurate as they are now believed to be. It has been thought proper to append to certain passages, the Latin text, from which they are derived. This, though a useless arrangement to some, will be satisfactory to others, who will deem the value of the book thereby enhanced. The Introduction is from the graceful and polished pen of a clergyman. He may deem an apology due for the manner in which it has been condensed and adapted to its present position. If so, it is hoped he will find a sufficient one, in the prospect of its continued usefulness.

THE AUTHOR.

Festival of the Immaculate Conception, 1854.

The Immaculate Conception by Guido Reni (1627)

Introduction

THE SUBJECT OF THE IMMACULATE CONCEPTION of the Blessed Virgin has often engaged the particular attention of the Catholic world. The Supreme Pontiffs have at different times brought it before our view; and recently, in his Encyclical Letter proclaiming the general Jubilee, Pope Pius IX asked all the faithful to unite in praying that he may be guided by the divine assistance to give soon a decision which may be to the glory of God and of that same Virgin our well-beloved Mother. This rendered it sufficiently evident that the Holy See was actually occupied with the question of publishing a dogmatical decree, defining it to be an article of Catholic faith that the Holy Mother of God was conceived without the stain of original sin. That decree has now been issued; and it is solemnly published to the world that Mary was Immaculate in her Conception.

But the question is sometimes asked, and perhaps oftener thought of, how such a decree can be made at this late period in the history of the Church? The faith of the Church is said to be unchangeable; is it not a very important change, if it be extended to embrace a truth which it did not embrace before? And then in the very nature of faith, it cannot receive any new truth except by a new revelation: for it contains only what has been revealed by God, and taught by His Church on His authority. If this doctrine were revealed to the Apostles and taught by them, it has always been of faith: if it were not so revealed, then the Church would not now define it to be of faith.

A little reflection will show that these objections do not apply exclusively to this one question of the Immaculate Conception. They equally pertain to every other doctrine that has ever been made the subject of an express definition from the Church: to various truths defined in the Council of Trent concerning the Sacraments, Grace, and Free Will; and to those regarding our Divine Savior and the Adorable Trinity, that were defined in the earlier councils of Nicæa, Ephesus, Chalcedon, etc. If these truths were revealed by God, they belonged to the faith before they were defined; and if they were not revealed, they never could be made to belong to the faith, because faith embraces only those truths that God has revealed.

To give a direct answer, we say that all these truths did belong to the faith before they were defined. The question immediately arises, of what value, then, is a dogmatic definition of an article of faith? What is the difference in the position of any doctrine before such a definition and after it? — Its value is that of an authentic declaration that the truth does belong and always did belong to the faith, because it was revealed by God, and taught by His Church.

To understand this more clearly, we must observe the difference between the Church *teaching* a matter of faith, and her *defining* it. The terms are sometimes used synonymously: before the definition, it was often said that the Church does not teach that the Blessed Virgin was conceived without sin, meaning that she does not teach it in the form of a solemn declaration. But if we take teaching in the more general sense of simply imparting knowledge, there is a wide difference between the Church teaching and defining truths of faith. Her teaching is done by many divers persons, and in different ways. Parents teaching their children, pastors catechizing their flocks, professors instructing their scholars, authors writing books on Christian doctrine.

These and many other channels are continually transmitting Catholic truth from generation to generation. And in this ordinary teaching, God displays a wonderful providence and love of His holy Church, by taking care that such a body of truths should be communicated to more than two hundred millions of people, and handed down through so many centuries, by so many different means, among persons so various in dispositions, interests, and habits of mind; and yet that these truths should be preserved without loss and without mixture of error. This is a standing miracle that attests the divinity of the Catholic Church, a miracle which no sect dares to claim. This method of teaching is ordinarily sufficient, under that heavenly providence, to keep the faithful acquainted with the truths important for their salvation, and for the glory of God, and to preserve them from dangerous errors. But cases arise from time to time in which this method of teaching does not suffice; and then she makes a definition of her doctrine which is done by her chief pastors, the successors of the Apostles, under the guidance of her supreme head on earth, the Bishop of Rome.

We have heard the question asked, as a serious difficulty, whether there is any instance on record of the Church defining a doctrine after an express declaration had been made that it was not an article of faith. We presume that the question had reference to the Bull of Pope Sixtus IV, *Grave nimis*, published in 1483 A. D. The document itself removes the difficulty. It forbids anyone to accuse of heresy those who should deny the Immaculate Conception, "since it has not yet been decided by the Church of Rome and the Apostolic See." — *Cum nondum sit a Romana Ecclesia et Apostolica Sede decisum.* The Bull may be found in the Corpus Juris Canonici, *Extrav. Com., l. iii, tit. 12.*

If it still appear strange that a truth should be taught by the Church, that is, transmitted through many generations of her children, and yet be questioned by learned and holy men, we reply that: A truth may be taught in general terms, which do indeed convey it, but do not express it clearly to every mind. Our present subject furnishes us with an illustration. When the Angel styled the

Blessed Virgin "full of grace" (*St. Luke, chap, i, 28*), this expression, if taken in the greatest extent of its meaning, would imply that there was nothing in her, present or past, which could lessen her favor in the eyes of God. But certainly original sin, existing in her though only for a moment, would have made her for that moment a child of wrath; and then for all eternity it would be true, that she had once been an object of God's displeasure. To many minds, therefore, that expression of the Angel Gabriel conveys quite satisfactorily the doctrine that the Blessed Virgin was stainless in the first instant of her conception. To other minds those words do not convey this meaning. Since men are continually using general expressions without intending them to be understood in all their vigor, — as when we say that a house is full of people — so many interpret this title of " full of grace," to signify only that the Blessed Virgin possessed at that moment every virtue, and an abundance of graces above all other creatures. Now in teaching, men often make use of such general terms, particularly when they have no doubt concerning the doctrine, and do not suspect that any Catholic will understand their words in a different sense from that in which they themselves understand them.

In any case like this, it might in the course of time excite attention, that some Catholics held a different belief from others on such a subject. The question then arises, which of these beliefs is really the truth received from God and taught by the Church. Perhaps on inquiry it may be clear, from a simple comparison of numbers, that the one doctrine is held by the great body of the faithful, and the other by a few individuals. If this be not quite clear, it remains to look back for evidence of what was believed and taught by the Church in some preceding period. Whatever it was at any one time, that it must be now. The text of Sacred Scripture, the writings of the holy Fathers and of theologians, are the chief sources from which this evidence can be drawn; but ancient liturgies, monumental inscriptions and other documents may also furnish some. In some cases this evidence will point so clearly to one conclusion, as to satisfy every sincere inquirer; but in others it may not be so.

It is often a very complex and very delicate work to examine and compare historical evidence. Even when a writer's sentiment is clearly expressed, it may be difficult to determine the value of his testimony; to judge whether he might have willfully misstated the doctrine, or might have misunderstood those from whom he received it, or might have unwittingly imbibed the error of the few, and thought that it was the doctrine of the Church. And when the writer uses general terms, it is still less easy to determine what sense he intended to convey by them. It may be necessary to compare other passages in his writings, to consider the object that he had in view, the place and times in which he wrote, the peculiarities of his style, etc. And then all these testimonies must be brought together, that the evidence on each side may be weighed and the balance struck. Is it strange if in some one question of the Church's teaching, this process should become difficult enough for men of learning to make an error in it, and not find proof to give them absolute certainty that the doctrine was taught by the Church as of divine authority?

As far as we have the means of judging, this is a sufficiently correct view of the case in regard to the doctrine of the Immaculate Conception.

Great numbers of the faithful, being taught that the Blessed Mother of God was perfectly pure, the holiest of all His creatures and "full of grace," never thought of imputing to her the stain of original sin. Others, bearing in mind the great doctrine of original sin, never thought of regarding her as an exception to this common lot of all the children of Adam, but understood her graces to be as abundant as they could be without setting aside this law. How early this difference existed among the faithful, and, how widely it was spread, it would not be easy to ascertain. As all Catholics were agreed in reverencing her as the most excellent of the creatures of God, the Church did not see any practical evil to result from some individuals being under a mistake with regard to one of her privileges. It was not necessary therefore that the divinely appointed pastors of the flock should make the examination and pronounce officially under the infallible guidance of the Holy Ghost, what was her teaching on the subject.

But for some time past the matter seems to have been growing in importance. Commonly the Church is induced to define a doctrine, because of the contrary error being taught by evil men, to the danger of the people — *contra errorem insurgentem*; but various other circumstances may make it equally expedient for her to publish a solemn profession of some particular truth. And at the present day such circumstances seem to be multiplied. The general increase of impiety, the deplorable tendency of the whole un-Catholic world towards the denial of the Incarnation, with which this mystery is so closely connected, and towards the rejection of all that is truly holy in religion, and the multiplication of all kinds of blasphemies against our Divine Savior and His Blessed Mother; — these seem to show that it is an appropriate time for the Church, His affectionate spouse on earth, to offer both to Him and her, some great act of reparation of honor. Such an act would be the publishing in the face of scoffers and of the worldly wise, this solemn declaration of the most precious of Mary's privileges; that which constituted perhaps the brightest of her ornaments in the eyes of her loving Son. And such a declaration would immediately be followed by innumerable acts of public worship and private devotion, all over the earth, amid the universal exultation of the faithful on this happy proclamation of their Mother's glory; a sweet perfume of praise and love ascending from every portion of the earth, to the Queen of Heaven; a tribute most gratifying to her Son, and glorious to the Divine Majesty, and drawing down innumerable blessings on this vale of tears.

If it be asked whether this particular act is best suited to the exigencies of the present time, the question would seem to be answered by the continually swelling voice of the faithful throughout the world, many of them calling expressly for the desired definition, but all uniting in extolling this privilege of Mary, and thanking God for this particular glory of His Holy Mother. And there is the voice of heaven itself, heard most distinctly in the numerous miracles and supernatural favors granted in return for devotions in honor of the Immaculate Conception.

It is heard particularly in the history of the medal which commemorates this mystery; a medal which was made under instructions brought from heaven by Mary herself and which has been the instrument of so many divine favors that it is known by the common name of the Miraculous Medal. After just a few years this medal has come into such general use, as almost to supersede, in some places, the use of all other medals. When we hear all these testimonies from heaven and earth mingling in a chorus of praise to the Immaculate Mother of God, we cannot wonder that the Vicar of her Divine Son on earth should draw the attention of all his flock to this consoling truth, and feel inspired with a holy wish to make it the subject of an especial tribute to her honor and the glory of God.

It is a solemn act of praise and thanksgiving: a solemn avowal that Catholics at least acknowledge the supreme dominion of God, and their sole dependence on the merits of the Son of Mary; that they are not of that impious world which is not only increasing every day in sin, but — unless wickedness belies herself, and pretends to be more wicked than she is — is actually reviving the horrid worship of that same devil whose pride was so crushed by this very event of the Immaculate Conception of the Infant Mary.1 It is a comforting assurance from the Holy Ghost, that the evil spirit has no power to touch a soul that God protects against him. It is a sounding of Mary's dearest privilege, in words so clear that no Catholic shall mistake them, and no voice shall be longer silent of the two hundred millions of the faithful, who glory in fulfilling the prophecy uttered by her own sacred lips: "Behold from henceforth, all generations shall call me blessed."

"The Blessed Virgin is ever ready to listen to those who invoke her in justice and truth; she especially assists those whom she perceives have made sincere efforts to become, like her, chaste and humble; if, at the same time, they add to these virtues, charity." —St. Bernard

---

1. Our daily papers furnish abundant grounds for this belief. To consult with evil spirits is an act of worship; and to make inquiries by table-rappings and other mediums seems to be either a real consultation with them, or a piece of trickery under that pretense. But the evidence becomes truly frightful when we read *The Spirit Rapper* of Dr. Brownson.

Painting of the Assumption of the Blessed Virgin Mary by Diaz Tavares

CHAPTER I

Preliminary Observations — The Statement of the Doctrine — And the Nature of the Proof which Sustains It

HAD THE DOCTRINE OF THE IMMACULATE CONCEPTION of the Most Blessed Virgin stood prominently forward in the history of Redemption, as does the doctrine of the Incarnation, or that of the Holy Trinity, without belief in which, no man might hope for salvation, doubtless long before this it would have been like those, not merely taught in the Church, but also solemnly defined, as now, an article of Faith. But, in the words of St. Bridget, "as the Church was not principally founded upon Our Lady, but upon her Son, our Lord, it seemed good to God, who makes His light to shine in an admirable manner, and causes it to appear, as sings the Psalmist David, from the tops of the mountains, He elucidates first the fundamental truths necessary to our salvation, and after that, in the abundance of His mercy, He causes us to see clearly other things, which, though of less importance, serve to direct our minds, and inflame them with more ardent love." (*Rev. lib. vi., cap. 61.*)

There wanted nothing to the perfect and complete triumph of our blessed and ever-venerable Mother, the Immaculate Virgin Mary, but this act of the Catholic Church, declaring her exempt from every, even the least stain, of sin. Each successive age of Christianity has been adorned with multitudes of pious souls, who have sighed and longed to be eye-witnesses of this inevitable decree, which pronounces Mary never for one instant to have been the enemy of God, the ally of the devil, and the heiress of eternal damnation. That, which their pious hearts sighed for in vain, and which their longing eyes strained to behold, without the fruition of their desire, we now have the unspeakable happiness of hearing, seeing, and assisting to proclaim to the world. Happy they, who fail not to understand their privilege, and who invite it to influence their devotion!

Viewed apart from every prejudice, and in the full light of God's plan for the redemption of fallen man, nothing would seem to be so absolutely clear, so essentially true, so necessary a part of that plan, as the exemption of His Virgin Mother from every taint of sin. What was that plan by which mankind was to be redeemed? It was, that the Son of God, descending from heaven, should assume our flesh, sinless, and die for us. But how should He assume sinless, untainted flesh, if she, through whom He condescended to derive it, had already been tainted with and subjected to His mortal enemy — Sin? The Blessed Virgin was pre-ordained from all eternity to co-operate with God the Holy Ghost to provide the human nature of our Lord. Was He, who out of nothing had created worlds, and out of the dust of the earth the sinless, unspotted flesh of our first parents, impotent to provide a holy tabernacle of flesh, in which to veil the glory of the only begotten One? It is not reasonable to suppose it. If, therefore, He had the power, which none denies, then must the inevitable conclusion subsist, that Mary, from the first instant of her creation, was, by prevenient[1] grace, preserved from even the least stain of original sin. "Who," asks St. Cyril, "hath ever heard of an architect building for himself a house, and yielding the occupancy and possession of it to his prime enemy?" Who, we in the same spirit ask, could suppose it consistent in the Omnipotent God, the Supreme Architect, to build for Himself the house, Mary, and let His chief, His mortal foe, Sin and the Devil, first take possession of and pollute it? If this be unreasonable in a human point of view, how much more would it be inconsistent in Him, who is infinite Purity itself, and who hath all power in heaven and in earth, and can do with His own as He wills, even as "the potter has power over the clay of the same lump, to make one vessel unto honor, and another unto dishonor. So hath God done, that He might show the riches of His glory on the vessels of mercy, which He hath prepared unto glory." (*Rom. ix.*) John the Baptist was filled with the Holy Ghost even from his mother's womb. (*St. Luke i.*) And of Jeremias it is said: "Before I formed thee in the bowels of thy mother, I knew thee; and before thou camest forth out of the womb, *I sanctified thee.*" (*Jeremias, chap. i., 5.*) Shall not a greater prodigy be wrought for her, who was actually to bring forth the Son of God, — who was to give Him flesh of her flesh, and bone of her bone, than to the mere forerunner and the prophet? Christ Himself hath said, "The servant is not greater than his lord, nor he that is sent greater than him that sent him."

We claim for the Blessed Virgin a higher prerogative, a loftier pre-eminence of grace, than is thought of for these. She was created especially to be the second Eve, and, like her, exempt in her creation from every stain of sin. By this is not meant that in her nativity only she was sanctified; or that before her nativity and subsequent to her creation, sanctifying grace was communicated to her; in this, as has just been shown, she would have been nothing greater than John the Baptist and Jeremias the prophet, and would still have had what the Fathers call *carnem peccati*, — flesh of sin, — from which the pure and stainless flesh of Christ could not have been derived. No one has ever doubted her to have possessed what had been granted to these. Neither is it meant that at the very instant of her creation the grace of pardon was communicated to her soul, by which the stain of Adam was purged away from her. Since even then, the foul, polluting taint, — the pestiferous and death-bearing stain, — would still, for the time being, however short, have rendered her a thing of loathing horror to Almighty God, the servant of the Devil, and a subject of eternal damnation. But it is meant

---

The Church teaches that God, knowing of his Son's Death, took its merits and applied its grace in an early, or prevenient, way to Mary at the very moment of her conception. https://cruxnow. com/commentary/2016/12/mary-requires-fancy-word-prevenient/

that, at the very moment of her conception, when the soul of the Blessed Virgin was infused into her body, special, preventing grace, participating, as it were, in the act of her creation, was present, and *exempted* her from the slightest stain of original sin; so that it could not be said that sin had dominion over her for the least interval of time.

It would be saying but little in regard to the evidences which sustain this doctrine, to affirm that, so far as the Sacred Scriptures are concerned, there is nothing in them repugnant to it. For, though there be no text which may explicitly, in so many words, declare it, — yet, if the texts upon which infant baptism, the doctrine of the Trinity, and some other articles of faith, are supported, were as clear and strong as those on which the doctrine of the Immaculate Conception may be based, it might be considered as indisputably established. When the Almighty God promised the advent of that woman, who should do that, which Eve, by sinning, had failed to do — crush the serpent's head — the inference is clear, that this could not be by one, who had been as frail as the woman who had already sinned. If the second Eve had had the taint of sin, wherein was she a better instrument for bringing forth Him who was to repair our loss, than she who was the cause of all our woe? And the words of the angel that saluted Mary as none had ever been before or since, "full of grace" (or, as the original Greek may be rendered, *"formed in grace"*), have a degree of intensity, as will be shown in its proper place, incompatible with any other idea than that of the Immaculate Conception. If to these be added the use of the word *"immaculate"* which, though it appears not within the sacred text, yet is used by the Apostle St. Andrew in a most remarkably pointed manner, and which, in the Liturgies originated by St. Peter and St. James, is also applied to the Blessed Virgin, it is clear to a demonstration, that the Blessed Mother of God is to be regarded as has here been stated,— wholly exempt from the least stain of original, as well as of actual sin. And when to these, again, is added the concurrent testimony of all antiquity, and of all succeeding time, — when the harmonious voice of the Saints of all ages, nations, and climes, unites in proclaiming her thus free from every stain, — he must be rash, indeed, who would venture to raise his feeble voice to contravene the overwhelming force of the evidence which meets him on every hand.

But were the evidence which so triumphantly vindicates the Immaculate Conception not so clear and so widespread as it is, — and were there not a text throughout the whole extent of the Divine Scriptures which pointed to the Blessed Mother of our Lord, — there would nevertheless be abundant reason for affirming and maintaining her prerogative — namely, the authoritative teaching of the Catholic Church. The former points or grounds of faith in regard to the Immaculate Conception will be exhibited and expatiated upon each in its proper place. But as to the latter, as it does not otherwise legitimately come within the scope of this volume, a few observations will be at once preferred.

Of all the characteristics of the Church of Christ, that of TEACHER is the most strongly marked. When our divine Lord commissioned His infant Church, He prefaced that commission with language which cannot fail to impress every believer as to its extent and power. As all the expressions He used in issuing His divine commission are not given by any one of the Evangelists, in order to exhibit them in their full force, we shall group them, leaving it to the reader to weigh them separately, if he please. Christ says: "All power is given to me in heaven and in earth. As the Father hath sent me, I also send you. Receive ye the Holy Ghost. (And) going, therefore, teach ye all nations, baptizing them in the name of the Father, and of the Son, and of the Holy Ghost; teaching them to observe all things whatsoever I have commanded you: and behold, I am with you all days, even to the consummation of the world." (*St. Mat., chap. xxviii, and St. John, chap. xx.*) Behold, then, the omnipotence of the Church! All power is given unto it.

The same power that Jesus Himself had from the Father. He sent it as the Father sent Him. And for what purpose? To teach. Such is the office, power and authority of the Church. It is the authority of Christ its Redeemer and head; who, prescient of this commission, had said: "And he that will not hear the Church, let him be to thee as the heathen and publican." (*St. Mat., chap. xviii.*) "And he that heareth you, heareth me; and he that despiseth you, despiseth me; and he that despiseth me, despiseth Him that sent me." (*St. Luke, chap. x.*) The promise of His own presence to the Church to the consummation of all things was a sufficient guaranty of its inerrancy; but He adds that of the Paraclete, the Spirit of Grace and Truth, to abide with it also forever, that all things which He had taught them might be brought to their minds, and that thus they might be always kept in the *truth*, and never fail in their office of teacher even to the end of the world. The keys of the kingdom of heaven, therefore, which were given especially to Peter, and the spirit of truthful teaching which were given to him, and to all the Apostles collectively, are equally given to Pius IX; for, if there was a moment when either could fail, then would the word of God be of no effect; and all certainty of possessing the true gospel must of necessity be lost, — a conclusion which no sincere Christian could for an instant admit.

Did the successors of the Twelve understand their commission as here described? St. Paul must so have understood it, when he called "*the Church of the living God,* THE PILLAR AND GROUND OF TRUTH." (*1 Tim., chap. iii.*) St. Clement so understood it when, at about the same date of the first century, he besought the seditious Corinthians, by every tender and loving appeal, to submit themselves to the priests. St. Ignatius thought so when he wrote to the Magnesians, "I exhort that ye study to do all things in the unanimity of God; *the Bishop holding the presidency in the place of God.*" And again, when he besought them, "*to be subject to the Bishop, as to Jesus Christ,*" and "Follow the Bishop, all of you, even as Jesus Christ the Father." So must St. Irenaeus have thought when he said: "They, therefore, who abandon the teaching of the Church, condemn the holy priests of ignorance; not considering," etc. And so have thought all the

Fathers, without interruption, to the present day. I will add only the remarkable words of St. Cyprian. He says: "Our Lord, whose precepts and admonitions we ought to observe, settling the honor of a Bishop and the nature of his Church, speaks in the gospel, and says to Peter, '*I say to thee, thou art Peter,*' etc. (*St. Mat., chap. xvi. 18, 19.*) Hence, through the changes of times and of successions, the ordination of Bishops and the nature of the Church flow on, so that the Church is settled upon the Bishops, and every act of the Church is regulated by these same prelates." (*Epis., chap. xxvii, Lapsis, p. 89.*)

To Pius IX, then, belonged the regulation of the present question, equally as any other question did to either of his predecessors, — even St. Peter himself. No prevarication, no sophistry, can overthrow the legitimate authority of the Church to teach. It is the very germ, the essence of the commission given to it, not only for the primitive times, but for all time — even to the end of the world.

But does this include authority to originate, to invent articles of faith? By no means. It involves no such power. The Church is to teach those things which it has been taught, — the depositum, — that which Christ himself had, either personally or by the inspiration of the Holy Ghost, committed to faithful men. It may, however, be further observed, that it is not said they should teach all things which had been written. Not one line of the gospel had at that time been written. Had the things which they were commanded to teach been all written, and had they been forbidden to teach anything else, it would scarcely have required the inspiration of the Holy Ghost to recall them to their minds. Hence it is that St. Augustine, not to oppress the page with many quotations, has said, in his sermon on the Assumption, "Where the Scriptures relate nothing concerning the Virgin, the reason must be sought whether what is alleged is conformable to truth; thus truth itself becomes authority, — without which there neither is authority, nor can it prevail."[2]

Hence, all things whatsoever which have been, from the first, always held in the Church, are the doctrine of the Church, and may, whenever the occasion arises, be solemnly and authoritatively defined by the Church teaching. And it matters not how remote from the origin of Christianity may be the occasion for such a definition. The commission is given for all days, even to the consummation of all things. It matters not, either, whether the question has been directly named in the written word of God; for the world itself would not contain the books, if all the things which Jesus did were written. (*St. John, chap. xxi.*) Hence, also, have the Apostles repeatedly enjoined it upon the Church, as a sacred duty, to keep the ordinances and traditions which had been delivered to it. "Let no man deceive you by any means," says St. Paul. "Brethren, stand fast; and hold the traditions which you have learned, whether by word, or by our epistle." (*2 Thess. ii.*) A prominent instance of the Church's faithful obedience to

---

2. Ubi Scriptura nihil commemorat de Virgine, inquirendum est ratione, quid conveniat veritati, fiatque ipsa veritas auctoritas, sine qua nec est, nec valet auctoritas. (*Sermo de Assump.*)

these injunctions has been already noticed, in regard to infant baptism. Nothing is found in Sacred Scriptures to enforce this practice, — yet it is religiously observed, and, as Origen says of it, "This, too, had the Church received as a tradition from the Apostles, to give baptism to children." *(In Epist. ad Roman.)* Hence, also, the more general observation of St. Augustine: "But those things which we observe, not because written, but transmitted, — things which are indeed observed throughout the world, — it is to be understood *that they are retained as commanded and decreed*, either by the Apostles themselves, or by general councils, the authority of which is most wholesome in the Church." *(Tom. IV. Epist. liv.)*

But is the definition of the Immaculate Conception of the Most Blessed Mother of God, as a dogma of the Catholic Church, included in this commission to teach? Most certainly it is, unless the Apostle St. Andrew could have erred; unless St. Peter and St. James, in originating their Liturgies, could have ascribed to the Blessed Virgin more than was due to her; and unless the entire Church of all ages could have departed from the faith, and thus ceased to be the pillar and ground of truth.3 For, besides the inference drawn from Holy Writ, such is the scope of the evidence which has long rendered it imperative upon the Church to define the Immaculate Conception as a doctrine of faith. It was the opinion of the ancient Fathers;

- it is so alleged in every ancient Liturgy and Menology;
- it was the belief of the Saints and medieval writers, and of the whole line of Roman Pontiffs, so far as they have given expression to their belief;
- Councils have so decided it;
- and the common consent of all faithful Christians affirms it as the belief of the Catholic Church. It is, therefore, no novelty recently originated, — no fallacy of a sophist, seeking to palm off the spurious creation of his fevered brain for divine truth. But it is the decision of the unfailing, unwavering, unchanging Church; whose guide and preserver in truth is the Holy Ghost, and whose ever-present head is the Lord Jesus Christ, its Founder and Redeemer.

3. See Chapter V.

CHAPTER II

Definition of the Doctrine — Its Reasonableness — Objections Answered

CONCEPTION IS BOTH *ACTIVE* AND *PASSIVE*. *Active* conception is that by which the body, with all its members, is constituted. *Passive* conception is that in which the rational soul unites with, or is infused into, the physical organization. It is the latter — *passive* conception — which is understood when we speak of the Immaculate Conception of the Most Blessed Virgin. By the doctrine of the Immaculate Conception, therefore, is meant that, —

> The soul of the Most Blessed Virgin, in being united to her body, was, by virtue of sanctifying grace, in which it was created, preserved from all stain of original sin.

If nothing concerning this exalted privilege of the Blessed Mother of our Lord had ever been uttered by the inspired penmen in the Sacred Scriptures; if the Liturgies had made no intimation of it; if the illustrious Doctors and writers of the Catholic Church had not (as in every age they have) affirmed it; and, in fine, if the Church itself had not, time and again, expressed its favorable opinion of it, still must its reasonableness have recommended itself to, and forced itself upon, the conviction of Christian men. For;

1. In the mysterious plan proposed for the redemption of man, it pleased its divine Author to take upon Himself our human nature. Would it be reasonable, or what might be supposed fitting, in a holy God, in whose, sight the heavens are not clean, nor the angels pure (*Job, chap. xv, 14*), to clothe His immaculate Godhead in flesh, sullied with the faintest trace of sin — of that mortal enemy of infinite Purity and infinite Holiness, which hurled myriads of angels from heaven, and which drove our first parents from Paradise? To have united Himself to that which had been thus polluted would have been a violation of his infinite sanctity: it would have been a union of Himself with that which He abhors — a body contaminated with sin; and it would have been an abnegation of Himself.

2. The Blessed Virgin, in the quality of Mother of God, is exalted above the angels and all the hosts of heaven. God, the Redeemer, sits at the right hand

of the Almighty Father, clothed in her sacred flesh. That she, therefore, should not be the highest of all created intelligences, Queen of Angels and Saints, is totally repugnant to all our ideas of the relation between mother and son. But had the Blessed Virgin ever been contaminated with the least stain of sin, she must of necessity be inferior to the angels, who never have sinned. Therefore she ever has been free from such a stain.

3.   Mary was predestined, in the councils of God, to be the second Eve, through whom life and immortality was a second time to be proffered to men. God had created the first Eve a sinless soul. Seeing that it was impossible that the Savior should unite His Godhead to sinful flesh, and seeing that it must be by His becoming man that man could alone be redeemed, could He do less than create the second Eve as He created the first — sinless? His power to do this is not denied. If, therefore, His was the power, and it comported with His infinite purity and dignity, where is the difficulty of admitting that He has made the second Eve equal to the first; and that, applying by anticipation to the holy Virgin the merits of the passion and death of her blessed Son, He has exempted her from the necessity of being, even for an instant, the slave of sin.

It is objected that by the fall of Adam the blight of original sin has included all our race — "in Adam all die." This does not weaken or impair the exemption from original sin in regard to the Blessed Virgin. The Immaculate Conception need not be maintained as an exception to the common rule; Mary being, as it is expressed in the Liturgy of the Apostle St. James, "Most holy, most glorious, Immaculate, and WITHOUT THE RANGE OF SINFUL MEN IN EVERY RESPECT." (*Bergier, lib. iv.*) But how, then, it may be asked, extend to her the benefits of Redemption? As already stated — by anticipation. Christ died for her, and for her chiefly; applying His merits to her by anticipation, as whose preservation was necessary to supply that life which He was to lay down for all.

But if Mary was Immaculate, why subjected to the common sufferings of life? Was she, because Immaculate, to be deprived of the common privilege of the just? But are not the sufferings of this life the consequences of original sin? True; but, under the decree of reparation, they become heaven's choicest favors. Was Mary, then, to be deprived of them; and, because Immaculate, therefore above all others worthy of them? The sword that pierced her heart was the brightest jewel in her crown.

That *in Adam all die* is the common rule; still, it does not follow that Mary was included under it. On the contrary, it therefore follows that she was not included under it. Besides, a common rule does not necessarily comprise every individual of the class specified.

1.   By the common rule, our species increase and multiply only in the commerce

of the sexes; yet the Blessed Virgin was exempt from this law, since she conceived, not by man, but by the operation of the Holy Spirit. "And the Angel said to her: The Holy Ghost shall come upon thee, and the power of the Most High shall overshadow thee. And therefore also the Holy which shall be born of thee shall be called the Son of God." (*St. Luke, chap. i, 35.*) "Fear not to take unto thee Mary thy wife, for that which is conceived in her is of the Holy Ghost" (*St. Mat., chap. i, 20.*)

2.   By the common rule, women, in becoming mothers, cease to be virgins. And yet, that there might not be even this taint upon the purity of the vessel which God had chosen, the Virgin Mother had not her virginal integrity impaired in bearing the Son of God. For "Behold a virgin shall be with child, and bring forth a Son, and they shall call his name Immanuel." (*St. Mat., chap. i, 23.*)

3.   The Blessed Virgin is, so to speak, an order in herself. She stands alone in the entire range of intelligent beings. Though infinitely below the Deity, yet is she, as the Spouse of the Holy Ghost, and Mother of God, exalted infinitely above all created beings. And, since she has been exempted in so many respects from the common rule in virtue of her dignity, where is the difficulty in admitting that, by special privilege, she was exempt from original sin? "The contrary opinion," says Cardinal Lambruschini, "appears to me so repugnant to the sublime dignity of the Mother of God, that I think we ought to regard it as theologically absurd."

The objection which alleges that the Blessed Virgin, being a child of Adam, is necessarily subjected to original sin, loses all its force in view of these considerations. And even though there had never been a solitary exception in the administration of those general laws to which Divine Providence subjects our race, still the exemption of Mary from original sin must subsist, whether regarded as to its reasonableness or its necessity. But when we reflect that the Sacred Scriptures abound in instances where, to effect His own divine purposes, the laws of nature and of grace are set aside, every objection founded upon such a basis must fall to the ground. The waters of the Dead Sea parted, and stood as a wall upon the right hand and upon the left; and the children of Israel passed through dry-shod. At the command of Joshua, the sun stood still and moved not toward Gabaon, nor the moon toward the valley of Ajalon. The fire burned not the three children, Sidrach, Misach, and Abdenago. And in the kingdom of grace the dead have been brought to life again after having once paid the debt of nature.

These, together with the prodigies already mentioned, *especially those experienced in the person of the Blessed Virgin herself,* are a sufficient answer to whatever may be alleged in support of the contrary opinion.[1] Why is it that so many privileges have been accorded to the Holy Virgin, dispensing her from the common laws to which our race is subjected? Is it not because her incomparable dignity of Mother of God rendered it proper, and even necessary, that she should be thus exempted; and could anything be imagined more necessary or more proper to this dignity than the most perfect innocence? The conclusion is unavoidable, that, if there be any law from which the dignity of Mother of God demanded exemption, it is that of original sin, with which all the other children of Adam are tainted.

---

1. It is a common law that all the children of Adam are defiled in their conception by the sin of their first father, and so the Blessed Virgin is omitted. Why? Because it is the privilege of the Mother of God not to be subject to almost any of the common laws which extend to all of Adam's children. For example, it is a common law that all women conceive their children in the ordinary way. The Blessed Virgin is exempt from it and conceived her only Son by the operation of the Holy Spirit. It is a common law that all mothers cease to be virgins when they are mothers. The Blessed Virgin is exempt from it, for she is a virgin mother who lost nothing of her virginal integrity for having produced the Son of God; on the contrary, she perfected it. It is a general law that all mothers give birth with pain: *In dolore paries*. The Blessed Virgin is exempt from this law, for St. Thomas expressly says that she felt no pain but very great joy when she gave birth to her divine Child. It is a common law that all children of Adam are subject to some actual sin: *Non est homo, qui non peccet*. The Blessed Virgin is not included in this law because it is the common belief of the Church, and a ruling of the Council of Trent, that she never committed any actual sin in all of her life. It is a common law that human bodies are reduced to ashes after death: *Pulvis es, et in pulverem reverteris*. The Blessed Virgin was not subject to this strict law. After her death, following the example of her only Son, her body having remained three days in the tomb, she resuscitated like Him and on the day of her Assumption, was received in triumph into heaven in body and soul. This is the general belief of the whole Church." *Cerri Triumphus B. M. V.*, p. 32.

CHAPTER III

The Doctrine Considered in the Light of the Sacred Scriptures

THE INTIMATE RELATIONS WHICH SUBSIST between the Son of God and His Virgin Mother, render it impossible that she should ever have been tainted with original sin. Mary has been called the first-born of His creatures — the beloved one of God, in whom is no spot — the tabernacle which the Most High hath sanctified. And it is in perfect consistence with what we know of the divine attributes, that the Blessed Virgin should have been created in a manner and with such perfections as He, the source of infinite holiness and infinite purity, might, without making a covenant, so to speak, with sin, unite His divinity to her virginal flesh — for it was an integral part of her body He took. Except the hypostatic union of the divine nature of Christ with his humanity, no union of the divine and human natures could be so intimate as that which Christ had with the Virgin. In the former, the divine nature was inseparably and indivisibly united with the human nature, and constituted "one Christ." In the latter, the divine person, at the very instant of conception, was so made one with the blessed Virgin — as to become substance of her substance — blood of her blood — flesh of her flesh.

From that moment it became impossible to separate the Virgin Mother from her divine Son, and equally impossible to regard the human nature of the Virgin, of which He thus made His own, as ever having been the property of His chief enemy, the devil. St. Paul tells us, "It was fitting that we should have such a High Priest, who is holy, innocent, undefiled, and separated from sinners." (*Heb., chap. vii, 26.*) The Apostle did not speak of separation by companionship; for it was these whom He sought out. Magdalen knelt at His feet, and the thief suffered by His side. He spoke of an essential characteristic of His nature. How could this be said, then, if this great High Priest drew his very life-blood from a sinner? On the other hand, how true is it, and how harmoniously does it blend with the attributes of a redeeming God, and with the whole gospel plan, to regard the Blessed Virgin as immaculate from the first instant of her creation? No text of Sacred Scripture is repugnant to this belief; but, on the contrary, there are so many passages which, by the common consent of all the sacred interpreters, point to this prerogative of Mary, and from which it may be lawfully inferred, that it cannot be regarded as destitute of scriptural support.

"God hath mercy on whom He will have mercy," is a sentiment expressed by St. Paul. The same Apostle tells us that He maketh one vessel to honor; and holy Job, in the same spirit, asks, "Who can make him clean that is conceived of unclean seed? Is it not Thou who only art?" (*Job, chap. xiv, 4.*) He created the angels clean, and also man. What should forbid the like purity to her, whom He had created to be His own Spouse?

1. The first prophecy was that which, uttered by God himself, referred to the Blessed Virgin, and the offspring of her virginal womb. In cursing the malign serpent, He said: "I will put enmities between thee and the woman, and thy seed and her seed. She shall crush thy head, and thou shalt lie in wait for her heel." (*Gen., chap. iii.*) Many of the Fathers, conformably to the Latin, so render this passage of the sacred writings. But whether *ipsa*, she; *ipsum*, the seed; or *ipse*, Christ, as the Hebrew and the Septuagint have it, be adopted as the true reading, the sense is the same, since it is by her seed, Jesus Christ, that Mary, the second Eve, crushed the serpent's head. But if she herself had been subject to this mortal enemy of man, — if she had ever, even for an instant, been impregnated by its baleful influence, — this prophecy fails; since, for that period of time at least, the enmity ceased, and she was in bondage to the devil. He who uttered the prophecy was the God, who thus proposed to take upon Himself our human nature through this promised woman. Is it credible that He, who could create, at a word, pure from impure, clean from defiled, — He who is bound by no law, and can except from law whom He will, — would clothe His immaculate purity with sinful flesh? If it be thus repugnant to all our perceptions of the fitness of things, of right actions in the divine Being, then must we conclude that she, the woman Mary, was created immaculate and pure. The Fathers and Theologians of the Church have so interpreted this text. St. Augustine has thus commented upon it: "The head of the devil is original sin; Mary hath crushed this head, because no sin hath entered the soul of the Virgin, and therefore, she hath been exempt from every stain." And St. Bonaventure has spoken still more clearly. He says: "It had been determined that the Blessed Virgin Mary, through whom our opprobrium was removed, should conquer the devil, so that she should not succumb to him, *ad modicum*, for an instant." The learned P. Tirin has also commented upon it thus: "By the 'woman' is particularly designated the Blessed Virgin Mary, who, by bringing forth Christ to us, has been made a most pure Eve, that is, the mother of all living."

2. "But thou hast upheld me by reason of my innocence; and hast established me in thy sight forever." (*Psalm xl, 13.*) Lorin, in commenting upon this psalm, says, "When God determined to provide himself with a Mother, He wished to appropriate her, wholly to Himself, so that she might be entirely and forever free from all dominion of the devil; whom, unless by prevenient

grace he had thus freed, she had been obnoxious, and actually would have been subjected to, the demon's power. Christ was always God; but His humanity did not exist before it was united to the divinity, so that it might be assumed on account of its innocence; for, I say, it was not before it was assumed. God made His Mother such, as I have said, that therefore He might choose her for His Mother; or, because He wished to choose her He made her such a Mother."

3. The following passage is also applied to the Blessed Virgin. "Glorious things are said of thee, O city of God. Shall not Zion say, This man and that man is born in her? And the highest himself hath founded her." (*Psalm lxxxvi, 3 and 5.*) St. Augustine explains this passage as mystically applied to Mary and her divine Son. She is the city of God, whom the Most High hath built for Himself; and Christ is the Man born in her. And in another place, commenting upon the following, "Concerning his Son, who was made to him of the seed of David according to the flesh," (*Romans, chap. i, 3,*) he introduces Christ, as it were, speaking against the Manicheans. He says, "I have created the Mother from whom I have been born; I have prepared the way for my journey, I have built it. She whom you despise, O Manicheans, is my Mother; she hath been made by my hand. Could I have been able to defile her whom I have made and from whom I have been born?"[1] Upon *Proverbs, chap. ix, 10,* "Wisdom hath built herself a house," St. Thomas says, "The Blessed Virgin was the divinely elect Mother of God, and it is not therefore to be doubted but that God hath rendered her by His grace suitable to this purpose."

4. The following, from the sublime Canticle of Solomon, is applied by St. Ildephonsus, St. Thomas Aquinas, St. Bernard, and by many others, to the Blessed Virgin: "Thou art all fair, O my love, and there is not a spot in thee." (*Cant., chap. iv, 7.*) St. Augustine, as quoted by Sophronius (*Sermo. de Assump.*) says, upon this text, "*Ideo Immaculata, in nullo corrupta.*" "She is therefore immaculate, and in nothing corrupt." If so, then must the Blessed Virgin have been exempt from original sin. The Church, moreover, has, in the Divine Office, applied these words to the same privileged Being. So also the eighth verse of the sixth chapter: "One is my dove, my perfect one is but one, she is the only one of her mother, the chosen of her that bore her." The Hebrew, instead of *perfect one*, reads *Immaculate one*.

5. "Give ear, ye islands, and hearken, ye people, from afar. The Lord hath called me from the womb, from the bowels of my mother he hath been mindful of me." (*Isaiah, xl, 1.*) St. Germanus, and many others, apply these words both

---

1. There is some question whether this latter passage came from the pen of St. Augustine; but whether or not, it is certain to have come down to us from most remote antiquity, and is an evidence of the opinion then entertained of the Immaculate Conception.

to Christ and the Virgin; being applicable to the former by nature; to the latter, by grace.

6. The salutation of the angel Gabriel, "Hail full of grace," (*St. Luke, chap. i, 28,*) implies the Blessed Virgin's exemption from original sin. The words, Χαίρε, κεχαριτωμένη, which are rendered in the Latin vulgate, *Ave, gratia plena*, are the medium of this remarkable announcement. There is no other instance of this form of salutation having been addressed to man. It is peculiar to the Blessed Virgin — Full of grace. It intimates that she, above all other creatures, was endowed with its sanctifying influence. The expression was reserved for, and especially suited to, her alone. Its peculiarity alarmed her; for, "Having heard, she was troubled at his saying, and thought with herself what manner of salutation this should be" (*verse 29*). But the original Greek has a more intensive signification than either its Latin or English translation. It also signifies *Formed in grace*. Origen gives it this signification; and in his first Homily (cited by St. Alphonsus de Liguori), he further says of Mary, "*Nec serpentis venenosi afflatibus infecta est.*" If, according to this, Mary was not tainted by the breath of the poisonous serpent, the devil, it follows, as above, that she never was stained with original sin. St. Sophronius, in his sermon on the Assumption of the Blessed Virgin, also remarks, upon the Angelical salutation, that "It is well said, *Full of grace*, because she excels all others. The entire plenitude of grace was poured out upon her."

There are many other texts which in their mystic signification have been applied to the Blessed Mother of God; and though none of them, in so many words, declare the doctrine of the Immaculate Conception, neither its integrity nor its truthfulness is thereby in the least impaired. This, the following considerations on what has already been advanced will sufficiently attest.

1. The Sacred Scriptures were not intended to contain all the things which the Christian Church was to believe and do. If all had been written, the world itself would not contain the books thereof. (*St. John, chap. xxi, 25.*) Much was left to oral instruction, with the injunction to hand it down from one generation to another. "Therefore, brethren, stand fast; and hold the traditions which ye have learned, whether by word or by our epistle." (*2 Thess., chap. ii, 14.*) "The things which thou hast heard of me by many witnesses, the same commend to faithful men, who shall be fit to teach others also. (*2 Tim., chap. ii, 2.*)

2. It is the universal custom of all Christians to consecrate the first day of the week to the worship of God, contrary to His written ordinance, which commands the observance of the seventh day. No one questions the propriety of this transfer, though it has not the slightest scriptural warrant.

3. There is no express authority in the Scriptures for infant baptism, nor for infusion, nor sprinkling; and yet, with an insignificant exception, the whole of Christendom affirms its validity, and commonly practices these modes of administering the rite.

Now, if these important points, together with many others not here mentioned, are obligatory upon Christians to believe and to observe, without express mention of them in the Sacred Scriptures, the doctrine in question — the Immaculate Conception — would not be necessarily weakened or impaired in consequence of a like omission. When, therefore, nothing is found repugnant to it, and much that renders it fit and proper, and, indeed, necessary, the conclusion drawn in its favor would be unavoidable. The merits of the redeeming blood of Christ were applied to two of His saints before their birth, and it is no disparagement of its efficacy to suppose it carried one degree higher. On the contrary, it magnifies and exalts it to say that it procured another privilege for her, who was to be — not a prophet, or a forerunner, but — the Mother of the Redeemer. Those texts which indicate the prevalence of sin, as already proved, are in no sense applicable to this highly favored Virgin.

The question is well put by a learned writer, who says: "It is not permitted to other children to select a mother according to their good pleasure; but if this were ever granted to anyone, who would choose a slave for his mother, when he might have a queen? Who a peasant, when he might have a noble? Who an enemy of God, when he might have a friend of God? If, then, the Son of God alone could select a mother according to His pleasure, it must be considered as certain that he would choose one befitting a God." St. Bernard so expresses it when he says: "The Creator of men, to be born of man, must choose such a mother for Himself as he knew to be most fit." Could it be otherwise, then, that a pure and holy God would choose other than a pure and holy Mother? He knew not sin Himself, and in order to take of her flesh, He must have created her without sin also.

St. Paul says: "The first man was of the earth, earthly; the second man from heaven, heavenly." *(1 Cor., chap. xv, 47.)* St. Ambrose, commenting upon this text, says: "That Mary is a celestial vessel. Not from the earth, but from heaven, did Christ select this vessel through which he should descend, and consecrated the temple of modesty." He called the Blessed Virgin a celestial vessel, not that she was other than earthly as to her nature, as some of the ancient heretics have affirmed, but celestial through the peculiar grace communicated unto her, in virtue of the high prerogative she was to enjoy in being the mother of the eternal Word. This exalted her above all creatures, even the angels of God; and hence St. Gregory has said of her: "Whom the perfection of merit hath exalted above the choirs of the Angels even to the throne of the Deity."2 But this certainly

---

2. "Meritorem verticem supra omnes Angelorum choros usque ad solium Deitatis erexit." — *De Expos, in lib. Regum.*

could not be, had any stain of uncleanness ever tainted the vessel which had been chosen to receive the King of heaven. God himself declares that he will never enter into a malevolent soul or a body subject to sin. *(Wisdom, chap. i, 4.)* His dispensations always accord with the rules of eternal justice; and it is not possible that He would violate them in this case, which involves principles so essential to His nature — infinite purity and infinite holiness. This is the more certain, in view of His omnipotence, which renders all things alike easy, to Him, — whether it be the cleansing of a vessel tainted with sin, or exempting it entirely from any taint whatsoever.

Hence St. Peter Damian says: "We should hold it for certain that the incarnate Word selected for himself a befitting mother, and one of whom He need not be ashamed." And also St. Proclus: "He inhabited those bowels which He had created, so as to be free from any mark of infamy." Our divine Lord, therefore, felt it no reproach when the Jews sought to degrade Him as the son of a poor woman. He ordained her position in life as well as her perfectibility of nature. He placed her in an humble sphere, because He came to set us an example of humility. But it would doubtless have been a subject of reproach, if the malign spirit could have said, that the woman pre-ordained to crush his head, in being the Mother of the Redeemer, was once, like the other descendants of Eve, a sinner and his slave. It was a divine ordinance that none of the tribe of Levi should serve as a priest, who was maimed or marked upon the body, even with so much as a mole; and the perfection of unblemished beauty was the chief pride of their daughters, inasmuch as they were the chosen mothers of this royal race of unblemished priests. Would it not, therefore, have been thought a signal reproach in the Mother of our Lord, the great High Priest, had she been deformed or maimed in body or mind? How much more, then, must it have appeared unseemly in the eyes of God, that His chosen Mother should have been deformed in soul, and tainted with sin!

CHAPTER IV

The Ancient Liturgies and Menologies[1] Prove the Doctrine — The Abstract Value of the Terms Do Not Impair their Force

THE ANCIENT LITURGIES AFFORD THE MOST COMPREHENSIVE and, in some sense, the most satisfactory evidences of certain doctrines and practices of the Christian Church. They are the most comprehensive, inasmuch as the evidences they contain are not those of individuals simply, but, as it were, of entire communities; and exhibit to us, therefore, not the private judgment of private persons, but the universal, public expression of the belief of large sections of the Christian Church. They afford the most satisfactory proofs, in so far as that the concurrent testimony of multitudes is superior to that of individuals. However numerous may be the exceptions to the expression, *vox populi, vox Dei*, in this connection at least, it may be truly said that the *voice of the people is the voice of God*. Their evidences are, moreover, the most satisfactory, since the points presented in them are *incidental*. They are not presented to us, so to speak, as from the lips of an advocate, seeking to enforce some particular point. The language flows smoothly on — and the "*Amen*" pronounced by the multitudinous worshippers is consentaneous. "So be it," "it is so," "So we believe," is their unanimous response; and no one doubts the truth of the thing expressed. We, moreover, resort to them with confidence, because of their undoubted antiquity, some of them dating back even to the Apostolic age — certain of them bearing the names of the Apostles, who are believed to have originated them — while all of them are of such early date, that whatever they contain, must be esteemed the exact impress of the mind of the primitive Church.

Another consideration, to mention no more, inspires the utmost confidence in these ancient formularies — namely, they have never, in any essential point, been altered or corrupted. The primitive Christians received their faith from the Apostles; and with it their Liturgies. Each Church had its own Liturgy. These were written and recited in the vulgar tongue; and the people were perfectly familiar with their phraseology. So that no one has ever had the temerity to

---

1.   An ecclesiastical calendar of festivals celebrated in honor of particular saints and martyrs; also a register of saints or outstanding religious personages.

engraft upon them doctrines which the Church did not believe.[2] In all of them the real presence, transubstantiation, the term sacrifice, the breaking of the host, incense, prayers for the dead, the invocation of saints, and, which most concerns us now, the Immaculate Conception of the Most Blessed Virgin Mary, stand forth in bold relief as the universal faith of the entire Church.

1. The Liturgy which first invites our attention is that of the Apostle St. James. This Liturgy is well known. There are many copies of it extant. That here quoted is taken from *Bibliotheca Veterum Patrum, Tom.* ii. No one doubts its antiquity. It is quoted by St. Cyril of Jerusalem, in 347 A.D. It is this Liturgy which is in most common use among the Orientals. They follow it first and chiefly; and all others are required to be accommodated to it; and from this alone is it lawful to copy. The Orientals have never doubted that it is the work of St. James; and when the Patriarchs of Constantinople suppressed in their jurisdiction all the Liturgies except those of St. Basil and St. John Chrysostom, they retained this of St. James in the churches of Syria. This Liturgy, so well attested, describes the Blessed Virgin as "*Sanctissima, gloriosissima, IMMACULATA, Deipara et semper virgine*" "Most holy, most glorious, *Immaculate*, Mother of God and ever Virgin." It also adds the very marked expression, "In every respect out of the range of sinful men." This is precisely the doctrine which the Vicar of Christ has solemnly defined as a doctrine of the Catholic Church — *Immaculate*, and *in every respect* outside of, beyond the range or ranks of sinners. *In every respect*; that is to say, all mankind are subject to the common law of being born tainted with original sin; but Mary is, in every respect, outside of this law; for she is "most holy, Immaculate."

2. The Liturgy of St. Mark, the Evangelist, has the following expressions: "*Sanctissima, IMMACULATA, et benedicta, Deipara et semper virgine Maria.*" Most holy, *Immaculate*, and blessed Mother of God, and ever virgin Mary." Can it be possible that these men, the Saints of the primitive Church, who were instructed by the Apostles, learned these forms of expression from them, and recorded them in their Liturgies, could have thus glorified the Virgin Mother if she had ever been sullied with the least stain of sin? Could she have been styled Immaculate, and yet have been spotted with the

---

2. It is a striking evidence, as well as guaranty, of the unchangeableness of the Faith — as far as the ancient Liturgies indicate points of faith — that age after age they remain the same as they were originally composed. The Latin and Greek rites were the prevailing ones; and though nations have melted away, and languages have changed, they continue to be celebrated as they were nineteen centuries ago. Doubtless the English Reformers felt the rebuke these Liturgies convey against the novelties they were inventing; and hence the true reason of their having invented a new one, containing doctrines not known to antiquity, and in every essential point totally different from those of the primitive Church. As a test of this fact, it may be asked, in what part of the English Liturgy can the sentences relating to the Blessed Virgin be found?

leprosy of sin even in her Conception? We must then conclude that it was the belief of the primitive Church that the Blessed Virgin was conceived without sin.

3. The Liturgy of St. John Chrysostom varies the expressions. In this the Blessed Virgin is named as absolutely free from every stain. She is there declared to be "*ex omni parte inculpata*" "In every part — wholly, altogether — untainted." How could this be if tainted with original sin? That St. John Chrysostom, and that portion of the Greek Church which used this Liturgy, believed the Immaculate Conception, these words sufficiently prove.

4. The Liturgy of St. Basil contains the following form: "*Præcipue cum sanctissima, illibata, super omnes benedicta, gloriosa Domina nostra Deipara et semper Virgine Maria.*" "Chiefly with the most holy, *spotless*, above all blessed, our glorious Lady, Mother of God and ever Virgin Mary."

5. The Alexandrine Liturgy of St. Basil has, "*Præcipue vero sanctissimæ, gloriosissimæ, immaculatæ, benedictionibus cumulatæ, Dominæ nostræ Deiparæ et semper Virginis Mariæ.*" "But chiefly of our most holy, most glorious, Immaculate, most blessed Lady, Mother of God, and ever Virgin Mary."[3] These expressions, daily on the lips and in the hearts of the primitive Christians, were repeated as acts of solemn worship, and were wholly inappropriate to the object of them if she were infected, even for an instant, with original sin.

6. The Greeks, in their calendars of the Saints, have recorded many equally unequivocal expressions indicative of their belief in the doctrine of the Immaculate Conception. Father Wangnereck, a Jesuit, in a learned work (now very rare) entitled *Pietas Mariana Græcorum*, printed at Munich by Wagner, in 1647, has collected many of the most ancient of these Menologies, which speak of Mary as "*omni nævo intacta,*" — intact; free from every stain as one who "*ab æterno munda fuisse dignoscitur*" — "is known to have been *wholly unsullied;*" and again, as "*sola ab æterno digna quæ Deipara fieret*" — "alone *wholly worthy* to become the Mother of God."

Such are, in brief, some of the undoubted genuine monuments of the Immaculate Conception, everywhere to be found throughout the eastern portion of the universal Church. Monuments which clearly indicate the mind of the Church, and which, as soon as the keen edge of the primitive persecutions was blunted, and the Church, under Constantine, was permitted to breathe freely, developed themselves in Festivals in honor of this Mystery.

---

3. The reader who may wish to examine these Liturgies more closely is referred to *Lebrun, Tom.* iv; also, to *Lienhart, De Antiquis Liturgiis.*

It would be but a repetition of the evidence to quote other Liturgies. They may vary the expressions, but they all unite in testifying to the Immaculate perfection of the most Holy Virgin. As in the East, so also in the Western portion of the Church, the same unity of faith prevails, and the same expression of it. There are commonly recorded four Occidental Liturgies; namely, the Roman, that of Milan, the Gallican, and the Spanish. Of these, the Roman Liturgy is the chief. It is of undoubted antiquity; and is believed to have had no less a distinguished author than St. Peter. All the others yield to it the precedence, and more or less strictly conform to its ritual. So far as relates to the question now under discussion, we find in it the same expressions as those contained in the Liturgy of St. James. We also find the same exalted description of the sublime virtues and privileges of the Blessed Virgin. She is there, as in the latter, denominated "*gloriosissima, sanctissima, IMMACULATA, Deipara et semper virgine Maria*" — "Most glorious, most holy, *Immaculate*, Mother of God, and ever Virgin Mary."

We have thus before us the united voice of the primitive Christian world, unanimously ascribing to the Virgin Mother of our Lord — and that in the most solemn acts of worship — characteristics which, if she were not a perfectly sinless creature, even from her very Conception, would be wholly unwarranted.

Can it be (as some have thought) fairly objected to the phraseology upon which, so far as the Liturgies are concerned, the claim of exemption from original sin in the Blessed Virgin, is based, that intrinsically considered, the expressions used convey no such force as is claimed for them? A moment's reflection will be sufficient to cause everyone to decide this question in the negative. For, without admitting that the objection is a just one, the following considerations may serve as a sufficiently conclusive response.

1. Supposing the objection to be just, it in no sense diminishes their force, that, totally isolated from the object towards whom they are directed, and irrespective of her supernatural history, some of them may not intrinsically convey the meaning affirmed of them. That is to say, the simple terms — *intacta, illibata, inculpata, munda,* and even the more intensive *immaculata,* isolated, do not necessarily and of their own innate force refer to the Conception. But neither is there anything in them forbidding such a reference. Any objection, therefore, predicated against the doctrine upon the abstract terms, falls to the ground; and we must resort to other reasoning, in order to ascertain their true value. But we do not admit the supposition. For;

2. The terms are absolute — "wholly undefiled," "intact, free from every stain" "most holy, spotless, above all blessed," "in every part, altogether, *wholly* untainted," "*Immaculate.*" They are therefore utterly inapplicable to ordinary persons; and still less so are they, when offered in the most solemn acts of divine worship, — the *Memento* of the Holy Sacrifice. *Thus,* to address any being as "most holy, most glorious, spotless, wholly untainted, Immaculate," who is tainted with the stain of

any, even original sin, would be an exaggeration of language, scarcely admissible in a solemn act of religious faith and worship.

3. The Blessed Virgin, to whom alone this language is applicable, is an exceptional being; exceptional in her life, in her perpetual Virginity, in her Maternity, in her Assumption, in her place among the daughters of Eve, and among the bright intelligences of heaven. Being thus supernaturally endowed and raised above all creatures, both human and angelic, she must, even aside from the evidences which so triumphantly sustain it, enjoy the presumption of being, in like manner, supernaturally exempt from the ordinary taint of conception. Any other conclusion would place her beneath those, above whom she is acknowledged to be, and confessedly render her inferior to that Eve, whose fault she was to repair, and whom she was so to excel in the perfectibility of her nature that she might truly be "*sola ab æterno digna quæ Deipara fieret.*"

4. The Liturgies, as at first noted, afford the most comprehensive and satisfactory evidences of certain points of faith. They, for example, expressly state the miraculous change of the bread and wine into the body and blood of our Lord, *vere et reipsa*; they offer the consecrated Host as a propitiation to the Father, for the sins of the living and the dead; they contain prayers for the repose of the faithful departed, and of course endorse the doctrine involved. But they do none of these things more distinctly, or more emphatically, than they proclaim the prerogative of the Immaculate Virgin. On the contrary, when speaking of her, there is in them a certain intensity of expression, a repetition of the same idea under various forms of language, which indicates an ardor, an earnestness, a want, as it were, of some stronger term, wherewith to portray in characters comporting with her dignity, the exalted Being of whom they speak. If all these expressions were a mere rhetorical flourish, sound without sense, it would be as empty and vain, as sinful. But being, as it is, the solemn, deliberate, formal, premeditated, daily act of religious worship, begun in the days of the Apostles, and by them, and thus perpetually continued, the Church meanwhile constantly attaching this idea to the expressions, it would violate every rule of correct analysis, to interpret them in any other sense, than that the Blessed Mother of God was wholly exempt from every stain of original as well as of actual sin.

*Saint James the Apostle by Lorenzo D'Alessandro da Sanseverino,
exhibited at the Great Masters Renaissance
in Zagreb, Croatia.*

CHAPTER V

Remarkable Document — The Testimony of St. Andrew and St. James, Apostles — St. Mark, the Evangelist — The Fathers of the First Five Centuries

IF THE INFERENCES DRAWN IN THE PREVIOUS CHAPTER from the testimony contained in the Ancient Liturgies were erroneous, then might we expect to find a universal silence observed upon the subject of the Immaculate Conception by all the writers of the primitive ages. But if, on the contrary, these inferences be correct, and the Immaculate Conception was the belief of the Primitive Church, as the strong language of the Liturgies clearly indicate, then might we confidently expect to find the corroborating testimony of its faith more or less scattered over the monuments which have survived the lapse of time. This latter expectation is precisely what is realized. Every age has its evidences of this belief. The writings which have come down to us; the primitive Rituals; the Festivals instituted in honor of the Immaculate Conception, all give distinct proofs of the prevailing sentiment of the Church. Strictly conforming to St. Vincent's rule, it has *always, everywhere,* and *by all*, been taught, held, and received.

The Sacred Scriptures enjoin upon us to "Inquire of the former generation, and search diligently into the memory of the fathers." (*Job, chap. viii, 8.*) It is a privilege, to be able to obey this injunction; and a duty, to avail ourselves of the light and knowledge thus to be derived. It was in this spirit of obedience that St. Hyppolitus wrote: "These testimonies are sufficient for believers, who study truth; as to unbelievers, they believe no one. Let us therefore, blessed brethren, believe according to the tradition of the Apostles." — *Contr. Hæres, Noet. n. 7.*

THE FIRST AGE — There is a letter extant, known to the Priests and Deacons of Achaia, which contains an account of the martyrdom of the illustrious Apostle St. Andrew, and a discourse which he pronounced in presence of the proconsul, Egeus, just previous to his suffering. In this discourse the holy Apostle speaks thus: "And moreover as the first man was created from *immaculate earth, it was necessary that from an Immaculate Virgin* should be born a perfect man; namely, the Son of God."[1] This reciprocal conversion of the terms *immaculate earth* and *Immaculate Virgin* exhibits the Apostle as declaring Mary to be as immaculate in her creation or Conception, as was Adam when he issued perfect from the hand of his Maker.

---

1. "Et propterea, quod ex *immaculata terra* creatus fuerat primus homo, *necesse erat ut ex Immaculata* Virgine nasceretur perfectus homo, quo Filius Dei."

The most ardent friend of the Immaculate Conception could wish for no stronger testimony than this.

This remarkable document was at first regarded by some with suspicion, in consequence of the Latin copy only being known. But since the Greek original has been found in the Bodleian Library, and published by Charles Christian Woog, a Protestant writer, all doubt has ceased. Baronius proves this letter to be genuine; as does also N. Alexander, in his *Ecclesiastical History, vol. 1.* M. Edvoy, professor of History and Antiquities at Leipzig, follows the same opinion in some learned dissertations which he published in 1748-51. Abdias Babilonicus also adds the weight of his name to its authenticity; and the celebrated Morcelli has inserted it, as authentic and true, in his Calendar of the Church of Constantinople, under the date of November 30.

St. Andrew suffered martyrdom in the year 96, and his discourse incontestably proves that the Immaculate Conception was believed and professed in the Apostolic age.

1. We have already quoted the Liturgy of St. James. The text of this Liturgy exists as recorded by Thesiphonius, a disciple of the Apostle, whom Vincartius praises. We have there seen the Blessed Virgin styled "most holy, most glorious, *immaculate, in every respect* outside of, beyond, the range of sinful men."

2. St. Mark the Evangelist, to whose Liturgy also reference has been made, besides the expressions there quoted, again denominates the Blessed Virgin, "*Sanctissimam super omnes angelicos spiritus.*" "Most Holy above all angelic spirits." St. Ignatius of Antioch, and Dionysius, the Areopagite, accord her the same praise. Could this be possible if she had not been created, through sanctifying grace, entirely free from the least stain of original sin?

THE SECOND AGE — Whether tested by the strong language of the foregoing documents, or viewed independently of them, the testimonies of the second age vindicate with no less force the sublime prerogatives of the Immaculate Virgin. Justin Martyr, St. Irenaeus, Tertullian, and the whole army of saints and martyrs of this age received the sacred truths of the Gospel immediately from the Apostles; and in turn transmitted them, as they had received them, to their successors. They used the same Liturgical forms; and made no exception to the glorious privileges which we find in them accorded to the Blessed Virgin. They daily offered the Spotless Victim which taketh away the sins of the world; and they as often hailed the divine Mother, as wholly unsullied, untainted, most holy, Immaculate, and in every respect out of the range of sinful men.

1. Justin Martyr styles her, "*Virginem Sequestram;*" The Mediatrix between God her divine Son, and our fallen race.

2. St. Irenaeus utters the same sentiment concerning her. (*Decret. lib. 3, cap. 22,* and elsewhere.) He also says: "If Eve disobeyed God, yet Mary was counselled to obey God; that the Virgin Mary might become the Advocate for the Virgin Eve. And as the human race was bound to death through a Virgin, it is saved through a Virgin; the scales being equally balanced; *virginal* disobedience by *virginal* obedience." — *Advers. Hæres. lib. v, cap. xix, p. 879.*

3. Tertullian speaks of her under the name of "*Consolatrix.*"

THE THIRD AGE —

1. St. Hyppolitus, in his celebrated oration upon the end of the world, uses the same language respecting the Blessed Virgin, as did the holy Apostles, St. James and St. Andrew, and the Evangelist St. Mark. He styles her: "*Sanctam et Immaculatam*" — "Holy and Immaculate."

2. Origen says: "*She has not been tainted with the breath of the venomous serpent.* For why should the Blessed Virgin Mary have been deprived of this prerogative in her conception, (in ortu suo,) with which, not only all the Angels, — even the bad (angels) — were adorned, in their original creation, but which our first parents, whom God created upright and innocent, also possessed?"[2]

Hence it is that St. Anselm also says: "God hath preserved the Angels from sin, among the others sinning, hath He not been able also to preserve the Mother pure from the sins of others?"[3]

3. St. Cyprian says: "Neither did justice suffer that vessel of election to be open to the common injuries, for being far exalted above others, she was a partaker of their nature, but not of their sin."[4]

4. St. Dionysius of Alexandria, commenting on the words "The Lord possessed me in the beginning of His ways," (*Eccles. chap. xxiv, 5*), exclaims; *una et sola filia vit*[], (*Epis. Contra. Pa. Samos.*) "One and sole daughter of life;" differing in this from others, who being born in sin, are daughters of death.

5. St. Methodius declares: That our Lord, "who hath said, 'honor thy father and mother,' would certainly keep the decree promulgated by Himself, and

---

2. "Nec serpentis venenosi afflatibus infecta est. Etenim et quomodo carere potuerit B. V. Maria in ortu suo ilia prærogativa, quæ non tantum Angeli omnes, etiam mali a prima eorum creatione ornati fuerunt, sed et primi parentes, quos Deus rectos finxit et innocentes?" — Horn. 1, de B. V. Maria.

3. "Angelos aliis peccantibus, a peccato reservavit; et Matrem ab aliorum peccatis exortem servare non potuit?" —*Sermo. de Conceptione.*

4. "Non sustinebat justitia, ut illud vas electionis communibus lacesseretur injuriis, quoniam plurimum a cæteris distans natura communicabat, non culpa." — *Lib. I, De Carne Christi.*

bestow upon his Mother every grace and honor."[5]

1. St. Ephraem says: "Mary is Immaculate, and most remote from every taint of sin."[6] He also salutes her; "*Ave orbis terrarum Conciliatrix.*" — "Hail! Conciliatrix of the world." And again, speaking of the Blessed Virgin he describes her as: "Immaculate, undefiled, incorrupt and holy in every particular; and *wholly exempt* from every stain of sin."[7] St. Anselm to this subjoins the following: "Was the wisdom of God impotent to construct a pure habitation with *every blemish* of the human condition removed?"[8]

2. St. Basil also exclaims; "*Ave Dei hominumque Sequestra constituta.*" "Hail! thou who art appointed Mediatrix between God and man."

3. St. Amphilochius says: "Who created the first virgin (Eve), perfect; He himself created the second (Mary), without blemish and without sin."[9]

   And who, indeed, in view of this remarkable language, can persuade himself that she, who was chosen from eternity to become the Mother of God, and to bruise the old serpent's head, should for a moment be under that demon's power?

4. St. Epiphanius calls the Blessed Virgin, "*Lilium Immaculatum*" — "*Ovem Immaculatam;*" "the Immaculate Lily," "the Immaculate Lamb;" and adds: "The Blessed Mary is worthy above all creatures, that angels and men should prefer her before all others."[10] In a short treatise, "*de Laudibus Virginis*" he expresses himself still more beautifully. He says: "God alone except, she is superior to all; she is more beautiful than the cherubim and seraphim, and the whole army of angels. (She is) the Immaculate One, who hath brought forth the Lamb Christ."[11]

5. St. Athanasius calls Mary, "*Nova Eva, Mater vitæ,*" — (*Orat. de Sancta Deipara.*) — "The new Eve, the Mother of life." Mary was the new Eve, mother of life,

---

5. "Qui dixit, honora patrem et matrem ut decretum a se promulgatum servaret, omnem Matri gratiam et honorem impendit." — *Orat. in Hypap.*
6. Maria Immaculata, et ab omni peccati labe alienissima? Tom. 5, Orat. ad Dei Gen.
7. "Immaculata, intemerata, incorrupta omnibusque modis sancta, et ab omni labe peccati alienissima." — Tom. 3 or 5, Or. ad Dei Genit.
8. "Impotens ne fuit sapientia Dei mundum habitaculum condere remota omni labe conditionis humanæ?" — *Sermo de Conceptione.*
9. "Qui antiquam virginem sine probro condidit, ipse et secundam absque nota, et crimine fabricatus est." — *Orat. 4, in S Deip. et Simeone.*
10. Digna est Beata Maria inter omnes creaturas, ut eam præ cæteris homines et angeli suscipiant. — *Orat. de Carn. Virg.*
11. Solo Deo excepto cunctis superior extitit, natura formosior est ipsis Cherubim, Seraphim, et omni exercitu Angelorum. Ovis Immaculata, quæ peperit Agnum Christum.

because she was the means by which the spiritual life of the soul, destroyed by the first Eve, was restored to us.

6. St. Ambrose says: "Not from earth, but from heaven, Christ selected this vessel, through which He should descend, and consecrated the temple of modesty."[12] Again, "Receive me not from Sarah, but from Mary, as an uncorrupted virgin; a virgin through grace, preserved from every stain of sin."[13] And in another place, he makes use of the following figure: "The Virgin Mother of God is the rod in which was neither original knot (original sin), nor bark of actual sin."[14]

7. St. Jerome, commenting upon those words of the Psalmist, "He conducted them with a cloud by day" (*Psalm lxxvii, 14*), says: "The Blessed Virgin was that cloud of day, because that cloud was never in darkness, but always in the light." And he afterwards adds: "It is not doubtful concerning the Mother of the Lord, but that she was such, that she could not be reproached with sin. She is the enclosed garden, the sealed fountain, into which no treachery hath been able to enter, nor fraud of the enemy to overcome; but she hath remained holy in mind and body."[15]

"It would be an infinite task," says the author of the *Fall and Rise of Man*, "if I should attempt to enumerate all who have called the Blessed Virgin immaculate, uncontaminated, undefiled, above all blessed, never reproached, altogether beautiful, wholly without spot, free from every contamination, untainted, and exempt from every stain of original and actual sin."

THE FIFTH AGE —

1. In St. Augustine we have an illustrious advocate for the Immaculate Conception. Pelagius had erroneously taught that the children of all baptized persons were born exempt from original sin. In refuting this error, St. Augustine says: "Except the Holy Virgin Mary, concerning whom, for the honor of the Lord, I wish to entertain no question, when sin is the subject of discussion; since we know that more grace hath been given to her to overcome sin in every respect (*ex omni parte*), who was worthy to conceive

---

12. Non de terra, sed de coelo vas sibi hoc per quod descenderet, Christus elegit, et sacravit templum pudoris. — *De Inst. Virg. cap. 5.*
13. Suscipe me non ex Sara, sed ex Maria, ut incorrupta sit virgo, sed virgo per gratiam ab omni integra labe peccati. — *Sermo 22, in Psalm cxviii.*
14. Deiparam Virginem, virgam esse, in qua nec nodus originalis, nec cortex actualis culpæ fuit.
15. Non dubium est de Matre Domini quin talis debuerit esse, quæ non posset argui de peccato. Hæc est hortus conclusus, fons signatus ad quem nulli potuerunt doli irrumpere, nec prævalere fraus inimici, sed permansit sancta mente, et corpore. — *Epist. 10 ad Eust.*

and bring forth Him, whom it behooved to have had no sin."[16]

This passage from St. Augustine merits more attention than is implied in its mere quotation. It has been well said of this holy doctor that he is worthy to be esteemed as a representative of the genius, wisdom, and piety of the primitive Church. Every word, therefore, that he utters upon this momentous question is a treasure, a mine of wealth, to the friend of the Blessed Virgin. These words clearly favor the doctrine of the exemption of the Blessed Virgin from original sin. "I wish," says St. Augustine, "to entertain no question concerning the Blessed Virgin, when sin is the subject of discussion." By this general mode of speaking, he declares his unwillingness to connect even her name with sin, actual or original. He does this "for the honor of the Lord." If the honor of the Lord demands that His mother, through her whole life, should be exempt from actual, even though it be but venial sin, how much more does it demand that she should be exempt from original, which is *mortal sin*, on account of which she would have been hateful to God, a servant of the devil, and the subject of eternal damnation!

He says that the Blessed Virgin "had grace given to her to overcome sin in every respect." How could this be said if she had formerly been tainted with original sin? He says she had this grace, "because she was the mother of Him whom it behooved to have no sin." She received this grace that she might be exempt from every sin from which Christ was free. But Christ was free from all sin, both actual and original. Therefore, the Blessed Virgin was also free. But let us grant that St. Augustine disputes with his adversary concerning actual sin alone — still, even under this view of it, he exempts the Blessed Virgin from original sin. For, he constantly teaches that actual sins have their origin from original sin, *as from a root*. That this is no private interpretation of the text, or a wresting of it from its legitimate force, St. Augustine himself sufficiently shows in several places. In his second sermon, *"In Natale Domini"* commenting upon the words, *"Hail full of grace,"* he says: "By which words he shows her to be *entirely* excluded from the wrath of the first sentence, and restored to the full grace of benediction."[17]

The word *renascendi*, which St. Augustine uses, has been alleged by some to militate against the Immaculate Conception. It does not this necessarily; and the whole context shows that the Saint does not at all mean to be so

---

16. Excepta Sancta Virgine Maria, de qua propter honorem Domini, nullam prorsus, dum de peccatis agitur, habere volo quæstionem; unde enim scimus quod ei plus gratiæ collatum fuerit ad vincendum ex omni parte peccatum; quæ concipere et parere meruit Eum, Quem constat nullum habuisse peccatum. — *Lib. de Natura et Gratia, cap.* 23.
17. Quibus ostendit *ex integro* iram primæ sententiæ exclusam, et plenam benedictionis gratiam restitutam.

understood. Julian had objected to St. Augustine, that he had "subjected Mary herself to the devil by the condition of being born." St. Augustine immediately replied: "We do not subject Mary to the devil by the condition of being born; for the condition itself is freed by the grace of the new birth."[18]

St. Augustine, as just stated, had exempted Mary from all imputation or question of sin, *ex omni parte*; and he here adds force to his previous declaration by saying that *the very condition itself*, that is, the condition of being subject to the devil at any time, is absolved in regard to the Blessed Virgin. Any other interpretation would imply a contradiction too palpable for such a writer as St. Augustine to commit. Besides, other passages of the Saint's writings show with sufficient plainness that his prevailing sentiment was in favor of this doctrine. In his twelfth sermon, "*In Natale Domini*," he institutes the following comparison between the Church and the Blessed Virgin: "The Church, as well as Mary, has perpetual integrity, and incorruptible fecundity."[19]

Both terms of the comparison are equal; and if the Church was never, at any one moment, in its origin or progress, peccable, then, according to St. Augustine, neither was the Blessed Mary peccable, or subject to sin at any one moment of her existence; and consequently, not at the moment of her conception. Again, this illustrious Saint and friend of Mary says: "As the devil was the head from whence original sin proceeded, that head Mary crushed, because no sin ever entered the soul of the Virgin, and therefore she was exempt from every stain."[20] He moreover testifies to the incorruptibility of the flesh of the Blessed Virgin. He says: "Corruption is the reproach of the human condition, from which, since Jesus was exempt, the nature of Mary was exempted; for the flesh of Jesus is the flesh of Mary."[21] Again: "Mary is the only one who hath merited to be called Mother and Spouse of God." — *Serm. de Assump.*[22]

When St. Augustine, in other parts of his writings, makes use of general expressions, which seem, without exception, to include all the human race, it is manifestly unjust to suppose (his positive declaration being to the contrary) that he includes in them the Mother of our Lord. It stands, therefore, that St. Augustine himself has declared that he exempts the blessed Mother in *every*

---

18. Non transcribimus Mariam diabolo conditione nascendi; sed ideo, *quia ipsa conditio solvitur gratia renascendi. Oper. Imp. contra Julianum, Lib.* IV, 122.
19. Ecclesiæ, sicut Mariæ, *perpetua integritas* et incorrupta foecunditas.
20. Cum peccati originalis caput sit diabolus, tale caput Maria contrivit; quia nulla peccati subjectio ingressum habuit in animam Virginis, et ideo ab omni macula immunis fuit. — *In Gen.* iii, 15.
21. Putredo namque humanæ est opprobrium conditionis, a quo cum Jesus sit alienus, natura Mariæ excipitur; caro enim Jesu caro Mariæ est. — *Sermo de Assump. B. V.*
22. Some of the learned doubt whether St. Augustine wrote this sermon. Others maintain that he did. This remark applies also to the passage from St. Jerome.

question of sin.

2. The testimony of St. Cyril, of Alexandria, is decisive. He says, "All men, He who was born of the Virgin excepted, *and the most sacred Virgin also being exempted,* by whom the God-man came into the world, are born with original sin."[23] He also, in another place, illustrates the wisdom of this exemption of the Virgin from original sin. He asks, "Who ever heard of an architect who has built a house for himself and first yielded the occupancy and possession of it to his enemy?"[24] Christ is the Architect, Mary the house, sin His enemy. Would Christ so have built for His enemy, or thus have permitted his occupancy of that sacred tabernacle constructed for Himself?

3. St. Maximus furnishes us with the following remarkable passage. He says, "Mary was evidently a fit habitation for Christ, not on account of habit of body, but on account of *original grace.*"[25]

4. St. Proclus, the disciple and successor of St. John Chrysostom, affirms that "Mary was formed from a pure essence." "*Formata est Maria ex essentia pura.*" (*Orat. v, Laud. Sanc. Genitricis.*)

No word of comment is needed in summing up these testimonies of the first five ages of the Christian era. Their clearness, their point, their beautiful and apt illustrations, are too plainly indicative of the meaning to be attached to them. Other witnesses might be added to those here presented; but it is needless. The faith of the Primitive Church stands confessed: Mary, the Blessed Mother of God, was conceived without the least stain of original sin. "Therefore, brethren, stand fast; and hold the traditions which ye have learned, whether by word or by our epistle." (*2 Thess., chap. ii, 3, 14.*) "Keep the good things committed to thy trust by the Holy Ghost who dwelleth in us; and the things that thou hast heard of me by many witnesses, the same commit to faithful men, who shall be fit to teach others also." (*2 Timothy, chap. i, ii, iii.*)

---

23. "Omnes homines, excepto illo, qui de Virgine natus est, *et sacratissima etiam Virgine*, ex qua Deus homo prodiit in mundum, *exempta*, cum peccato originali nascimur."
24. "Quis unquam audivit architectum, qui sibi domum ædificavit, ejus occupationem et possessionem primo suo inimico cessisse?" — *In Concilio Ephesino*, n. 6.
25. "Idoneum plane Maria Christo habitaculum, non pro habitu corporis, sed pro gratia originali." — *Hom. v, ante Natale Domini.*

CHAPTER VI

"She shall crush thy head." — "Thou hast upheld me by reason of my innocence." — "Hail, full of grace!"

BY DISOBEDIENCE OUR FIRST PARENTS LOST the original holiness and justice in which they were created, incurred the righteous anger of God, placed themselves under the dominion of the devil, and involved all their posterity in their guilt and its penalty — spiritual, temporal, and eternal death. "Wherefore," says St. Paul, "as by one man sin entered into this world, and by sin death; and so death passed upon all men in whom all have sinned." (*Rom., chap. v, 12.*) This fearful penalty and alienation from God is incurred by every child from the first instant of animation. Hence the exclamation of the Psalmist: "Behold I was conceived in iniquities; and in sins did my mother conceive me." (*Psalm 1, 7.*) This is the origin and source of that universal proclivity to evil, that depravity and naughtiness of our corrupt nature, which is evinced from the earliest moment each new being of our race is capable of action. It is this, also, which is denominated original sin, because it is entailed upon us in Adam, who is our natural and moral representative. God hath made of one, all mankind, to dwell upon the face of the earth (*Acts, chap. xvii, 26*); and as the whole human race was represented by Adam, so was it involved in his transgression. Hence the Apostle institutes a comparison between Adam and Christ: "For as by the disobedience of one man, many were made sinners; so also by the obedience of one, many shall be made just." (*Rom., chap. v, 19.*)

This state or condition of sin is mortal, deadly; banishes the grace of God from us; renders us hateful and abominable in His sight; and, if not effectually removed from the soul by grace, condemns it to eternal punishment. It is not possible for man to realize all its guiltiness. None but God Himself can estimate it fully, as none but the life of a God could atone for it. It violates the sanctity of the soul, which should be wedded to Jesus Christ; it profanes the temple of the living God; and it thus involves the unrenewed in the awful denunciation conveyed by the Apostle in these words: "If any violate the temple of God, him shall God destroy." (*Eph., chap. vi, 12.*) Innumerable are the evils of which original sin is the poisoned source. Their magnitude is thus expressed by David: "There is no health in my flesh, because of thy wrath; there is no peace for my bones, because of my sins." (*Psalm xxxvii, 4.*) He marks the virulence of the disease by declaring that it left no part of his frame uninfected. The poison of sin entered into his very bones. In other words, it infected his understanding and his will —

the two great faculties of the soul. The Sacred Scriptures, describing this widespread and destructive contagion, speak of it as a leprosy, which pervades every part of our being; as a paralysis, which disables us from doing any good thing; as a condition which deprives us of the proper use of our faculties; rendering us lame, dumb, deaf, and blind. It places us in an attitude of war against Almighty God; and the soul which enters the presence of its Creator still poisoned with its venomous breath shall surely die eternally.

Such being the incompatibility between sin and holiness; the essential enmity between the devil, our corrupt nature, and God; the redemption of man would have been impossible, unless a special dispensation of Divine Providence, so exempted some one of His creatures, from the deadly taint, that He might be able to unite His Godhead to our human nature, and thus repair the violated law.

Whoever, therefore, contemplates the Divine Being in His infinite and immaculate holiness, must feel that it would be incompatible with His nature to incorporate Himself with a body, which had been thus tainted with sin. He cannot endure sin in His presence. The Angels, for one fault, were hurled from the battlements of heaven; and man, for one transgression, was thrust forth from Paradise. How then should He enter into, and dwell within, a body disfigured with that deadly evil; and over which Lucifer had once held his fell dominion?

But the Merciful Creator had resolved, not to leave fallen man entirely without hope. A horn of salvation was to be raised up in the house of David His servant, (*St. Luke, chap. i, 69,*) that He himself might be just and yet the justifier of the penitent believer. (*Rom., chap. iii, 26.*) It was therefore by the operation of free and undeserved grace, that God designed to save man from merited death; and thus reverse, and undo the sad effects of the fall. Through the efficacy of the infinite sacrifice, which, in the fullness of time, was to be offered up, sanctifying grace is infused into the soul, which is thereby more and more assimilated to the likeness of God; and restored to the original state of holiness in which it was first created. Every stain of sin is purged away, and it is united to God forever. This is the usual process by which grace operates to the perfection of the Saints. But God, who is boundless in His mercy, and infinite in the outpourings of the richness of His grace, has been pleased to except in this, some of the more privileged of His Saints, by lavishing upon them at once a superabundant measure of grace; in order that they might be, in an especial manner, fitted for the peculiar mission they were to fulfil. He has by prevenient grace in some instances anticipated their birth, and sanctified them while yet in the womb. "Before I formed thee in the bowels of thy mother, I knew thee;" saith the Lord to Jeremias; "and before thou camest forth out of the womb, I sanctified thee, and made thee a prophet unto the nations." (*Jer., chap. i, 4, 5.*) Thus was Jeremias specially prepared for his plaintive mission to the people of God; being, in his mission, in his life, and in his violent death, peculiarly a figure of the Man of Sorrows, and acquainted with infirmity.

A similar privilege, though of an inferior degree, seems to have been conferred upon another servant of God. It was foretold to the mother of Sampson; "Thou shalt conceive and bear a son, and no razor shall touch his head; for he shall be a Nazarite to God, from his infancy and from his mother's womb." (*Judges, chap. xiii, 5.*) But as the dispensation of types and shadows, drew towards its close, and the great Antitype was about to make His advent into the world, His coming was heralded by superior measures of grace, than had yet been poured out upon any of His most favored prophets. An Angel is sent from heaven to that servant of God, the High Priest Zachary, to announce the birth of the forerunner of the Redeemer; "who should be great before the Lord, and who should be filled with the Holy Ghost even from his mother's womb." (*St. Luke, chap. i, 15.*) Thus was foretold the birth of a Prophet, than whom, "there is not a greater born of women." (*St. Luke, chap. vii, 28.*)

High as were the missions of these illustrious prophets and servants of God, that of Mary was confessedly still higher, and far more glorious. They were but to prepare the way before Him; She, to give Him a body, wherewith to appear. They, to preach repentance in His name; She, to afford Him that life, which He was to lay down for their redemption. And if they received a special degree of grace above others for their mission, how infinitely greater must have been the degree of grace conferred upon her who was actually to receive within her, the Lord of life and glory, the Prince of Peace, the Desire of the nations! Consider the attributes of the Deity, whom she bore within her virginal womb. His infinite purity, His sanctity. Consider His abhorrence of sin, upon which He cannot look with the least degree of allowance. He sanctifies even his forerunners before their birth; so that, even in them, He may have perfection. How much more her, whose flesh He took; whose blood was His life; whose milk His sustenance! Consider His infinite love for her; infinite, not in the general sense only, but in that especial manifestation of it, whereby He had from all eternity predestinated her to be His Mother. What an infinitude of graces must He have poured out upon her!

No gift has been conferred upon any creature, but Mary hath received of it more abundantly. Hence St. Bernard declares: "We certainly cannot suspect that, what has been bestowed upon the chosen among mortals, should be withheld from the Blessed Virgin." (*Epist.* 174.) And as St. Thomas of Villanova says: "Nothing was ever given to any of the Saints that did not shine more pre-eminently from the beginning of her life." (*Serm. 2, de Assump.*) If Eve was created holy to be the worthy spouse of Adam, what must have been the perfection of Mary, created to be the Spouse of God the Holy Ghost? Well hath St. Augustine, — meditating upon the salutation of the Angel, "*Hail, full of grace,*" — said: "By these words he shows her to be *entirely* excluded from the wrath of the first sentence, and restored to the full grace of benediction." And St. Amphilochius also says: "He who created the first virgin without reproach, also created the second without stain or crime." And St. Ildephonsus: "It is certain that she was exempt from original sin."

Is there question of His power? He created the Angels perfect at a word, and after His own image, man. "Let it be; and it was;" "He spake, and it was done;" is the simple and sublime record of Almighty power, by which a host of Angels and a myriad of worlds were ushered into being and set their appointed course.

Was He, who made the Angels pure and man intact, impotent only to ordain and constitute the sacred vessel from which to take His sacred flesh and blood, sinless, immaculate, and pure? His power is confessed; and, in view of His divine perfections, the infallible inference must be drawn that He could do no less. *Necessity* impelled that when the first Eve, perfect, failed, a second perfect Eve should be found to crush the Serpent's head. God Himself deigns to utter the first prophecy concerning this peerless one. Inspired by Him, the Psalmist sings, and Prophets prophecy her coming, her glory, her innocence, and spotless perfection. "She shall crush thy head." "Thou hast upheld me by reason of my innocence; and hast established me in thy sight forever." "Thou art all fair, O my love, and there is no spot in thee." And when, in the fullness of time, the heavenly messenger, winged with love, flew to the abode of the Immaculate Maid, he hailed her, *"Full of grace."* Like salutation never saluted mortal ear; and she trembled while she heard that she was the predestined Spouse of the Holy Ghost, ordained to bring forth Him who is styled the Savior, the Mighty God, the Prince of Peace, the Immaculate Lamb.

In view of so heavenly a presage, what might be expected of the Church founded and established by her divine Son? That it should forget the Immaculate Mother! Dishonor the Spouse of the Holy Ghost! and ignore the unblemished perfection of her nature! Should it not rather place her where God hath done — next to Himself? Should it not honor her as He hath? — "Hail, formed in grace!" and address her as He hath, with filial reverence and perfect love? Accordingly, as we have seen, that Church, in her divine Office, failed not to honor whom the King hath honored; and whenever it commemorated the spotless Victim, slain for our redemption, it forgot not to mention the Immaculate Virgin that brought Him forth; that fondled Him upon her knee; nourished at her breasts; and followed to the cross. Wherever the voice of the sacred Liturgies went forth, whether from the mountain-tops, within the peaceful vales, or from the depths of the caves and dens of the earth, their voice was still attuned to Mary's praise. There was she called "Most holy, most glorious, above all others blessed, immaculate and pure." And when the holy Apostles finished chanting these sacred Liturgies here, Saints and Martyrs took up and prolonged their dying strains, until the glories of the Mother of God became as familiar as the story of redeeming love. "Unpolluted, undefiled, forever blessed, altogether beautiful, without spot, immaculate, entire, free, exempt from every stain of sin," was the doctrine that they taught, and the theme which ever inspired their tongues.

Some of the evidences of this, found in the monuments of the first five centuries, have been adduced. That which is to follow may serve to show that the Church has been ever true to the first lessons it had learned from those Apostolic men.

Interior of the Basilica of the National Shrine of the Immaculate Conception in Washington, D.C.

CHAPTER VII

Festivals Instituted in Honor of the Immaculate Conception

IN EVERY AGE OF THE WORLD THE PEOPLE OF GOD have observed certain days of the year as Festivals; on which occasions to express in a more solemn manner their gratitude and holy joy for special favors and blessings received. Usually, the anniversaries of these events have been so observed. God Himself has instituted festival days for the observance of His people; and Christ our Redeemer has been pleased to institute a perpetual festival of His infinite bounty and love in the life-giving Sacrament of the Altar. The Apostles and the disciples of our Lord, who though their lives were one perpetual scene of fervor and zeal, soon began to set apart certain days for the special commemoration of certain events which particularly marked the history of the infant Church. The Jewish Sabbath gave place to the festival of the Lord's Day, and the anniversary of the Day of Pentecost was devoutly observed in commemoration of the descent of the Holy Ghost. And as many of the most solemn and awful passages in the Redeemer's life occurred during the Paschal season, Christian observances were substituted for those of the Jewish calendar. Hence Easter was, from the earliest date, a prominent festival of the Christian Church.

Nevertheless, joyous as were the occasions which prompted these seasons of special devotion, yet, in consequence of the fiery torrent of persecution, the sacred joy of the Christians mostly glistened on their faces through blood and tears. They came not forward in open day, nor raised their voices on high in their hymns of thanksgiving and praise; but shrank within the dens and caves of the earth; or, perchance, sang Glory to God in the Highest from the depths of some lonesome dungeon, or while expiring from the pangs of torture. It is not surprising, therefore, that some of the minor festival days of the early Church are not with much distinctness traced upon the page of history of the first four centuries. For even the gleam of sunshine which overspread the Christian world on the accession of Constantine was not of sufficient duration to permit the Church to deck herself in her garments of joy. There cannot be a doubt, however, that, from the very first, the anniversary festivals of the saints were always celebrated. St. Gregory informs us that the anniversary of St. Theodore was thus celebrated: he says, "Though we celebrate this day" (that of St. Theodore) "with a yearly festival, yet does the crowd of comers, filled with zeal, never cease; but the road which leads to this place keeps up the appearance of an ant-hill; some ascending, and others making way for new comers." (*Tom. iii, De St. Theodor., p. 580.*) Tertullian, also, as early as the second century, enjoins the observance of the annual festivals (*De Monogam. n. x,* and in many other places). And though these passages relate to obituary rather than natal festivals, they so far answer our purpose as to indicate the inclination of the mind of the primitive Church, and prepare us for what is immediately to follow.

1. The exalted dignity of the Virgin Mother, and her intimate relation to our Lord, forbid us to believe but that festivals in her honor bear as early date as any which relate to the saints. The Festival of the Immaculate Conception of the Blessed Virgin is known to have been celebrated in the Oriental Churches about the year 406. This, Andrew, Archbishop of Crete, who composed the Ecclesiastical Canons of the Greek Church, 560 A.D., renders undoubted.

2. Bergier also affirms that the Festival of the Immaculate Conception was celebrated, and, even in the seventh century, was regarded as of very ancient date. He instances the testimony of George, Archbishop of Nicomedia, who lived at that epoch, during the reign of Heraclius. The Greeks, he says, have constantly called the Blessed Virgin *wholly pure, spotless, without sin.* Neither have they, he adds, borrowed the idea from the Roman Church, since they still preserve it.[1] P. Combeficius has published several sermons that George, Archbishop of Nicomedia, had written upon this Festival about the year 610, in which he says, "This Festival is not of recent institution, but ancient" — "*non novissime institutum, sed antiquum.*"

3. Among those who about this period celebrated this Festival, as cited by Card. Barronio, in his notes upon the Roman Martyrology, was the Emperor Leo Augustus, surnamed the wise. (*In Notis ad Martyrol. Romanum.*)

4. The Emperor Comnenus, who ascended the throne about the year 1143, naming the Festivals to be celebrated, speaks of the ninth of December as one, "because then is celebrated the Conception of the Mother of our God." He says, "*Nonus dies Decembris, Quia tum Genitricis Dei nostri Conceptio celebratur.*"

5. Matthew of Paris relates of the Archbishop of Armenia, that, on going into England about the year 1228, he was interrogated whether they celebrated the Conception of the Blessed Virgin in Armenia. The Archbishop replied,

---

1. "Already in the seventh century under the reign of Heraclius, George of Nicomedia regarded the Immaculate Conception of the Blessed Virgin as an ancient feast, and at least since that time, the Greeks have constantly called Mary *Panachrante,* all pure, spotless, without sin. They did not borrow this belief from the Roman Church; since they still keep it. " — *Bergier,* on the word *conception.*

"*It is celebrated*; and this is the reason: because the Conception was made (known) by an Angel announcing it to Joachim, sorrowing, and at that time dwelling in a desert."[2]

6. Joseph Assemani is said to have demonstrated from the marble calendar of Naples, engraved in the Ninth Age, that the Festival of the Conception was then kept in that city; and that the Church of Naples was the first in the West which adopted it in imitation of the Orientals. But it is affirmed, on the most ancient authority, to have been observed in Spain even from the time of the Apostle St. James. And it is certain that St. Ildephonsus, Bishop of Toledo, celebrated it with hymns, and prayers, and sermons, 667 A.D.[3]

7. Another illustrious monument of the antiquity of this Festival is furnished by a work containing the laws of the Visigoths under king Ervigis; which extends back to 851 A.D. The passage referred to in this book, according to Thomassin, (*De Festis, lib. 12, c. 7*), is as follows: "The Festival of the Holy Virgin Mary, in which is celebrated the glorious Conception of the same Mother of (our) Lord."[4] "This evidently seems to me, says Cerri, (*Triumphus, B. M. V. page 58*), both an old and manifest monument of the Festival; hence I am the more astonished at the interpretation of Thomassin, who thinks the law should be understood of the Festival of the Conception of Christ by the Virgin, concerning which there are some vestiges in the ancient Calendars. But who could cause '*Conceptio ejusdem Genitricis Domini*' to bear such an interpretation, which plainly refers to 'the Blessed Virgin's own Conception'?"[5]

8. Another notable example in favor of the Immaculate Conception is derived from the Mozarabic Liturgy. In a work concerning the use of the Liturgies, (*chap. ii, page 3*), by Francis Anthony Zaccaria, the Blessed Virgin is called *Incorrupt*. "The Lord Jesus Christ, who came to assume a true body of the *Incorrupt flesh* of (His) Mother."[6]

---

2. "*Celebratur*, et hæc est ratio; quia Angelo nunciante Joachim dolenti, et desertum tunc inhabitanti; ipsa *Conceptio* facta est."
3. The Churches of Spain "did not give up their Liturgy until the arrival of the Goths. In the 11th century, and until the year 1080, the Christians who remained there after the invasion of the Moors or Arabs remained attached to the Gothic Mass. The mixture of Christians with Moors is what gave the name to the early Mozarabs. The popes had to work for more than 30 consecutive years to establish the Roman Liturgy use in Spain. All these facts show that in no century or place around the world has it ever been easy to introduce changes in the Liturgy." — *Bergier*, on the word *liturgie*.
4. "Festum S. Virginia Mariæ, quo gloriosa Conceptio ejusdem Genitricis Domini celebratur."
5. See *Ex Alexio, Aurelio, Pellicia de Christianæ Ecclesiæ primea, mediæ, et novissimæ ætatis politia. Tom. iii, cap. 11, sec. 9.*
6. "Dominus Jesus Christus, qui venit de *incorrupta Matris* carne, corporis veritatem assumere."

9.　The learned Mabillon affirms, that there is no doubt that this Festival was celebrated in Spain, in the tenth century. (*Annot. Epis.* 174, *St. Bernardi.*) Vincartius also confirms the same. (*Eleg. Marian. ad litt. 1.*) Long before the revision of the Breviary, by Pius V, it was the uniform practice of all the Churches of Spain, to recite the office of the Conception of the Blessed Virgin. This is affirmed on the testimony of Thomas de Argentina and others. (*Ger. Serm. de Concept., Bosius, lib. de Signis Ecclesiae, c. 8, Baronius in notis ad Martyrol. Rom. Decem, viii,* also testify to the same.)

In 1394, Don Juan the First, King of Aragon, instituted, by royal patent, the Feast of the Immaculate Conception, in all the provinces then under his government. And while this ordinance shows that all his predecessors had encouraged and celebrated this Festival by suitable solemnities, it also proves the great importance attached to its appropriate observance in that most Catholic empire. The ordinance is as follows:

"We, Don Juan, by the grace of God, King of Aragon, &c.:

"Why is it that some persons feel astonished that the Blessed Mary, Mother of God, should have been conceived without original sin, whilst they entertain not the slightest doubt that St. John the Baptist had been sanctified in his mother's womb by that same God, who, descended from the highest heavens, and from the throne of the Most Holy Trinity, was made flesh in the blessed womb of the Virgin? What favors, think we, could the Lord have refused to a woman who brought him forth by means of her fruitful Virginity? Loving His Mother equally as Himself, he must have encompassed her conception, her nativity, and the other phases of her holy life, with illustrious prerogatives.

"Why call in question the glorious conception of a virgin, whose extraordinary privileges and favors, which cannot command sufficient admiration, Catholic faith forces us to acknowledge? Is it not the greatest subject of wonder to all Christians, that a creature should have given birth to her Creator, and that she should have become mother without the loss of her virginity? How can the human mind adequately sound the praises of this glorious Virgin, whose prerogatives of divine maternity, combined with the luster of stainless virginity, and her elevation above the prophets, and all the saints, and all the choirs of angels, the Omnipotent destined her the possession of, without the slightest corruption. To cast on her the imputation of original sin, on her, to whom the angel commissioned by heaven addressed these words: '*Hail, Mary, full of grace; the Lord is with thee; blessed art thou amongst women;*' it must follow that at the first instant of her conception she stood in need of some special grace and favor. Let those who speak so improperly, then, be silent; let those who have only vain and frivolous objections to propose against the Immaculate Conception, so privileged and pure, of the Blessed Virgin, feel a blush of shame at giving them publicity, because it was only meet that she should be endowed with purity so spotless, as to be inferior only to the purity of God Himself. It is only meet that she who had brought forth a Son, the Creator and Father of all things, should have been ever, and should be now, most pure, most lovely, most perfect, having, by a divine decree, been chosen before all ages, to bear in her womb Him, whom the whole world and the highest heavens cannot contain.

"But we, who, among all Catholic kings, without any merit on our part, have received so many graces and favors from this Mother of mercies, firmly believe that the Conception of this Blessed Virgin, in whose womb the Son of God deigned to become man, has been entirely holy and spotless.

"Thus with a pure heart we will honor the mystery of the Immaculate and glorious Conception of the Most Holy Virgin, Mother of God, and we, and all those of our royal household, shall every year celebrate its Festival with solemnity, in the same manner that our illustrious predecessors, of glorious memory, have celebrated it, having established in honor of it, a perpetual association. It is for this purpose we ordain that this Festival of the Immaculate Conception shall be celebrated with all possible solemnity and respect every year in perpetuity, in all the kingdoms subject to our obedience, by all the faithful, whether religious or secular, by all Priests and all other persons, whatsoever may be their condition and state; and that from henceforward we strictly prohibit all preachers, and all those who deliver public lectures on the Gospel, from saying, publishing, and advancing anything, which in any manner may act prejudicially to, or derogate from, the purity and sanctity of this glorious Conception; but, on the contrary, we ordain that preachers, and all others, who may have formed opposite opinions, shall maintain strict silence, as the Catholic faith requires not that the contrary opinion should be either supported or professed; and that such as hold in their hearts our pious and salutary opinion, should, by discourse, make it known, and earnestly show forth their devotion, in celebrating by the praises of the Most High, the glory and honor of the Blessed Mother, who is Queen of Heaven, the Gate of Paradise, the Help of Christians, the assured Port of salvation, and the Anchor of the hope of sinners, who place their trust in her. By the tenor of these presents, we expressly ordain in perpetuity, that if, henceforward, any preacher or any other person among our subjects, of whatever rank or condition he may be, should not faithfully observe this general ordinance, he shall be expelled from their convents and houses; and that so long as they maintain this adverse opinion, they shall, as our enemies, remain without the bounds of our kingdoms. So willing and ordaining, with full knowledge and deliberation, under pain of incurring our displeasure and anger, all and every one of our servants, who are, or who will be, on this or the other side of the sea, to observe and cause to be observed with the greatest diligence and respect our present edict, as soon as it shall be made known to them, and that each, in his district, shall, in the usual places, publish it solemnly and with the sound of the trumpet, so that no person can show cause of ignorance, and that the devotion of the Immaculate Conception of the Most Blessed Virgin, which the faithful have long preserved in their hearts, may be increased more and more, and that we may no longer hear certain persons of the opposite opinion giving expression to their sentiments. In faith whereof we ordain that these presents be dispatched, authorized by our seal attached.

"Given at Valencia, February 2nd., the day of the Purification of the Most Blessed Virgin, in the year of our Lord, 1384, and the eighth of our reign.

"Don Juan, Rex, &c."

In 1506, an association of the Immaculate Conception was formed in Spain by Cardinal Ximenes; where the Festival of the Conception is celebrated with great solemnity. Almost every sermon is commenced with an invocation in honor of this mystery, and of the Blessed Sacrament, as follows: "Praise be to the most Holy Sacrament of the altar, and to the Immaculate Conception of the Virgin Mary, our Lady, conceived without original sin at the first instant of her life. Amen."[7] But it is not only in festivals, and solemn acts of religion, that the people of Spain exhibit their devotion to this belief. It has incorporated itself with their daily life; and the most ordinary form of salutation of one entering a house, before wishing good day, is; *Ave purissima*; to which the proprietor returns answer; *Sin peccado concebida sanctissima*.

> **V.** "Hail most pure."
> **R.** "Without sin conceived, most holy."

10. From the time of Henry I, King of England and Duke of Normandy, the Festival of the Immaculate Conception was celebrated at Rouen with extraordinary solemnity. An ancient copy of the history of Rouen says, "From the time of the first institution of this Festival, an association was founded of the most illustrious persons of this city; who even yet, on every year, select from among themselves the head of the Confraternity; which, erecting a platform

---

7. "Praised be the most holy sacrament of the altar and the Immaculate Conception of the Virgin Mary, Our Lady, conceived without original sin at the first moment of her being. Amen."

for all orators, in every language, offers a valuable premium to those who, in the most ornate, appropriate, and perfect style, should celebrate the praise of the Virgin Mary, on the subject of the Immaculate Conception, by hymns, odes, sonnets, ballads, royal chants, &c. (*Antiquities of Rouen, by N. Taillipied.*)

11. Through the zeal of St. Anselm, Archbishop of Canterbury (who died 1109 A.D.), the Festival of the Immaculate Conception of the Blessed Virgin was celebrated in England. Hence the Fathers of the Council of London, in the year 1328, issued the following mandamus concerning it: "Adhering to the example of our venerable predecessor, St. Anselm, who, among some other more ancient festivals, thought proper to add the solemnity of the Conception, we ordain, and command that the *Festival of the Conception*, published in all the Churches of our Province of Canterbury, be celebrated appropriately and with the usual solemnities."[8]

There is an epistle of St. Anselm's extant which corroborates the evidences of the prevalence of the Festival. It commences, "*Conceptio Dei Genitricis*," "It will delight you to hear me narrate, with many evident proofs, in what manner the Conception of the venerable Mother of God is celebrated and declared in England, France, and other countries." Whether or not there be just reason to doubt the genuineness of this epistle, it dates from St. Anselm's time, and it is certain that the Festival of the Conception was celebrated in England during the eleventh century — the period when he flourished.[9] From thence it was translated to Normandy, Gaul, and to the Church at Lyons.[10] It was this which gave occasion to the celebrated letter (alleged of St. Bernard) to the Canons of the Church of Lyons, complaining against their addition of a solemn festival in their Church, for which they had neither the counsel nor example of the Church of Rome to substantiate it. Some have, from this, supposed that St. Bernard was not favorable to the Festival itself. He was one of the most ardent friends and advocates of the privileges of the Blessed Virgin. He had no thought of derogating from her

---

8. "Venerabilis Anselmi prædecessoris nostri qui post alia quædam ipsius antiquiora solemnia, Conceptionis solemne superaddere dignum duxit, vestigiis inhærentes statuimus, et firmiter præcipiendo mandamus, quatenus *Festum* Conceptionis prædictæ cunctis Ecclesiis nostris Cantuariensis provinciæ festive, et solemniter de cætero celebretur." — *Concil. Angliæ, Tom.* ii, p. 494.

9. The Festival had already been established in Hungary 800 A.D, two centuries before St. Anselm's death.

10. Christianus Lupus, *ad Concilium Moguntinum, sub Leone IV, tom, iii, Vet. Edit.*, p. 497.

honor, and this letter will be vindicated in the proper place.[11]

He was jealous of the least semblance of innovation, and zealous to oppose it wherever and in whomsoever it appeared. But suppose he doubted the Immaculate Conception, and disapproved of the Festival — St. Thomas, the Apostle, doubted the resurrection of Christ. Nevertheless he confessed Him and adored when he put his hands into His wounds. So did the Saints — as St. Anselm — who, when they learned this truth, strenuously labored that the Festival of the Immaculate Conception should everywhere be celebrated throughout the world. Neither did St. Bernard's epistle avail anything against it. It steadily increased and spread; so that Germany and Belgium were added to the number of those countries in which it was observed, and none questioned that the Blessed Virgin was conceived without original sin. In 1136, St. Norbertus instituted a religious order under the invocation of the Immaculate Conception of the Blessed Virgin.

12. The Festival of the Immaculate Conception began to be celebrated at Rome about 1221 A. D. as Praeses, Bishop of Albania, and Cardinal, testifies. (*In Sent. Dist. lib. iii, p. 31.*) Speculator, in the thirteenth, and John Andrew, in the fourteenth century (both renowned Canonists), testify that the Festival of the Conception was habitually solemnized and approved. Bazilius corroborates their testimony. (*Ad Vitam. Papar. Avenion. p. 370.*) Sixtus IV attained the Chair of Peter in 1471 A. D., and soon after decreed the public veneration of the Mystery of the Immaculate Conception. He instituted a special Office and Mass in honor of it, and sanctioned by indulgences the solemn observance of the rite throughout the Christian world. In a second Constitution, published in 1483 A. D., we read the following in reference to the Office and Mass of Leonard di Nogaroli of Verona: "Whereas the Holy Roman Church publicly celebrates the solemn Festival of the Conception of the undefiled and ever Virgin Mary." This Office was afterwards removed from the Breviary by Pope Saint Pius V, and the one now used substituted in its place; the reason of this change being to obtain uniformity of worship throughout the Church, which the multitude of offices then in use forbade. Clement VIII elevated this office to a rite of the *Double Major*. Clement IX added the observance of the *Octave*; and Clement XI, 1700 A. D., so amplified the privileges of this Festival, that it was thenceforward numbered among those which are, throughout the universal Church, observed by *Precept.*

---

11. Chapter IX, St. Bernard. It may, however, be here stated that this interpretation of the letter seems unreasonable; since he could not be ignorant of the fact that many Churches of the West had, from a very remote date, observed this Festival, and that the Eastern Churches had very generally observed it with great devotion; and that it was among them deemed a holy day long before the Emperor, Emmanuel Komnenos, enforced its observance by an edict — 1150 A. D. — *Apud. Balsam, in nomoncan. Photii.* There are many probabilities that St. Bernard never wrote this letter, and that it has been erroneously attributed to him.

(*In Constitut.* 40, *ejus Bullar.*, p. 90.) Benedict XIV formally established the Festival by Consistorial Decree.[12]

Such was the ardor and devotion of the Church, in regard to the Immaculate Conception, that it had now, for a long time, been earnestly desired that it should be solemnly defined as a Dogma of faith. With this view, the Cardinal Princes, Prelates, and Theologians; the Catholic Kings, and Christian people, supplicated the Supreme Pontiffs, solemnly to define it. Popes Paul V, Gregory XV, Urban VIII, Alexander VII, and Clement, both the XI and XII of this name, and others, were importuned to this end. But the time had not yet arrived, in the councils of the Most High, for this happy consummation of the question; and, while they renewed the Constitutions which had been issued in previous reigns, in regard to the Festival of the Conception, they resolved not to exceed the bounds which had limited their predecessors. Not that they held any opinion contrary to the Immaculate Conception; for they all declared with Benedict XIV: *Toto Nos animo Immaculatæ Conceptionis B. Mariæ sequi sententiam;*" "With all our heart we follow the opinion of the Immaculate Conception of the Most Blessed Mary." The succeeding pontiffs also, as it will presently appear, availed themselves of every season of sunshine and peace in the Church to enlarge the spiritual favors and blessings originally attached to the devout recital of the Office and Mass, appropriate to this Festival. And, happily for the Church and the world, the clouds and storms which obscured the atmosphere have been dispersed: "the winter is past, the rain is over and gone," and the great sign, which appeared in the heaven, clothed with the sun, the moon under her feet, and crowned with twelve stars, now appears in the full glory of her majesty; adorned with those immaculate perfections with which it pleased God to endow her from the first instant of her creation; and the voice of millions in heaven and on earth hails her, as did the Angel Gabriel: "Begotten in grace: Blessed among women; conceived without the least stain of sin."[13] It is a mystery of love and benediction to man; in which, as Alban Butler beautifully remarks, "the Blessed Mary appears, pure and glorious, shining among the daughters of Adam, as 'a lily among thorns.' (*Cant. xi, 2.*)

---

12. The following is that portion of the Decree more immediately relating to the establishment of the Festival. "In Festo Conceptionis B. V. in Liberiana Basilica deinceps sacra solemnia peragenda coram Papa, DD. Cardinalibus, et Prælatis quibus in Capellis Pontificiis certus constitutus est locus; eumque diem inter illos, quibus ejusmodi sacra solemniter ad eundem modum celebrantur, adnumeravimus."

13. It is a remarkable fact, which should excite the attention of every reflecting mind, that the Catholic Church alone, of all that call themselves Christian, fulfills the prophecy recorded in *St. Luke, chap.* i, 48: "From henceforth all generations shall call me blessed." All sects not only do not venerate the Blessed Virgin, but they ignore all her prerogatives. Even that one, which affects to be most primitive in its faith and mode of worship, and which is said to be reformed the least, makes no more account of her. Scott, a favorite commentator with that denomination, calls her "a poor sinful mortal," and indulges in other dishonoring terms respecting her. *See his commentary on St. Luke, chap.* i, 28. It is not strange, therefore, that many of his brethren are rank Socinians. They who are taught to dishonor the Mother, are not likely to reverence the Son.

To her, from the moment of her Conception, God said: 'Thou art all beautiful, my love, and there is no spot in thee.' (*Cant. iv, 7.*) She was the 'enclosed garden' which the serpent could never enter; and 'the sealed fountain,' which he never defiled. (*Cant. iv, 12.*) She was the throne and the tabernacle of the true Solomon, and the Ark of the Testament to contain, not corruptible manna, but the Author of the incorruptible life of our souls. Saluting her with these epithets, in exultation and praise, let us sing with the Church: 'This is the Conception of the glorious Virgin Mary, of the seed of Abraham, sprung from the tribe of Judah, illustrious of the house of David, whose life by its brightness, illustrates all Churches.'" (*Feast Concep. L. Sts. Dec. 8.*)

That the Conception of the Blessed Virgin was Immaculate is sufficiently attested by the institution of this Festival; for the Church celebrates no event as a festival which is not perfectly holy. To conclude this point, therefore, we say with Hugo of St. Victor: "The tree is known by its fruits. If the Lamb was always Immaculate, always Immaculate must the Mother also have been." (*Coll. iii, de Verb. Imm. Con.*) And again, with the same: "*O Digna Digni;*" "The worthy Mother of a worthy Son." None but an Immaculate Mother could be worthy of such a Son; and none but Jesus could be worthy of such a Mother.

CHAPTER VIII

Testimony of the Saints and Eminent Writers Subsequent to the Fifth Century, and During the Medieval Times

IT IS CLEAR FROM THE EVIDENCE ALREADY ADDUCED in favor of the Immaculate Conception of the Blessed Virgin, that the doctrine is no novelty of the nineteenth century; and that the trivial sneer, "I thought your Church never changed!" is a solemn and everlasting truth. The Church is the pillar and the ground of truth; to keep and preserve it in which, it is impressed with the divine signet of "the Father of lights, with whom there is no change, nor shadow of alteration." (*St. James, chap.* i, 17.) Did no other evidence exist, therefore, than that which has been already adduced, this doctrine would be triumphantly established as the ancient belief of the Catholic Church. But, as already intimated, it is not only the sacred Liturgies, and solemn Festivals, and the writers of the primitive ages, that, beyond all controversy, establish it as a living, tangible fact. Innumerable writers, and the Christians of every rank, and in every age, unite in this confession of Faith. The remains of the Apostolic age, and the four centuries immediately succeeding, affording, as they do, an ample range of undeniable proof, it is only necessary to complete the golden chain of testimony, by adding some new links for every century since those times, in order to show that the doctrine once, delivered to the Saints, has been committed to faithful men, who have never betrayed their trust. The mine is rich and inexhaustible. To elaborate the material is the simple task before us. And if in the mouths of two or three witnesses, a truth shall be established, on how firm a foundation does this truth rest, in the concurrent testimony of the Saints of every age!

1. St. Fulgentius, Bishop of Ruspia (501 A.D.), says: "The full grace of benediction was restored to Mary, which grace indeed, Eve, having been created without sin, lost by sinning."[1] Again: "Mary was created in the state of original innocence, which original innocence Eve had lost on account of sin."[2] In another place he says that, "the Angel in saluting Mary, *full of grace,* indicated that the original sentence of first condemnation was absolutely

---

1. "Plenam benedictionis gratiam restitutam fuisse Mariæ, quam quidem gratiam Eva, sine peccato condita, peccando amiserat."
2. "Conditam in statu innocentiæ originalis fuisse Mariam, quam originalem innocentiam amiserat ob peccatum Eva."

destroyed in her." (*Sermo. de Laudibus Mariæ.*)

2. St. Sophronius, Patriarch of Jerusalem (630 A.D.), says: "The Virgin is therefore called immaculate, because she is in nothing corrupt."[3]

3. St. Ildephonsus, Archbishop of Toledo (667 A.D.), says: "The flesh of the Virgin assumed from Adam, did not admit of the taint of Adam; and it is certain, that she (Mary) was free from original sin."[4]

4. St. John of Damascus (700 A.D.) writes: "When the time had arrived that the Mother of God and Virgin should spring from Anne, nature dared not prevent the offspring of Grace, but waited until grace had produced its fruit."[5]

    He expresses himself more plainly in the second discourse concerning the Assumption. He there beautifully says, in regard to the Blessed Virgin: "*Ad hunc paradisum serpens aditum non habuit.*" — "Into this paradise the serpent hath not entered." St. John of Damascus in another place says: "*Matris Dei et servorum Dei infinitum est discrimen.*" *Orat. i, de Assump.* — "There is an infinite distance between Mother of God and servant of God." Again he still more plainly says: "He preserved the soul as well as the body of the Virgin, as was befitting her who was about to receive God into her womb; for He being holy, dwells only with the holy."[6]

5. Idiota, who, according to Bellarmine, lived about 800 A. D., agrees with St. Thomas, St. Ildephonsus, a Lapide, St. Bernardine, St. Lawrence Justinian, and many others, in applying those words of the Canticles to the Virgin's Immaculate Conception: "Thou art all beautiful, O my love, and there is no spot in thee." He says: "Thou art most fair, O most glorious Virgin, not in part, but wholly; and the stain of sin, whether mortal, or venial, or original, is not upon thee."[7] He adds: "Thou hast found peculiar grace, O most sweet Virgin, for thou wast preserved from the original stain." (*Contemp. B. M., vol. 3, cap. 2.*)

6. St. Nicephorus of Constantinople (811 A.D.) says: "The Blessed Virgin Mary

---

3. "Virginem ideo dici immaculatam, quia in nullo corrupta est." — *In Epist., cap. 6, tom. 3, p. 307*
4. "Caro Virginis ex Adam assumpta, maculas Adam non admisit; et constat eam (Mariam) ab originali peccato fuisse immunem." — *Sermo. ii. de Assump. B. Virginis.*
5. "Quoniam futurum erat, ut Dei Genitrix ac Virgo ex Anna oriretur, natura gratiæ foetum antevertere minime ausa est, verum tantisper expectavit dum gratia fructum suum produxisset." — *Orat. 1, de Nativ., B.V.M.*
6. "Cum Virginis una cum corpore animam conservasset, ut earn decebat, quæ Deura in sino suo exceptura erat; sanctus enim ipse cum sit, in Sanctis requiescit." — *Lib. iv, de Fide Orth., cap. 15.*
7. "Tota pulchra es, Virgo gloriosissima, non in parte, sed in toto; et macula peccati sive mortalis, sive venialis, sive originalis non est in te." — *In Contemp. B. V., cap.3*

was pre-sanctified in soul and body."[8]

7. St. Peter Damian lived during the tenth age. He entirely disproves that the Blessed Virgin was stained with any sin, actual, venial, or original. (*See Serm. ii, de Nativ. Mariæ.*) And in his sermon on the Nativity of John the Baptist, he teaches that "the Blessed Virgin was more perfect than John the Baptist and Jeremiah, since she was created without original sin, while they were sanctified in the womb."

8. St. Bruno, Patriarch of the Carthusians (999 A.D.), explaining the 20th verse of the 101st Psalm, "From heaven the Lord hath looked upon the earth," has the following: "From heaven the Lord hath looked upon the earth; when, from his royal throne (descending), He entered the Virgin's womb. This is the incorrupt earth which the Lord hath blessed, (being made) free, therefore, from every taint of sin."[9]

9. St. Anselm (1040 A.D.) says: "If Jeremiah, who was destined to prophesy in lamentations, was sanctified in the womb, and if John, the forerunner of the Lord, was filled with the Holy Ghost from his mother's womb, who will dare to affirm that the Mercy-Seat of the whole world was destitute of the illumination of the Holy Ghost at the very instant of her conception? Was the wisdom of God impotent to build (for Himself) a pure habitation, free from every stain of human imperfection? He preserved the Angels from sin, amidst the others sinning: was He not able to preserve His Mother free from the sins of others?" He adds in the same sermon: "If the two Prophets, on account of the dignity of their office, were sanctified before their birth, the dignity of Mother of God, which is far greater than theirs, demands that the Blessed Virgin should be sanctified, not only before her birth, but at the very beginning of her Conception, that she might possess grace suitable to her dignity; for if she was subsequently restored through grace, what more would God have conferred upon her than upon Jeremiah and John?"[10]

10. St. Arnold of Chartres says: "The flesh of Mary and of Christ is one, and hence I esteem the glory of the Son to be, not so much common to both, as

---

8. "Beatam Virginem Mariam in anima, et corpore præmundatam fuisse."

9. "Dominus de coelo in terram, aspexit dum de regalibus sedibus, in uterum Virginis venit. Hæc est incorrupta ilia terra cui benedixit Dominus, ab omni propterea peccati contagione libera."

10. "Si Jeremias, qui in gemitibus prophetaturus, in vulva est sanctificatus, et Preacursor Domini Joannes, Spiritu Sancto ex utero matris est repletus, quis disserere audeat totius sæculi propitiatorium, mox in suæ Conceptionis exordio Spiritus Sancti illuminatione destitutum? Impotens ne fuit Sapientia Dei mundum habitaculum condere, remotum omni labe conditionis humanæ? Angelos, aliis peccantibus, a peccato reservavit, et Matrem ab aliorum peccatis exortem servare non potuit?" — *De Conceptione Virginis.*

the same."[11] This had been already forcibly expressed by St. Augustine, who says: "That the flesh of Jesus is the same as that of Mary, in such a manner that the flesh of the Savior after His resurrection was the very same which He received from his Mother." (*Sermo de Assump.*)

11. St. Yvo Carnotensis. (1115 A.D.) Among twenty-four sermons of this saint, still extant, there is one concerning the Nativity of Christ, in which he says: "In what manner Christ hath sanctified the Mother of His flesh we may perceive, so that thence the Catholic may rejoice, and the Heretic be confounded; since he hath erased from it every spot, both of original and of actual sin, and assuming flesh of her flesh He hath made it divinely pure."[12]

12. St. Dominic (1201 A.D.), thus speaks: "As the first Adam was formed of virgin earth, never accursed, so it behooved the second Adam, Christ, whose Virgin Mother was never accursed."[13]

13. St. Bonaventure (1275 A.D.), in his second sermon, *de Beata Virgine*, says: "Our Lady was full of grace in her sanctification; that is to say, grace preservative against the dishonor of original sin."[14] Again, in another place: "It is the special privilege of Mary, that above all men she was most pure from every sin."[15]

14. Dennis the Carthusian (1320 A.D.) says: "God the Creator of all things, about to construct a worthy habitation for His Son, adorned her with all pleasing gifts."[16] This accords with the language of the Church; which, in her prayer, in the Office of the Immaculate Conception, thus expresses the same belief: "Omnipotent and eternal God, who by the co-operation of the Holy Ghost, didst prepare the body and soul of the glorious Virgin Mother, that she might become a worthy habitation for thy Son," The Greek Church also, in the Mass for the Annunciation, asserts the same privilege of Mary. It says: "By a singular providence, God hath ordained that the Most Holy Virgin should be perfectly pure from the very beginning of her life, as was

---

11. "Una est Mariæ et Christi caro; atque adeo filii gloriam cum matre non tam communem judico, quam eamdem." *De Laud. Virginis.*
12. "Quomodo Matrem carnis suæ sanctificaverit, audiamus, ut inde lætetur Catholicus, et Hæreticus confundatur, omnem quippe nævum tam originalis, quam actualis culpæ in ea delevit, sicque carnem de ejus carne sumens in divinam munditiam transformavit."
13. "Sicut primus Adam fuit in terra virgine, et nunquam maledicta formatus, ita decuit in secundo Adam fieri, id est Christo, cujus Mater Virgo nunquam fuit maledicta."
14. "Domina nostra fuit plena gratia in sua sanctificatione; gratia, scilicet, præservativa contra foeditatem originalis culpæ."
15. "Primum Mariæ privilegium est, quod super omnes homines ab omni peccato sit purissima." — *In Speculo, B. M. Virginis.*
16. "Omnium artifex Deus, filio suo dignum habitaculum fabricaturus, eam omnium gratificantium charismatum copia adornavit." — *Lib. ii; de Laud. Virginis, Art. 2.*

becoming her who was to be a Mother worthy of Christ."

15. St. Vincent Ferrer (1417 A.D.), while expounding these words of Genesis, *Let there be light*, says: "Let it not be believed that it was as in us, who are conceived in sins; but, as soon as the soul (of the Blessed Virgin) was created, it was sanctified, and immediately the Angels celebrated the Festival of the Conception in heaven."[17]

16. St. Bernardine of Sienna (1438 A.D.), says: "It is certain that God created Adam and Eve without sin; but it is not to be believed that the Son of God Himself wished to be born of a Virgin, and to take her flesh, which should be stained with any original sin. Rather, it is to be believed that He wished to assume most pure flesh, and that His Mother was more (pure) than Adam and Eve, who were created without original sin."[18]

17. St. Lawrence Justinian (1440 A.D.), speaks thus concerning the Blessed Virgin: "From her very Conception, she was anticipated with benedictions; no one is excepted from original sin but her, who hath begotten the Savior."[19]

18. St. Thomas of Villanova (1488 A.D.), says: "Nothing was ever given to any of the Saints, that did not shine more pre-eminently in Mary, from the beginning of her life."[20] Speaking of the fitness of such immaculate perfection in her, who was preordained to be the Mother of God, he says: "When God elects anyone to a certain dignity, He also fits him for it; hence, God, having chosen Mary for His Mother, rendered her worthy of it by His grace, according to what the Angel said to her; 'Thou hast found grace with God.'[21] From this he concludes that the Blessed Virgin never committed even so much as a venial sin; otherwise, he says, she would not have been a worthy mother of God, since the ignominy of the Mother would be that of

---

17. "Non credatur quod fuerit sicut in nobis, qui in peccatis concipimur; sed statim, atque anima fuit creata, fuit sanctificata, et statim Angeli in coelo fecerunt festum Conceptionis."

18. "Certum est, quod Deus creavit Adamum et Hevam sine peccato; modo non est credendum, quod ipse Filius Dei voluerit nasci ex Virgine, et sumere ejus carnem, quæ esset maculata aliquo peccato originali. Imo credendum est quod voluerit sumere carnem purissimam, et quod ejus Mater fuit plusquam Adam et Heva, qui creati fuerunt sine peccato originali." — *Vol. 3, lib. 4, serm. 4.*

19. "Ab ipsa Conceptione fuit in benedictionibus præventa; ab originali delicto nullus excipitur præter illam, quæ genuit Salvatorem."

20. "Nihil unquam alicui Sanctorum concessum est, quod a principio vitæ cumulatius non præfulgeat in Maria." — *Sermo ii, de Assump.*

21. Beata autem Virgo fuit electa divinitus, ut esset Mater Dei; et ideo non est dubitandum, quin Deus, per suam gratiam, eam ad hoc idoneam reddidit, secundum quod Angelus ad eam dicit — *"Invenisti gratiam apud Deum!"* — St. Luc., i, 30. In Corp. 3 p. q. 27.

the Son.[22]

19. St. Thomas, Archbishop of Valentia (1530 A.D.), says: "As the sun brightly shining, thou hast gone forth into the world, O Mary, since by the brightness of the true Sun, thou hast been illuminated (*Adumbrata* — overshadowed) in thy Immaculate Conception."[23]

20. The eloquent voice of Bossuet (1627 A.D.), that incomparable writer and defender of the faith, is raised in favor of the Immaculate Conception. He says: "There is in the opinion of the Immaculate Conception, a certain innate force, which brings conviction to devout souls. After articles of faith I see nothing more certain. It is for this reason that I feel no surprise, that the school of the Parisian Theologians, obliges all her children to defend this doctrine. As for me, I feel joy and satisfaction in following, at this time, her intentions. After having been nourished with her milk, I willingly submit myself to her ordinances; and particularly so, as such ordinances seem to me to be in accordance with the wishes of the Church. The sentiments of the Church redound to the honor of the Conception of Mary." (*Sermo de Conceptione.*)

Such is the evidence, such the saintly names, of men, who have illustrated every age, and their glorious lives, by the most pious and tender devotion to the Immaculate Mother of God; men, who have approached the Altar of the Immaculate Conception, with prayers, and vows, and hymns of thanksgiving; men, who have exhausted every figure, every verse and beautiful trait of human language, to express, their faith in the Immaculate Conception; men, who have thought it no injury to the honor of God, to love, and venerate, and praise His Mother; men, who, on the contrary, have believed that they amplified and extolled the Divine Majesty by magnifying the prerogatives of her, who was chosen before the foundations of the earth were laid, to cradle the Divine Architect upon her knee; and who, on this account, have thought it more easy to err, in falling short of giving her due praise, than to blaspheme God by praising her too much; since, as it is not possible to comprehend her exalted dignity; so, is it not possible for the tongue of men or angels to praise her enough. The golden chain of evidence is complete. No link is wanting. Every age has its representatives of Mary's Immaculate Conception. It is easier to continue the narrative than it is to decide where to pause. St. Camillus de Lellis, St. Francis Regis, St. Fidelis of Sigmaringen, St. Joseph Calasanctius, St. Vincent de Paul, John Duns, Peter Aureolus, Francis de Mayronis, John Bassoli, William de

---

22. Non fuisset idonea Mater Dei, si peccasset aliquando, quia ignominia Matris ad filium redundasset. — *Sermo 3, Natal. Virginis.*

23. "Sicut aurora valde rutilans in mundum prodiisti, O Maria, quando veri solis fulgore adumbrata in conceptione tua immaculata fuisti." — *Serm. in Concept B. V. M.*

Rubione, Peter de Aquila Scotello, Thomas of Strasbourg, Francis Martini, Peter d'Ailly, John of Segovia, Alphonsus Tosta, Nicolas de Cusa, William Verilungo, Nicolas Orbello, Dennis Rickel, James de Valence, Gabriel Biel, Perbarto de Temeswar, Ambrose Spiera, Marsile d'Inghen, John Tritheme, Henriquez, Comitolo, Vasquez, Pinsanno, Salmeron, St. Aloysius Gonzaga, St. Francis Carracciolo, have all been distinguished children of Mary; whose evidence in favor of the doctrine of the Immaculate Conception, if mentioned here, might add beauty and weight to the mass of testimony, but would not intrinsically increase its force.

It is needless, therefore, to push the investigation further in this direction. The Immaculate Conception is clearly proved to have been, like all the Dogmas of the Catholic Church, ever taught by the Saints of all ages, and held in veneration by the Catholic world. With the exception therefore of St. Bernard, and St. Thomas Aquinas, whose testimony demands a special notice, this portion of the argument will be concluded in the beautiful language of St. Alphonsus Liguori. In demonstrating the dignity of the Immaculate Mother, and the necessity of her special prerogative, he says; "The Immaculate Conception was proper in reference to the Eternal Father, because Mary was His Daughter; it was proper in reference to God the Son, because Mary was His Mother; and it was proper in reference to the Holy Ghost, because Mary was His Spouse." (*Glories of Mary.*) How, with less than immaculate perfection, could Mary be supposed capable, or fit, to enjoy such intimate relations with the infinite Godhead, the Immaculate Three in One?

Engraving of Saint Bernard kneeling before the Virgin and Child by Claude Mellan, 1640.

CHAPTER IX

St. Bernard

ST. BERNARD, WHO FLOURISHED DURING the early part of the twelfth century, was distinguished not more for his piety and zeal, than for his tender affection and pious regard for the Mother of God. When she was the theme of his discourse, the singular sweetness and eloquence of his language, without losing any of its sublimity, became still more refined and purified. The Blessed Virgin was, in his view, the true symbol of purity and love; the tender Mediatrix between man and her divine Son. St. Bernard, therefore, is inexhaustible in the effusions of his love and gratitude towards the Virgin Mother. The following passage, taken from his fourth sermon upon the *Salve Regina*, though impaired by the translation, will give some indication of the glowing eloquence of this saint when speaking of her and her Immaculate Conception:

"Thou, Mary, hast been innocent of all sins, actual and original. Thou alone, of all the human race. Hence, with St. Augustine, when sin is the question, we wish no mention made of thee, Mary. We believe that greater virtue hath been granted to Mary to subdue sin in every part, because she merited and was destined to conceive and bring forth Him who had no sin. 'In every part,' he says; that is, on the part of original sin, and on the part of actual sin. She alone excepted, all others, then, can only exclaim, 'If we say that we have no sin, we deceive ourselves, and the truth is not in us.' I believe, with pious faith, that thou hast been absolved in the womb of thy mother from all original sin. This is no vain faith — no false opinion. Both reason and authority enjoin it. If others were sanctified before their birth, how much more thou, Mother of the Lord! Jeremiah was sanctified, and John the Baptist was filled with the Holy Ghost, from the womb. But thou alone, Mary, Mother of God, hast possessed the full grace of the Holy Ghost, which they had only in part; since the Angel Gabriel hath saluted thee '*Full* of grace.' Thy odor long before hath the Patriarch, Isaac, perceived, when, in blessing his son, he said, 'Behold the smell of my son is as the smell of a plentiful field which the Lord hath blessed.' (*Gen., chap. xxvii, 27.*) Thou art the plentiful field; full of virtue, full of grace. Thou dost bring forth the chosen fruit, which is the Bread of Angels. The Lord hath blessed thee. Thee, I say, the Lord hath blessed, so that, through thee blessed, life might come, as death proceeded through the malediction of Eve. Thou it is of whom Solomon hath said, 'Who is she that cometh forth as the morning rising, fair as the moon, bright as the sun, terrible as an army set in array?' (*Cant., chap.* vi, 10.) The morning ever follows the night; the night precedes the morning. But why is the night cheerless and dark, unless because of original sin — cheerless through concupiscence, dark through ignorance? Thou, therefore, goest forth as the morning, bright and rosy, because original sin hath been overcome by thee in thy mother's womb. Thou hast been born bright in the knowledge of truth, and rosy in the love of virtue. Hence is it that the Holy Church honors, with festivals, thy sacred Nativity; which she doth not for any others. She honors the nativity of none but thee, except that of thy divine Son, and of his forerunner, who was full of the Holy Ghost from his mother's womb. Since, therefore, so many clear, inspired authors, testify to thy innocence from the womb, who shall further doubt that thou art sacred, and begotten in this world Immaculate?"

The whole tenor of this beautiful passage asserts the Immaculate Conception. The saint first declares the Blessed Virgin "innocent of all sins, actual and original." Then, in support of his faith, he happily and forcibly adduces the testimony of St. Augustine, who would have no question of sin entertained when the Blessed Virgin was meant. For she had greater virtue — grace — granted to her, than any of the descendants of Adam, to subdue sin in every part; "on the part of original, and on the part of actual sin." Mary was, in his belief, absolved from the very imputation of original sin. And finally, after having adduced the examples of Jeremiah and John the Baptist, to show that they, though endowed with extraordinary grace before their birth, fell far short of the measure of grace which was conferred upon her, he triumphantly asks, "Who shall further doubt that she was begotten Immaculate?"[1]

It is a common maxim in theology that no grace has been ever granted to any creature, but with which the Blessed Virgin has been more richly endowed. This has been expressed by St. Bernard in the following manner: "We certainly cannot suspect that what has been bestowed on the chosen among mortals, should be withheld from the Blessed Virgin."[2]

St. Bernard therefore believed that Eve was not created more perfect than

---

1. It has been inferred, from the passage just quoted, that St. Bernard meant to affirm that Jeremiah and John the Baptist were on an equality with the Blessed Virgin in their sanctification before birth. Nothing could be farther from the saint's meaning, and, indeed, from his plain expressions. Jeremiah is represented as sanctified, and John the Baptist as filled with the Holy Ghost, from the womb. But the Blessed Virgin alone is represented as "innocent of all sins, actual and original," by the special favor of heaven: as, being the Mother of God, it behooved her to be immaculate, that she might communicate to, and afford an immaculate body for Him who was to conquer sin and death by His own death upon the cross.
2. "Quod vel paucis mortalium constat esse collatum, fas certe non est suspicari tantæ Virgini esse negatum." — *Epist.*, 174.

Mary. That such was his constant opinion is clearly inferred from the passage already quoted. Eve was created Immaculate. The saint, in his discourse, affirmed the same of Mary, because she was destined to conceive and bring forth Him who had no sin. He expressed the same idea in other words, when speaking of the necessity which must force, as it were, the Creator to choose such a Mother as, from her Immaculate perfections, should be worthy of Him who had no sin. He says: "The Creator of men, to be born of man, must choose such a Mother for Himself as He knew to be most fit."[3] Surely it is inconsistent to suppose that God, who sanctified two of his servants before their birth, and who has power over the clay, to make of it a vessel to honor, and who can make clean whom He will, would suffer her whom He had chosen for a Mother to be contaminated with sin. God created Eve Immaculate. He was certainly able to bestow the same grace on Mary; and without it, redemption would have been, impossible. And when St. Bernard afterwards exclaimed: "Thou alone hast been found worthy, that in thy virginal hall the King of kings should choose His first mansion," he could only be understood, consistently with himself, to mean that she had been ever exempted from sin; since, if she had been tainted with either actual or original sin, she would not have been "worthy" to have received the King.[4]

The Holy Ghost has figuratively called His Spouse, Mary, "A garden enclosed, a fountain sealed up." (*Cant., chap. iv, 12.*) These words have always been applied to the Blessed Virgin. St. Jerome's commentary upon them has ever been the accepted explication of their mystic meaning. Mary, he says, is this enclosed garden, and sealed fountain; for the enemies never entered to harm her, but she was always uninjured, remaining holy in soul and body. (*Epist. x, ad E. de Assump.*) St. Bernard has the following beautiful variation of this idea: "Thou art an enclosed garden, in which the hand of sin hath never entered to rob it of its flowers."[5] If so, it is equally as clear that St. Bernard believed the Immaculate Conception as it is when he said the Blessed Virgin was "innocent of all sins, actual and original;" or, when he said that she "was begotten Immaculate."

The passages here adduced are clear and decisive of St. Bernard's belief in the doctrine of the Immaculate Conception. It is both false and unjust to impute to him the contrary opinion. The only foundation alleged for such an assertion is the celebrated letter addressed, as it is alleged, by the holy Doctor to the Chapter of the Church at Lyons, which had determined, after the example of other Churches, to adopt the custom of celebrating the Festival of the Immaculate Conception of the Blessed Virgin. The holy Abbot opposed the institution of this Festival in that Church. Without entering into a critical examination of the question as to whether this letter has been unjustly attributed to St. Bernard,

---

3. "Nascens de homine Factor hominum talem sibi debuit eligere matrem, qualem se decere scie-
bat." — *Hom. 3, Super Miss.*

4. "Tu sola inventa es digna, ut in tua virginali aula Rex regum primam sibi mansionem eligeret." —
In Deipara ad Virg.

5. "Hortus conclusus tu es, ad quem deflorandum manus peccatorum nunquam introivit."

as many eminent theologians affirm; but admitting it, on the contrary, to be authentic, it in no manner whatever disproves the belief of the holy Doctor in the Immaculate Conception. He censured the Chapter of the Church at Lyons for instituting the Festival without first consulting the authority of the Apostolic See; alleging the danger to be apprehended from the example of a Church so influential as that of Lyons taking upon itself so important an office.

At this date the Festival of the Immaculate Conception had not been enjoined by precept in the Church. The clergy and people of particular Churches had simply by their own private devotion, and in continuation of practices which had obtained from the earliest times, venerated the Mother of God under this title and by this Festival. St. Bernard, full of zeal for the authority of the Holy See, and anxious to prevent all innovations and errors from creeping into the Church through private fancy or the caprice of individuals; and considering that this Festival had never obtained at Lyons; and reflecting, on the one hand, that the Holy See had commanded nothing in regard to it; and, on the other, that if the rite were admitted in a Church so ancient and so illustrious as was that of Lyons, it being the first Church of Gaul, feared lest its eminent example, in assuming the authority of establishing new rites, without first obtaining permission from the Holy See, might be to the prejudice of its prerogative.

As already explained, the Church affirms the Conception of the Blessed Virgin in its *passive* sense. By an unauthorized institution of the Festival, there was danger of mistaking its proper object; and celebrating it, in a sense which the doctrine does not admit. That St. Bernard was thus apprehensive of the danger of mistaking the *active* for the *passive* Conception is evident from his mode of reasoning in the subsequent passages of his letter; and he therefore the more strenuously opposed it. He knew that if the Festival was duly authorized, and its object defined by the Apostolic See, there would be no cause of apprehension. He also considered, that the Conception, in its *passive* sense, was already celebrated in the Festival of the Nativity; and that the very title of *The Conception*, in addition to the former, might mislead them to regard it erroneously in its active sense. These considerations evidently swayed him; though, as before noted, he wrote chiefly to reprove the Chapter for their presumption in acting without the authority of the Apostolic See.

St. Bernard's letter, therefore, affords no reason for supposing that he disbelieved the Immaculate Conception as the Church holds it, namely, in the *passive* sense. It is not easy to comprehend how any should so charge him. Let us for a moment glance at the history of the question as he must have known it. It is certain that the Festival of the Conception was, from the earliest ages, celebrated by particular Churches, both in the East and in the West. In some places, as in Spain, it is traced to the Apostolic times. The Blessed Virgin is called Immaculate in every Ancient Liturgy; and the observance of the Festival continued to spread throughout the Christian world, though no precept had been issued by the Catholic Church enjoining it upon them. It was a pious devotion consonant to Ecclesiastical worship, to Catholic Faith, to right reason, and to the Sacred Scriptures. St. Bernard himself, as quoted above, has reasoned most eloquently upon it; and shown by various passages of Holy Writ, that it was foretold in the Old Law, and ratified in the New. As to the antiquity of the doctrine, we have seen it on every page of traditionary history; we have listened to it on the lips of every saint, and martyr, and holy Father, who has made the glories of Mary the theme of his discourse. We have heard St. Andrew, and St. James, Apostles; and St. Mark, the Evangelist; Justin Martyr, St. Irenaeus, Tertullian, Origen, St. Cyprian, St. Ephrem, St. Jerome, St. Chrysostom, St. Augustine, and an innumerable company of such men, exhaust the beauty and force of human language in illustrating and teaching this doctrine. And, as we have seen, St. Bernard, himself, who closes the series of Fathers of the Church, has said of the Immaculate Conception, "Mary is innocent of all sins, actual and original. This is no vain faith, no false opinion. Both reason and authority enjoin it." And he instances the evidence of St. Augustine, as a testimony of its being "commended by ancient tradition."

But the objection is repeated, that this holy Father disbelieved the doctrine. What then? High authority though he be, in matters of faith and morals, he is not the source of doctrine. We go far above and beyond him for a definition of the articles of faith. And if he had not believed it, which we disprove, it would have been but an error of judgment; and one, which, as in all other questions, he submitted to the decision of the Roman Church.

This consideration alone is sufficient to bring all controversy to a close; for, if St. Bernard was ready to admit his error, had he had any, and to conform to the decision of the Sovereign Pontiff, by his own confession, though he had been the strongest opponent and dishonorer of the Holy Virgin, he would, upon an adverse decision, have been the first to have supported her prerogative. But when we consider the tender devotion he always displayed towards the Mother of God, and know that he was ever one of the most ardent defenders of her privileges, it is impossible to believe, that he ever spoke or wrote, to detract in the least degree from her dignity. Had he lived to see the Festival of the Immaculate Conception universally celebrated by the authority of the Holy See, as it is today, and erected into a Dogma of the Church, he would have defended it with all the power of his incomparable eloquence; he would have rejoiced at the privilege accorded to the divine Mother, and, with renewed love would have exclaimed: "Thou art all beautiful, O Mary, and there is no spot in thee," since thou hast been conceived without the least stain of original sin.

A painting of scholastic philosopher Saint Thomas of Aquinas in St. Stephens Basilica in Jerusalem, Israel by Joseph Aubert.

CHAPTER X

St. Thomas Aquinas

WE NOW APPROACH THE TESTIMONY of another illustrious Doctor and Saint of the Church of God, who flourished in the thirteenth age — St. Thomas Aquinas, and who, from his learning, eloquence, sanctity, and zeal, has been beautifully endowed with the title of Angelic Doctor. St. Thomas was an advocate of Mary in the doctrine of the Immaculate Conception. The following passages amply vindicate this privilege of the Blessed Virgin, and the honor of this illustrious champion of her prerogatives.

"The Supreme Artificer, in the plenitude of His power, hath made an image (mirror) clearer and more faultless than the brightest Seraph; so that, God except, it is not possible to imagine anything more pure than the person of the most glorious Virgin; concerning whom Anselm says, 'It behooved that the conception of Him should be made of the most pure Mary; of that purity, than which, next to God, nothing could be esteemed greater.'"[1] What words could more clearly affirm the Immaculate Conception? The Blessed Virgin is here declared to be clearer and *more faultless* than the brightest Seraph; most glorious, and, God alone except, purer than anything which could be imagined. The word *speculum*, which occurs in the passage, is peculiarly forcible. It signifies a mirror; and hence, an image of one's self. In this case, therefore, the Blessed Virgin is called an image of her Creator. So was Adam called, when created in the image of God; immaculate, from immaculate earth. This could not be said of the Holy Virgin, if the deadly blur of original sin obscured the mirror God had made.

In the following, also, the Immaculate Conception is positively affirmed: "It is therefore possible, that some creature may be found, than who nothing can be more pure among created things, provided it is not infected (or sullied) by the contagion of sin; such was the purity of the Blessed Virgin, who has been exempt from original and actual sin."[2] Cardinal Lambruschini remarks, upon

---

1. "Fecit Summus Artifex, in ostensionem pleniorem artis suæ, speculum, unum clarissimo clarius, Seraphim tersius, ut purius intelligi non possit, nisi Deus esset, personam, scilicet, gloriosissimæ Virginis, de qua Anselmus; 'decebat illius Conceptio hominis de Maria purissima fieret, ea puritate, qua major sub Deo nequit intelligi." — *Opus, vi, De Dilect. Dei et prox.*

2. "Ideo potest aliquid creatum reperiri, quo nihil purius esse possit in rebus creatis, si nulla contagione peccati infectum (vel inquinatum) sit, et talis fuit puritas B. Virginis quæ a peccato originali, et actuali immunis fuit." — *Sentent. Distinc, 44, Lib. i, quaest. 1, art. 3.*

this passage, that the Angelic Doctor has not limited himself by saying, "*omni peccato originali caruisse;*" for this was verified in Jeremiah, in John the Baptist, and in every child upon the reception of Baptism. But he says: "*a peccato originali et actuali IMMUNIS FUIT.*" Now, if Mary was thus, according to St. Thomas, *exempt* from original sin, she could never have contracted it; for if she had contracted it, even for an instant, it could not have been said of her, that she was *immunis* — exempt. There is no ambiguity of speech in this passage; and it cannot be denied, that St. Thomas has thus recorded his positive belief in the Immaculate Conception. There is yet another passage, in this connection, in which he institutes a comparison between the Immaculate purity of God and that of the Blessed Virgin. He says: "Neither God, nor the Most Blessed Virgin, has had any sin; this being the difference, God is exempt from sin by nature, the Blessed Virgin is exempt by special privilege."

The following passage occurs in all the old editions of St. Thomas' works. Why it does not appear in some more recent editions, those who have tampered with their integrity must explain.[3]

In commenting upon the Epistle to the Galatians, *chap.* iii, he says: "Of all, no woman hath been found exempt, at least from original or venial sin, except the most pure and most renowned Virgin Mary, who was exempt from every sin, original and venial."[4]

The following is given on the authority of Bromiardo, a Dominican, who, in explaining the true sentiment of St. Thomas, expressed in the *Summa, part 3, quest. 27, art. 2*, says, "St. Thomas places the excellence of her sanctification as to priority of time in this: that she was sanctified in her animation; that is, in the conjunction of the soul with the body, in the womb of her mother."[5] This evidently affirms the Immaculate Conception in its passive sense, wherein the soul of the Blessed Virgin, being prevented by sanctifying grace, was rendered

---

3. Bishop Wielmo, in his work *Pro Defensione Sancti Thomae*, says: "Execrabilius est, quod nequam et scelesti homines quidam, vel ad Thomæ auctoritatem enervandam, vel, ut ego quidem arbitror, ad suam aliquam opinionem, quæ in controversiam vertebatur, tanti viri testimoniis fulciendam et comprobandam egerunt." Gilles of Rome, who was the devoted disciple of St. Thomas, some years after the death of the saint, wrote a work entitled, *Castigatorium in Corruptorem Librorum Thomae Aquinatis*. Richard Klapoel, Hervy Noel, William Messelech, John of Paris, William Bollionio, Nicholas Madense, Durandelle and Archbishop Hugues, members of the Order of St. Dominic, have all written with vigor against those who have altered the writings of St. Thomas. And another Dominican, John Nicolai, in the Preface of his edition of St. Thomas's works, published at Paris in 1663, attests that this edition has been, with much care and study, purged of those typographical and other errors, by which the legitimate sense and historical sincerity and truth, have been perverted.

4. "Mulierem ex omnibus non inveni, quæ a peccato omnino immunis esset ad minus originis, vel veniali, excipitur purissima, et omni laude dignissima Virgo Maria, quæ omnino immunis fuit a peccato originali et veniali." This passage may be found in the Venetian edition of St. Thomas, 1593 A.D., and in that of Paris, 1542 A.D.

5. "Sanctus Thomas ponit ejus sanctificationis excellentiam, quantum ad temporis prioritatem, in hoc, quod sanctificata fuit in sui animatione; id est, in conjunctione animæ cum corpore in utero matris suæ."

exempt from original sin.

In another passage, St. Thomas, speaking of the Blessed Virgin, says, "The Blessed Virgin is said to have merited to bear the Lord of all, not because she hath of herself merited the incarnation of the Word; but because, on account of the grace given unto her, she hath merited that degree of purity and sanctity that she might be rendered worthy to be the Mother of God."[6] What that degree of purity and sanctity was, of which the Saint speaks, we learn in his fourth *Opusculum de Salutatione Angelica*; where he says, "The Blessed Virgin was most pure, with respect to every fault; since she hath not incurred any sin, either original or venial."[7]

That the Angelic Doctor believed and taught the Immaculate Conception is conclusively proved by the passages here adduced. But the doctrine can, with no less force and certainty, be deduced from many of his general propositions. The following will serve as specimens of this: he says, *"Non posse festum celebrari nisi de sancto."* — "No festival can be celebrated except of what is holy." But the Church celebrates the Immaculate Conception of Mary; therefore, her Conception was holy. Again: *"Dubitari non posse Beatissimam Virginem sine peccato originali natam esse, quia Ecclesia ejus Nativitatem celebrat."* — "It cannot be doubted that the Most Blessed Virgin was *born* without original sin; *because* the Church celebrates her Nativity." But the Church also celebrates the Festival of the Conception of Mary; therefore, according to St. Thomas, she was, without doubt, conceived without original sin. To contradict himself was never a failing of so profoundly philosophic a scholar as the Angel of the Schools. His works all strictly harmonize with each other; his sequences logically flow from his propositions; and unless it could be supposed that St. Thomas wished to place himself in opposition with his own principles, it must be admitted that he as firmly believed as he eloquently expressed and resolutely maintained the Immaculate Conception of the Most Blessed Mother of God. Other grave and weighty questions occupied attention at the period in which he flourished; but had this one then assumed the prominence which it has since, or had he lived at the present epoch, doubtless he would not only have maintained the belief of the Immaculate Conception, but he would have brought the whole energy and force of his profound genius to bear upon this prerogative of the Blessed Mary; and he would have stood foremost among those who have solicited its solemn definition as a Dogma.

This conclusion is not drawn from a mere consideration of how he might be supposed to act in a given case; but it is derived from the Saint's own solemn declaration, made to the minister of religion from whose hands he was about

---

6. "B. Virgo dicitur meruisse portare Dominum omnium, non quia meruit ipsum incarnari, sed quia meruit ex gratia sibi data illum puritatis et sanctitatis gradum ut congrue posset esse Mater Dei." — *Summa*, part 3, ques. 2.

7. "B. Virgo Maria purissima fuit quantum ad omnem culpam, quia nec originale, nec veniale peccatum aliquando incurrit."

to receive the Viaticum. St. Thomas then said, "I have taught many things concerning the most sacred body of our Lord Jesus Christ and concerning the other sacraments; I have written many things in the faith of Jesus Christ and of the Holy Roman Church. I *subject all things to its correction; I submit all things.*"[8]

After this declaration, what more need be attempted in defense of this illustrious Saint? There is but one word which need be added, by way of a general conclusion, in regard to him and those who, as it is alleged, have not favored the doctrine of the Immaculate Conception: namely, even supposing it were true that they dissented from this belief, and made no virtual retractation of their error in their dying moments, still, they were but individuals, whose voice or numbers would weigh nothing in the opposite scale against the Universal Faith. Their opinion, however respectable, is of no avail against a defined Dogma and the perpetual current of testimony in the Church of every age. It is easy to estimate at their just value the arguments of those who maintain their dissent upon so slight a foundation as an incidental loose expression of a writer. No acknowledgment of the weakness of their position could be more decisive than the argument itself. We have every motive, therefore, to exult with joy and thanksgiving that Almighty God turns even the errors of man to the glory of His name, and evidence of His faithfulness in His promise of leading, guiding, and preserving His Church all days in the way of truth.

---

8. "Ego de sanctissimo Corpore D. N. J. C. et aliis sacramentis multa docui; multa scripsi in fide J.C. et sanctæ Romanæ Ecclesiæ, cujus correctioni cuncta subjicio, cuncta suppono."

CHAPTER XI

"Behold a Virgin shall conceive and bear a Son whose name shall be called Emmanuel, God with us."

"The sensual man perceiveth not these things which are of the Spirit of God; for it is foolishness to him because it is spiritually examined." (*1 Cor., chap. ii, 14.*)

"But God hath made foolish the wisdom of this world; and he hath chosen that which the world deems foolish to confound and bring to nought that which it deems wise." (*1 Cor., chap. i.*)

TO THE WISDOM OF THIS WORLD, the clearest demonstration of divine truth is an absurdity. The rays of light glancing from the throne of God serve not to enlighten, but only to strike with more hopeless blindness. It will prove to you, clearly as a problem in Euclid, magnetism, clairvoyance, or spiritualism; but will laugh to scorn the earthly life of the Son of God, and the story of redeeming love. With it, the scriptural scheme of creation, with all its mysterious appendages, and the intellectual beings with which it is inhabited, is but the wild vagary of priestly imposture; but, viewed without the great first Cause, and simply as the result of chance, the blind, fortuitous concurrence of particles of matter, is wisdom and science. The sensual man, the carnal man, the proud, the egotistical, comprehend not that which comes from God; that which it behooves them to know, to love, and adore. It is only the pure in heart, the humble, of whom the world thinks slightingly, and, it may be, passes by with a sneer, that God deigns to enlighten and bless with that wisdom which is unto salvation. To such we say, behold the finger of God in the Immaculate Conception of the Most Blessed and thrice revered Virgin Mother. Raise your hearts and voices in sentiments of profound gratitude, and bless God the Creator that the second Eve hath found grace in heaven to be created pure of heart and free from the least stain of sin; for it is through her obedience, and the power of God, that the wonderful mystery of man's redemption was finally wrought.

In view of this mystery of Divine love, who will not acknowledge that the hand of God hath wrought it? Who will not with eagerness and gratitude receive this pledge of peace that the Divine mercy hath lavished upon us in the

Immaculate Conception of Mary? Who will not permit his heart to be impressed with her incomparable perfections, filled with confidence in her powerful protection, and inflamed with zeal for her glory? Well hath the Church, inspired, by the angelical salutation, and in the spirit of fulfilling her prophecy, taught all her children to proclaim thee blessed, Mary; *Blessed art thou indeed among women*, and exalted above all the hosts of Heaven. All the graces which descend upon those who honor thy Immaculate Conception, are but the forerunners of those, which thy beloved Son, our Lord, longs to pour out upon those who have recourse to the Divine sources, which in our day are so abundantly opened for the pure and humble of heart. The heart must indeed be insensible to every motive of joy and gratitude, if it experiences no emotion of thanksgiving for the inestimable benefits which Mary, by her cooperation with the Divine Will, hath been the happy agent of obtaining for us.

Mary could with much greater reason than Isaiah, say: "The Lord hath called me from the womb; from the bowels of my mother he hath been mindful of my name." (*Isaiah, chap. xlix, 1.*) For, from the first instant of her being, He had prepared her to be His most holy tabernacle.

When Almighty God commanded a temple to be built to His honor in Jerusalem, what preparations did He not ordain? What purity did He not require in the things that belonged to that work, even in the persons and materials that were employed in it? David, though a great saint, was excepted against by God, because he had been stained by blood spilt in just wars. Again, what purifications, consecrations, rites, and ceremonies did He not order to sanctify all the parts of the building? This for a material temple, in which the ark was to be placed, and men were to offer their homages and sacrifices to His adorable Majesty. What, then, did He not do for Mary, in spiritually adorning her whose chaste womb was to be His living tabernacle; from whose pure flesh He was to derive His own most holy body, and of whom He would Himself be born? So tender a mercy was this great work to Him, that the Church, in her most earnest daily supplications, conjures Him, as by a most endearing motive, that He will be pleased to hear her prayers, and enrich her children with His special graces, by His effusion and liberality towards her, when He most wonderfully prepared and fitted both her body and soul, that she might be made a worthy dwelling for Himself.[1] She was made worthy to become the Mother of God; and the Church, though it has delayed to pronounce this doctrine as necessary to salvation, has never for an instant lost sight of, or ceased to proclaim, her prerogative.

But before proceeding onward in tracing the outlines of the evidences of the faith of the Church, in this long-cherished doctrine, let us pause and throw a retrospective glance upon the road over which we have so far journeyed. Let us look around and view the company we have joined and passed upon the way. What a glorious array of Saints, and Martyrs, and blessed souls do we see, all uniting in honoring and venerating the Virgin Mother in her Immaculate

---

1.   Butler's *Lives of the Saints*, Dec. 8.

Conception! Men of different nations born, of different tribes and tongues, of varied passions and tastes: men who, if considered in any point of view outside of the Church, have not, perhaps, one affinity which would unite them or cause them to embark in any single enterprise, but who, nevertheless, in the brotherhood of holy Faith, forget all distinctions of race, of nation, of family, and of rank, and unite in the profession of one Lord, one Faith, one Hope; men whose souls glow with that charity without which it is as impossible to be saved as without faith, but in the possession of which all things are easy, whether bonds, or persecution, or death. Such are they who unite, as if urged by one impulse of heavenly inspiration, to honor the Virgin who merited to bring forth Him who was to take away the sins of the world. No language, in their view, is too strong to express the high dignity of her position; no graces of expression too elegant or sweet to portray her unapproachable beauty and excellence; no emblems or figures too pure or too sublime to illustrate their idea of her whom all emulate to love.

Most holy, most glorious, Immaculate Virgin; high above the range of sinful men, and superior to all the heavenly hosts; Mother of God, Mother of Christ, Mother of our Lord, Mother of Him who had no sin; Daughter of God the Father, Mother of God the Son, Spouse of God the Holy Ghost. Consolatrix of the world; Mediatrix of sinful men; Virgin most pure, Virgin undefiled, Virgin most beautiful, Virgin conceived without the stain of sin. Thou art all beautiful, O my love, and there is no spot in thee. Beautiful as the morning rising, fair as the moon, bright as the sun, and terrible as an army set in array; purer than the Angels, clearer than the most glorious Seraph. Immaculate in thy conception, immaculate in thy birth, immaculate in every phase of thy holy life on earth, and immaculate in Heaven, where thou sittest Queen of all the heavenly citizens. Such are the glowing terms in which they utter the praises of the humblest and lowliest Maid of all the daughters of Eve; of the highest and most exalted creature whom God hath created. Such is the rapt eloquence with which they discourse of her whose wondrous maternity of God was foretold by him whose tongue was touched with a live coal from off the altar, that he might prophesy with a sublimity of eloquence and a minuteness of detail surpassing that of any other.

> "Behold, a virgin shall conceive and bear a Son, whose name shall be called Emmanuel," — God with us. (*Isaiah, chap. vii, 14.*)

Did they, whose inmost souls were thus inspired to exalt the merits of their Queen, detract from the honor due to God? Ask the Prophets, who were privileged to foretell her matchless worth, and who now reign with her in Heaven; ask the angel Gabriel, who was glad to be honored to visit her in her lowly cot; ask the Cherub Choirs, that sang around the stable at Bethlehem: ask her Redeemer Son, who loved to rest His sacred head upon her gentle breasts. Who were they who loved to honor whom the King of Heaven had honored? The disciples that sat at His feet; the Apostles, whom He sent to convert the world; the Martyrs who, for the love of Him, endured unspeakable torments and death; the Saints of all ages, who have thought the loss of all things gain, if they were but so happy as to win His love. These are they whose inspired tongues were early taught thus to address her who was foreordained to repair the loss sustained through Eve. Did they not know what was due to the God that bought them with His own blood upon the Cross; and what was due to her who brought Him forth to save mankind? Who would not rather follow them in their love and praise of Mary, than the driveling skeptics that laugh her to scorn, as they do the Son of God who died for them? If error were possible (which it is not) who would not rather even err with Cyprian, Ambrose, Chrysostom, Augustine, Dominic, Bernard, and the Angelic Doctor, in honoring Mary, than accord with the dissentients of every age, in casting disgrace and contempt upon the spotless, sinless one, who sits at the right hand of her Son in Heaven?

But it is not only these who, singly, in the fervor of their hearts, accord to the Holy Virgin her meed of praise. It is not only the whole army of Saints and Martyrs who, having washed their robes white, are now seated with her at the right hand of God, that once like us — when in the flesh — hail her immaculate, conceived without sin, the purest of created things. It is not these, I say, in their single capacity alone, but the whole Church militant collectively, that joins its universal voice; that pauses in the solemn Sacrifice of the spotless Lamb, to commemorate her, the *Virgo Deipara*, immaculate, spotless, pure, without the taint of sin. Does she, the Church, the Spouse of Christ, not know what is due to the Creator, and what to the work of His own hand? "Go, teach." Does she, the teacher sent, not know the lesson to be taught? She knows it well, and inscribes it upon her Ritual, upon her Liturgies, upon her mighty Tomes, and sounds it with her trumpet voice — Mary, Mother of God, immaculate, spotless, pure, without the taint of sin. "Thou art all beautiful, O my love, and there is no spot in thee."

CHAPTER XII

The Religious Orders, Academies, Universities, and Theologians Adopt the Doctrine of the Immaculate Conception

NO DISPUTES AROSE AMONG THE ANCIENT FATHERS and Doctors of the Church, concerning the Conception of the Blessed Virgin being immaculate, or without the taint of original sin. Nor did such arise until about the twelfth century. And it was long subsequent even to this date, that the celebrated contests arose between certain theologians; especially between the Fathers of the Order of Preachers, and the Order of Minors. From this time, the controversy waxed warm, and sometimes immoderate; the one party affirming that Mary was immaculate from the first instant of her conception; the other denying this, but admitting that before her birth she was by special grace sanctified. The fire of this controversy continued to burn until it was extinguished by the Constitutions of the Apostolic See. At that date, by common consent, almost all the religious orders celebrated and propagated the Festival of the Immaculate Conception; and the Academies of the entire Christian world bound themselves by a solemn vow to defend it. In some of them the theological degree was not conferred upon any who did not adhere to it.

The brothers of the Order of Minors, known as the Seraphic School, have always been especially devoted to the maintenance of the Immaculate Conception. This is proved by the testimony of Peter of Alliacus. (See his history of the fourteenth age to the year 1387 A.D.) This illustrious Prelate, who obtained the honors of the Cardinalate on account of his profound learning and piety, defended, in the name of his Order, the judgment of the University of Paris against one John of Montesone, a doctor of theology of the Order of St. Dominic. This latter (1387 A.D.), had advanced fourteen propositions against the Immaculate Conception. One of these propositions was: "To deny, that every man, except Christ, has contracted sin, is expressly contrary to faith." The University, in condemning it, said: "This proposition is revoked as false, scandalous, presumptuously affirmed, and offensive to pious ears." Peter of Alliacus, vindicating this judgment, said: "Many Saints, and Catholic Doctors, many Supreme Pontiffs, and Cardinals of the Holy Roman Church, and other illustrious prelates, and many individual members of the Church, indeed almost the universal Church, or the greater and wiser part of it, have asserted and publicly taught, that the Blessed Virgin was conceived without sin."

Montesonus, as narrated by Spondanus, about the same time shocked the public ear with similar propositions against the Immaculate Conception. But Peter of Ordeomente, Archbishop of Paris, opposed him, and sustained the opinion of the University. Montesonus did not submit. He appealed to Clement VII, who resided at Avignon. He went thither, and endeavored to sustain his propositions, and wipe off the disgrace inseparably adhering to those who denied the Immaculate Conception. He did not succeed in his endeavor. There had been sent from the Academy to Avignon, to meet him and his adherents, Peter of Alliacus, Ægidius de Campis, John of Novavilla, and Peter of Allianvilla. The discussion proceeded; Montesonus was condemned, and the judgment of the University of Paris sustained. He was ordered to return to Paris and abjure his errors. But seeing that his cause was lost, he left Avignon, and eluded the government by a precipitate flight to Aragon. For which reason, he was judged contumacious, and all who had followed and supported his errors recanted. (*Hist. Universit. Paris, Tom. 4.*)

The disputes, however, continued. The condemnation of the propositions of Montesonus aroused the whole Order of which he was a member. William de Valone, a bishop of this Order, "to his great disgrace and theirs," as Natalis Alexander says, reaffirmed the condemned propositions. The general of the Order placed all the members under obligation to support this bad cause, lest any of them should subscribe to the episcopal or academical censure. Montesonus also, by his audacity, inflamed them. And their perversity so increased, that finally the whole Order was deprived of their seats in the Academy, and was further interdicted from preaching and hearing confessions. "They not yielding, their Order was cut off from the body of the University, and the faculty of preaching and hearing confessions was wholly interdicted to it. (*Spondanus Hist. Univers. n. 12. Paris, 1387, Tom. iv.*) The rupture would have been even more serious, had it not been for the friendly offices of Ferricus Cassenellus and John Gerson. Through the zeal and charity of these eminent men, those who had been expelled from the bosom of the Church subscribed to the opinion of the Academy, and were most fondly reinstated in their former positions.[1] So that those who had thus been unwisely opposed to the general, ancient, and pious belief, and devotion towards the Immaculate Conception of the Most Blessed Virgin, now embraced, preached, and strove with all fervor to propagate it.

About the year 1494, a religious, named Trithemius, published a commentary upon the praises of St. Anne; in which he defended the Immaculate Conception of Mary. In reply to this, another religious, named Wigand, wrote, denying the Immaculate Conception. But he met with no greater success than did those whose bad example he had followed. For the Universities of Paris and Cologne,

---

1. "Curante Ferrico Cassenello episcopo Antisiodiorensi, propositiones publice revocarunt, et festum Conceptionis Beatissimæ Virginis Mariæ celebrarunt. *Spond. Ibid.* Annos solidos viginti quinque ab Academia manserunt exclusi, mutuis ordinis ipsiusque Academiæ ex ila tempestate incommodis, quæ deflet venerabilis Gersonius, qui Fratres nostros cum Academia parente, incredibili caritate reconciliavit." — *Nat. Alexander Hist. Eccl. Saec. xiii et xiv, cap. iii; art. xxiii.*

the Order of Carmelites, all the communities of the Brothers of the Order of Minors, most of the Cardinals, a great many Archbishops, the Bishops, and chief men, the entire body of the Clergy, and the learned men of Germany, vindicated the work of Trithemius and condemned his opponent.[2]

Three years after this (1497 A.D.), another theologian ventured in a sermon to deny the Immaculate Conception. This immediately aroused the usual opposition: and he was obliged, by the University of Paris, publicly to retract his proposition. And in order that all cause of dissension might thereafter be forever removed, the University published that celebrated decree, to the effect that no one should henceforth obtain the degree of Doctor of Divinity, who did not advocate the Immaculate Conception, to which the candidate bound himself by solemn vow.[3] Those who bound themselves by this decree declared "that the Blessed Mary was Immaculate in her Conception; and that the contrary opinion was to be judged false, impious, and erroneous." This obligation bound them also to accept the Decree of the Council of Basle as sacred. It was also declared (1496 A.D.), that, "If anyone should dare to entertain the opinion contrary to that of the Immaculate Conception of the Blessed Virgin Mary, he should be deprived of all the honors of the University, degraded, and expelled from their community." Similar enactments were made by the Universities of Toulouse, and the Neapolitan Academy in Italy; those of Vienna, Cologne, Louvain, and Mentz, in Germany; of Salamanca, Barcelona, Toledo and Alcala, in Spain; and Coimbra, in Portugal. In fine, there is scarcely a theological institution in the world but which has taught and maintained the doctrine of the Immaculate Conception of the Most Holy Virgin.

To furnish a complete catalogue of them, and of the Religious Orders, Congregations, and Confraternities which have been established under the auspices of the Immaculate Conception, would be an endless task. But it is not only these which have borne testimony to this ancient and pious belief. The common consent of the faithful is not less decidedly in its favor. Hence Alexander VII has said in his Constitutions: "The Faithful firmly believe that the soul of the Blessed Virgin has been exempt from the least stain of original sin, from the very first instant of her Conception; and would be grievously offended, if anyone should even whisper the contrary doctrine." And Paul V also takes occasion in his Constitutions to say: "The assertion that the Most Blessed Virgin has been conceived with original sin, has caused scandals, strife, and dissensions to spring up among Christian people."[4]

Hence, too, the Emperor of Germany, about the year 1276, bitterly complained to Innocent V against a decree issued by the chamberlain of the

---

2. See Spondanus as above quoted, and also Fleury's Ecclesiastical History, Tom. 24, p. 229.
3. Hist. Univers. Tom. v, p. 815, also Fleury, Tom. 24, p. 336.
4. Vasquez states, that in the fourteenth century the belief in the Immaculate Conception prevailed not only among Theologians, but universally among the people, and that it had become so strengthened by time, that no one could be withdrawn or diverted from it.

Sacred Palace, which seemed to detract from the spotless Conception of the Virgin. Hence, also, the Catholic King, with almost all the Bishops and Chapters of Spain, complained to Alexander VII against those who deformed the Festival of the Immaculate Conception. Philip III (1622 A.D.), sought to obtain from Paul V a definition of this question. Philip IV did the like with Gregory XV. They zealously, but at that time ineffectually, expostulated with the Holy See in favor of this doctrine. So also did the Emperor Augustus Ferdinand III, King of France, and Louis XIII and XIV, and also John I, King of Aragon. The time, however, had not yet arrived, when, in the secret councils of the Most High, this great question was to be finally and forever put to rest. But, after all these eminent testimonies in favor of the Immaculate Conception of the Blessed Mary, and in view of the increased light which every day beams upon us afresh, may we not, with St. Augustine, truthfully exclaim: "It is most insolent and insane to dispute whether that may be done, which the Church hath done." *Epis. 118.* The Church has now definitely declared, that Mary was in her Conception exempt from the stain of original sin; and she has forbidden any of her children to affirm the contrary. What, therefore, the Church hath done, we do; and with devout ardor and filial love exclaim: "Hail, Mary, conceived without sin, pray for us sinners, who have recourse to Thee."

Amidst so many Universities, Academies, Confraternities, Congregations, and Religious Orders, which have maintained the privilege of the ever venerable Mother of God, it is cheering to the pious heart to trace out those multitudes of individuals who have preeminently distinguished themselves by extolling her virtues and defending her prerogative in respect to her Immaculate Conception. These form a brilliant array of witnesses to the fact that the doctrine is no novelty of the nineteenth century. They dot every age; they raise the finger and point to every fragment of time; and they testify that the doctrine was believed then, and then, and then, from first, to last. Without the labor of searching through ponderous folios, you simply ask them, and they reply, this doctrine was believed and taught in our time, and ours. Thus have we asked them, and so have they replied, in every age, from the commencement of the Christian era. Let the following testimonies of eminent theologians, taken from the mass, serve to connect the primitive with the more modern times: —

1. Paschasius Radbertus (835 A.D.), Abbot of Corbei, says, "It is my great privilege to declare the chastity of the Most Blessed Virgin, uncorrupt and uncontaminate, and to confess her exempt from every stain of original sin."

2. Fulbertus, Bishop of Chartres (1000 A.D.), speaking of the Virgin in the Angelical Salutation, says, "Elect one, thou art chosen among the Virgins; thou hast ever been Immaculate, from the commencement of thy creation, who wast about to bring forth the Creator of all sanctity."

3. Peter Cela (1125 A.D.), says, "The plenitude of every grace was at once united in her; because, from the commencement of her Conception, the entire grace of the Deity was poured out upon her in the aspersion of the Holy Spirit."

4. Peter, the venerable Abbot of Cluny (1140 A.D.), says, "The Holy Virgin excepted, to whom it was impossible that any stain of sin whatever hath entered her."

5. Augerius, Abbot of the Cistertian Order (1140 A.D.), in a sermon *de Coena* (the thirteenth sermon among the works of St. Bernard), says, "Among the children of men, there is no one but hath been conceived in sin, *except the Mother of the Immaculate One.*"

6. Petrus Lombardus (1140 A.D.) says, "The Virgin, through the prevenient grace of the Holy Spirit, was made entirely chaste from every stain of sin."

7. Peter Comestor, brother of the former, commenting upon the words, "Glorious things are said of thee, city of God, The Most High hath founded it," concludes, "No vestige of the ruin of the old Adam remains; for the Most High himself hath built the City of God; which is understood to be said concerning the womb of Mary and the body of Christ."

8. Rupert, Abbot of Tuitia (1200 A.D.), introduces the Virgin, as it were, commenting on the text "In iniquities hath my mother conceived me." He represents her as saying, "There is no one who saith untruly 'In iniquities have I been conceived,' except myself and Him alone whom I have conceived without iniquity." (*In Cant. v, chap. 5.*)

9. Richard of St. Laurence (1265 A.D.), exclaims, "It is right that she should have been exempt from all original sin through whom not only the malediction of Eve was dissolved, but truth, also, and benediction was conferred upon all."

10. Jacob de Voragine, Archbishop (1290 A.D.), a prelate conspicuous for sanctity and learning, in his work concerning the praises of the Virgin Mother of God, and in explaining that text of Canticles, "Thou art all beautiful, O my love, and there is no spot in thee," says, "Thou art all beautiful, O Mary, because thou art without original sin."

11. Gerson (1429 A.D.), in his sermon *de Concept. B. M.*, says, "Since Thou, the Great Supreme, dost choose to have a Mother, Thou wilt doubtless honor her; but it doth not now appear that the law should be well fulfilled by permitting the abomination of original sin in her who was destined to be the habitation of infinite Purity."

12. P. Macedo, in his work *de Clavibus Petri, tom. i, lib. 4*, affirms "That the Blessed Virgin Mary hath been preserved wholly exempt from every stain of original sin."

13. Petavius, in *Theolog. Dogmat., lib. xiv, cap. 2*, says, "It is the common sentiment of all, that nothing has been created by God more chaste, pure, innocent, and finally, more foreign from every spot and stain of sin, than the Virgin."

14. John Maria Detorri, a celebrated professor of Moral Theology in the Royal Academy of Turin, expresses himself as follows: "From which, although you may have readily conjectured what is my opinion on this most famous question — namely, that the sentiment which vindicates the Blessed Mother of God from all stain of original sin is in the highest degree probable, and consentaneous to the piety not only of the simple and illiterate, but also the experienced and enlightened piety of the Sovereign Pontiffs. I wish, nevertheless, to declare (my opinion) more openly and more explicitly. Imbued with the doctrine of Gerson, that 'there is much greater danger of erring by blaspheming this Virgin than by praising her who cannot be sufficiently praised by human praise,' moved by singular reverence towards the most excellent Mother of God, obsequiousness towards the most august Queen of Angels, gratitude towards the most beneficent Patroness of men; excited by the almost unanimous agreement, suffrage, and voice of the faithful; in fine, compelled by the truth itself, or certain appearance of truth (which alone a theologian ought to consider), *I most cordially embrace the most prevalent sentiment of the Immaculate Conception of Mary*, as that which I judge to be supported by not a few probable arguments, opposed by none sufficiently strong, consentaneous to the mind of the Church, adapted to cherish the piety of the faithful, and most suitable to the dignity of Mother of God."

15. Lorin, commenting on *Psalm xl, 13*: "Thou hast upheld me by reason of my innocence; and hast established me in thy sight forever;" says: "Christ was always God; but His humanity did not exist, before it was united with the Divinity, so that it might be assumed on account of its innocence, — for, I say, it was not before it was assumed. God made His Mother such, as I have said, that therefore He might choose her for His Mother; or, because He wished to choose her, He made her such a Mother."

Many other eminent names might be added, of theologians and writers who have vindicated the Doctrine of the Immaculate Conception; men who by preaching, teaching and writing, have proved the antiquity, the universality, and the propriety of this belief; and the excellence, the reasonableness, and necessity of the subject of it — the Blessed Virgin's exemption from original sin.

Many great names might be added. Medina, Corduba, Galatin, Salaz, Navarino, De Lugo, Ægidius, Vasquez, Suarez, Segneri, Everard, Duvall, Rinaldo, Lossado, Baronio, Gonet, Bellarmine, Croiset and Valois, have rendered their own names glorious by displaying the evidences, which prove the Immaculate Conception of our loving and most venerable Mother.

We will, however, conclude this division of the subject with the testimony of Robert, a Camaldolese monk, who in the fifth chapter of his work, entitled *Amore di Maria SS. Madre di Dio*, thus reasons: "The Eternal God prepared from the flesh and blood of Mary, a body for the Word His own Son; for the Word, by the Incarnation, received His own body, formed in the womb of Mary, from her flesh and blood; so that it might be truly said, '*Bone of my bones, and flesh of my flesh.*', The Virgin was most near to the Son of God through identity of flesh, as St. Bernardino says, 'Because the same flesh which was the Virgin Mother's, was made the flesh of the Son of God.' And as Dionysius, the Carthusian (*Lib. 2, de Laud. v*), adds: "After the hypostatic union, no union is so intimate or close as the union of the Mother of God with her Son.' And, as St. Damian says, in his sermon on the Assumption; 'It is not true to say, that Christ is in the Blessed Virgin by identity, because He is the same as she — God dwelt in the Virgin, with whom He had identity of one nature. The flesh of Jesus is the flesh of Mary, which remains in Him the same as that, which he assumed from Mary.' Albertus Magnus, in continuation of this same idea, which was originally uttered by St. Augustine, says: 'The flesh of Christ is the flesh of Mary; and although it was glorified in the resurrection, it nevertheless remained the same as that which was assumed from Mary. And, it could not be more intimately joined with God, unless it became God Himself.'" It follows therefore that unless the Blessed Virgin was exempt from original sin, the Son of God was conceived of sinful flesh; receiving in His person, flesh, tainted with the sin of Adam. This is repugnant to infinite Holiness. Who then shall question its merit to be solemnly defined as a doctrine of the Catholic Church, that the Blessed Virgin Mary was conceived without the least stain of original sin?

Statue of the Blessed Virgin Mary in the Room of the Immaculate Conception in the Vatican papal apartments. This room was commissioned by Pope Pius IX following the Promulgation of the dogma of the Immaculate Conception.

CHAPTER XIII

Various Councils Favor the Belief of the Immaculate Conception

IN VIEW OF THE EVIDENCE ADDUCED IN FAVOR of the Immaculate Conception, proving that this doctrine has been the general belief of the Church in every age, the question, what have the Councils of the Church done in regard to it, naturally presents itself to our consideration. It is true that none of them have *explicitly* defined it as a doctrine; but it is not less true, that many of them have *implicitly* favored it, and that the Council of Trent desired to define it. Did the Immaculate Conception lie at the foundation of the Christian Faith, as a fundamental truth, necessary to salvation, doubtless it would long since have been so defined by the acts of the highest tribunal in the Church, and have been presented to believers for their veneration.[1]

The subject of the Immaculate Conception has often been named in various Councils; the universal belief of it has been well known; and the Church, which has condemned all heresies, however insignificant the subjects of such condemnation, would not have failed to condemn this doctrine, had it not been approved. Many doctrines, even of a fundamental character, have remained for long periods undefined, tacitly believed by all, until some special occasion, as a heresy, excited the attention, and elicited a formal definition. The Marianitæ were condemned in the first Council of Nicæa (325 A.D.), and yet, the Holy Fathers of the same Council, instituting a comparison between the Angels and Saints, and the Blessed Virgin, extolled her above them all, and declared her to be, "*omnino sanctam, puram, et castam.*" It is an oft-repeated error of the adversaries of the Catholic Church, that such and such a doctrine is a novelty, or an innovation, because it may not have been formally defined until such and such a period of the Christian era. A doctrine may, like this of the Immaculate Conception, remain for an indefinite period without a formal definition, and yet in all respects conform to the rule of St. Vincent, being believed in always, everywhere, and by all. When the occasion arises, the Church does not fail formally to

---

1. "As the Church was not founded mainly on Our Lady, but on her Son Our Lord, it was fitting that God would wonderfully enlighten her and make her light appear from the top of the mountains, as the Prophet David sings (Psalm lxxv.), clarifying above all the fundamental truths of our salvation. Later, by an abundance of His goodness, He made us see clearly several other truths which, although less consequential than the former, nevertheless lead our minds to know her better and love her more ardently"—*Revelations, lib. 6, cap. 61.*

declare her faith in every case. The first Council that invokes our attention in favor of this privilege of the Blessed Virgin is the general Council of Ephesus in 431 A.D.

1. The Fathers of the Council of Ephesus, under the celebrated Pope Celestine, thus speak concerning her: "That the Conception of the Word might reach above the choirs of Angels, she hath raised herself even to the throne of the Deity."[2] How could Mary be thus sublimely exalted, if she had ever been tainted with original sin? In this Council, Proclus, Bishop of Cyzicus, after having portrayed the Blessed Virgin as worthy of all praise, on account of the ineffable excellence of her dignity, says: "Mary is the weft, Virgin of unpolluted flesh; she is the weaver's distaff, bearer of immense grace."[3] And in the same Council this Prelate exclaims: "Whom (Mary) He hath formed without any stain, and from whom also He hath proceeded, no spot having been contracted."[4]

    In this Council also the Blessed Virgin is called *Deipara Immaculata, pura ab omni labe*; that is, "Mother of God, immaculate, pure from every stain," according to the ancient interpretation of St. Sophronius and St. Jerome; "immaculate, because in nothing corrupt." It is true there is nothing here said explicitly declaring the Blessed Mary immaculate *in her conception*; but does not the affirmation that she was *pure from every stain* exclude original sin? The Church, after the consecration of the Chalice, in the Canon of the Mass, causes the celebrant to say, upon the Oblation, "*Hostiam puram, Hostiam sanctam, Hostiam immaculatam.*" By these words it is understood that nothing more perfectly pure, nothing more perfectly holy, can be offered than Christ, who is God Himself. So the Sacred Council, when it calls the Virgin Mother immaculate, pure from every stain, means that she was absolutely so, both in her Conception and in her after life. That the holy Fathers themselves so explain it, and affirm it, has been already shown, and that the Church so understands it, we hope presently to be able more fully to establish.

2. The fourth Council of Toledo (634 A.D.), received and approved the Breviary revised by St. Isidore, Archbishop of Seville. In this Council, provision was made for celebrating the Festival and Office of the Conception of the Blessed Virgin, through the entire octave, and it affirms in every place that the

---

2. "Ut Conceptio Verbi pertingeret super Angelorum choros, se usque ad solium deitatis erexit." — *J. Aloysius de Froment. Serm. de Concept B. M. V., Vol. 8*

3. "Maria est trama, impolluta Virginis caro; radius textorius, immensa gestantis gratia." — *In Homil. cap. 7*

4. "Quam (Mariam) enim citra ullam sui labem formaverat, ex hac quoque nulla macula contracta processit."— *In Homil. Vol. 2, cap. 3, page 7.*

Blessed Virgin Mary was exempt from original sin because she was the chosen Mother of God; the truth of which may be found fully confirmed in the acts of this Council.

3.   The eleventh Council of Toledo (675 A.D.), accepted with applause this doctrine. In two places it is there taught that "Christ assumed flesh of the Holy and Immaculate Virgin Mary."[5]

4.   In the sixth general Council of Constantinople (680 A.D.), an Epistle of St. Sophronius, Patriarch of Jerusalem, was read, to the great joy of the holy Fathers, which contained these words concerning the Blessed Virgin: "Jesus entered the womb of the holy Mary, who was free from every stain, both of body and soul."[6] This epistle of Sophronius is found on the records of the Council of Constantinople, together with the following definition: "From the inviolable and virginal blood of the holy and immaculate Virgin Mary, the Word was truly made incarnate."[7] Again, it says and defines: "Christ hath entered the untouched womb of the Virgin Mary, holy and illustrious, and wise in the things of God, free from every taint of sin, both of body, of soul, and of mind."[8]

5.   The Fathers of the Council of Trullo (692 A.D.), in the seventy-ninth canon, which was approved in the seventh Synod of the second Nicene Council, *Act. 7, can. 1*, and cited by the general Council of Florence under Pope Adrian and other Pontiffs, constantly affirm, "The Blessed Virgin Mary was truly exempt from every penalty, and from the common stain."[9]

6.   The second Council of Nicæa, approved by Pope Adrian (787 A.D.), *art. 5*, thus defines, "Whoever does not confess the Holy and ever Virgin Mary, properly and truly Mother of God, to be more sublime than every creature visible and invisible, let him be anathema."[10]

The same Council called the Blessed Virgin "Most holy, immaculate, and purer than every sensible and intellectual nature." Moreover, this same seventh general Synod, Act. 7, says: "We define that venerable, holy images

---

5.   "Christum carnem de Sancta et Immaculata Maria Virgine assumpsisse." — *In cap. 2, page 546.*
6.   "Ingressus est (Jesus) uterum Mariæ sanctæ, et ab omni labe liberate corporis et animæ."
7.   "Ex inviolabili nanque, et virginali sanguine sanctæ atque Immaculatæ Virginis Mariæ, Verbum vere factum est incarnatum." — *Act. xii.*
8.   "Et uterum intactum ingressus virginitatis castitate lustratum Mariæ Sanctæ, præclaræque, et quæ Dei sunt sapientis, et ab omni contagione liberatæ et corporis, et animæ, et intellectus."
9.   "B. V. Mariam immunem fuisse prorsus ab omni poena ordinante ad culpam, atque labe communi." — *Roberto Amor di Maria, SS. cap. x, n. 11.*
10.   "Si quis non confitetur sanctam semper que Virginem Mariam proprie ac vere Dei genitricem sublimiorem esse omni visibili et invisibili creatura anathema sit."

are to be placed and had in the holy temples of God; but chiefly the images of our Lord and Savior Jesus Christ, and next, of our undefiled Lady, Mother of God."[11]

7. The national Council of Oxford, held in England (1222 A.D.), in the beginning of the thirteenth century, instituted and commanded to be observed the Festival of the Conception, after the example of many other Churches, especially those of the East. This it could not have done under any other view than that the Conception of the Blessed Virgin was Immaculate; since it is contrary to the perpetual maxim of the Church to institute a Festival in regard to anything that is not holy."[12]

8. The Council of London (1328 A.D.), affords us a similar testimony in honor of the Immaculate Conception. The Fathers of this Council, referring to the example of St. Anselm, revered for his piety, and for his devotion to Mary in the Immaculate Conception, issue the decree already quoted.

9. The general Council of Constance (1414 A.D.), approved the Revelations of St. Bridget, which affirm the Immaculate Conception of the Blessed Virgin. See the book of the "*Revelations*" of this Saint.

10. The Council of Basle (1439 A.D.), passed the following decree concerning the Immaculate Conception. The Bull containing this definition and declaration, given in the time of the Council, is still preserved at Rome. It runs as follows: "This doctrine, asserting that the glorious Virgin Mary, Mother of God, through the special preventing and operating grace of the divine Being, was never actually subjected to original sin, but was always exempt from original and actual sin, holy, and immaculate, *we define and declare* as pious, and consonant to Ecclesiastical worship, to the Catholic Faith, to right reason, and to Sacred Scripture; by all Catholics to be approved, and held, and embraced; (and also) that it is not lawful for anyone to preach or to

---

11. "Definimus venerandas sanctas imagines in templis Sanctis Dei collocandas et habendas esse; maxime autem imagines Domini et Servatoris nostri Jesu Christi, deinde intemeratæ Dominæ nostræ Deiparæ."
12. "The national Council of Ossone, held in England (1222 A.D.), established the feast of the Blessed Virgin's Conception, already celebrated in the East for several centuries, as I will tell you shortly. Could the Council have ordered this feast if it had not believed in the Conception of the Holy and Immaculate Blessed Virgin? For everyone agrees that one does not celebrate sinners." — *Les Grandeurs de la Très-Sainte Vièrge Marie*, Vol. 1, chap. 2.

teach anything to the contrary."[13]

"But the Council of Basle is illegitimate." This, though it deprives the decree of authority, does not diminish its force as evidence. On the contrary, at least with respect to those outside of the Church, it should rather add to its force; since, even though the Fathers placed themselves in the wrong as to obedience, they formally defined the Immaculate Conception. The Supreme Pontiff, Martin V, had summoned this Council; but he soon afterwards died, and the Council did not convene. Eugenius IV succeeded to the Pontificate, when the Fathers assembled, and the Session of the Council commenced. The subject of the Immaculate Conception occupied their attention. They debated it with considerable warmth; and were unable, for this and other reasons, to come to a decision. Eugenius, therefore, translated the Council to Ferrara; but a portion of the Prelates perversely remained at Basle, where they issued the decree above quoted. The Council was not, therefore, legitimate, certainly, but became a schismatical assembly; and the decree which it issued concerning the Immaculate Conception, though consonant with the general belief of the Church, had no other force than it could derive from that fact. As such, we have inserted it here. However, the Provincial Synod of Avignon, according to the testimony of Peter de Alliacus, sanctioned the decree, and commanded it to be observed, "as pious and wholesome." (*In Hist. 14 Sæc. 1387, p. 5.*) Besides, the doctrine itself was received and held by the theologians of every country — Italians, French, Germans, Poles, Flemish, English, Scotch, Spanish, Portuguese, and the Orientals; and also by most of the Academies and Universities. The decree was the precise expression of the Catholic faith in regard to this doctrine; and its not having been duly and authoritatively defined at that period must be attributed to the portentous character of the times, and to the weighty questions which distracted the deliberations of the Fathers, rather than to the mere force of any opposition that may have been brought against it.

---

13. "Doctrinam illam asserentem gloriosam Virginem Mariam, præveniente et operante divini Numinis gratia singulari nunquam actualiter subjecisse peccato originali, sed immunem semper fuisse ab omni originali et actuali culpa, sanctam, et immaculatam, tamquam piam, et consonam cultui ecclesiastico, Fidei Catholicæ, rectæ rationi, et sacræ Scripturæ, ab omnibus Catholicis approbandam, et tenendam, et amplectendam, *definimus et declaramus* nullique de cætero licitum esse in contrarium prædicare seu docere."

Entrance to the Church of Santa Maria Maggiore in the city of Trento, the site of the Council of Trent.

CHAPTER XIV

The Declaration of the Council of Trent

THE STORMY SCENES WHICH HERALDED THE ADVENT of the sixteenth century eventuated in the assembling of the Council of Trent (1542 A.D.) The turbulent spirits of that period aimed at nothing less than the undermining and total overthrow of the basis of civil and religious society. To define anew, and reenact, the whole body of Christian doctrine, was, therefore, the immense task which devolved upon the Fathers of this Council. And while, on the one hand, it became their duty thus to emphasize the main points of Catholic Faith, it was incumbent upon them to guard against an increase of the prevalent excitement, by refraining from the addition of a new definition to the points especially involving their attention. Nevertheless, they hesitated not to make such a declaration of the universal belief of the Immaculate Conception as was consistent with their sense of duty in regard to the general interests of the Church.

The learned and accurate Cardinal Pallavicini, in his History of the Council of Trent (*Book vii, chap. 7*), has given the following interesting account of the action of the Council, upon this important question.

"Besides the discussions upon Discipline, they examined with care the decrees for the definition of the dogmas upon original sin. And as Pachecco stimulated the Fathers to the end that they should define the question concerning the Mother of God, they believed that he had artfully proposed a subject too difficult to be thoroughly examined by the time of the approaching session. But it was, nevertheless, evident that he proceeded in the measure with a sincere devotion to the Blessed Virgin. There had just arrived two theologians of his own nation — Diego Lainez and Alphonsus Salmeron — sent to the Council by the Pope; who, say the ancient Memoirs of our Society, especially the former, often spoke eloquently in favor of Pachecco's measure. When, in a general assembly, especially convened on the eighth of June, the Decree concerning original sin had been read, Pachecco, seeing that a definitive decision of this question could not be accomplished in so short a time, requested that to the general proposition, which declares original sin to be common to all men, the following words should be added: 'Concerning the Blessed Virgin, the Holy Synod declares that it defines nothing, although it *piously believes that she was conceived without original sin.'*[1]

"The majority of the Fathers embraced his view; but the Bishops, and others who were present of the Dominican Order, opposed it with ardor, and had partisans in their opposition; saying, that if one of two sentiments was declared pious, the contrary must impliedly be declared impious; which would be a tacit definition of the question. In consequence, the Council sought the adoption of terms which would not prejudice either opinion, but leave them both in their actual state. The better to realize this object, the theologians, in their assemblies, drew up the Decree in the following terms: "The Holy Council declares, that in this Decree concerning Original Sin, its intention is not to comprehend the Blessed and Immaculate Virgin Mary, Mother of Jesus Christ; not intending to declare at present, upon this matter, any other thing than that which has been decreed by Sixtus IV, of happy memory."

"Cardinal de Jaen declared himself not satisfied. He alleged that, in the preceding assembly, more than two-thirds of the Fathers had consented to add the words *'concerning whom, the Holy Synod piously believes that she has been conceived without original sin.'* It cannot be denied, he adds, that this opinion is conformable to piety; since not only all the regular Orders, except one, and all the Academies, adhere to this belief as the most pious, but that the Church celebrates with solemn rites the Festival of the Conception. The Legates were divided in opinion. Cardinal del Monte made profession of his belief in the Immaculate Conception; Massarello relates of Cervin, that he held the contrary opinion. In regard to Pole, I have no information; but they all three agree that no debate should be enkindled between the two parties; and that no expressions should be used in the decree of which either party could take advantage. Cervin replied, that if, in the last assembly, any expression had been uttered by the Bishops, it had not been done at the instance of the Legates, nor in the form requisite for the Decrees; that, in the preceding assembly, of the twenty-eighth of May, it had been settled that, in regard to this controversy, no decision should be made, and no partiality shown to either of the advocates of the two opinions. He added, that if the formula proposed was considered prejudicial to the one or the other, they would alter it; but if it were not so, that it would be inconvenient to introduce another, by means of which they would arrive in an indirect way at that which the Council had refused to grant directly. Hereupon, the Bishop of Astorga proposed to suppress that clause in which it was said that *'the Council intended to declare nothing at present;'* which, it seems to me, had this effect: that it would remain, at the least, declared that the Blessed Virgin is not necessarily comprised in the general affirmation that original sin has been contracted by all men; and in consequence, the argument for the opposite side thence deduced, does not

---

1.   "De B. Virgine declaret Sancta Synodus, se nihil definire, etsi credat pie, eam sine originali laba esse conceptam."

render her exemption the less probable.

"Bertrano, however, and the others, in view of the imminent risk they ran, applauded the proposition of the Bishop of Astorga. But Cardinal Pachecco and his adherents were not satisfied. Moreover, further discussion was elicited, and this assembly was of unusual length. The conclusion, however, was, that although the majority believed the Conception really Immaculate, they thought it more expedient to abstain from arousing prejudice in regard to the contrary opinion. And this is the reason why the words of the decree, as it now stands, were, to the great regret of Pachecco, approved according to the correction proposed by the Bishop of Astorga."

Such is the interesting history of the debate which finally resulted in the adoption of the Decree on Original Sin, with the declaration appended, as it now stands in the Acts of the Council of Trent. This Council first re-affirms the dogma of the transmission of original sin to all the descendants of Adam, the means of its remission, &c, and then concludes with the following important clause: "Nevertheless, the Holy Synod has not the intention to comprehend in this Decree, *where original sin is treated of the Blessed and Immaculate Virgin Mary, Mother of God*; but the Constitutions of Pope Sixtus IV, of happy memory, are to be observed under the penalties contained in these Constitutions, which it renews."[2]

Several important considerations present themselves in view of this history of the debate of the Fathers of Trent, and in view of this Declaration.

1. It is evident that a majority (more than two-thirds) of the Fathers were in favor of a solemn definition of the doctrine of the Immaculate Conception. Prudential motives alone deterred them from proceeding to this happy termination of their wishes.[3]

---

2. "Declarat tamen hæc ipsa Sancta Synodus non esse suæ intentionis comprehendere in hoc Decreto, *ubi de peccato originali agitur, Beatam et Immaculatam Virginem Mariam Dei Genitricem*, sed observandas esse constitutiones felicis recordationis Sixti Papæ IV, sub poenis in eis constit-ntionibus contentis, quas innovat." — *Sess. V.*

3. These Fathers solemnly declared they did not intend to include the Blessed Virgin, true Mother of God, in the prepared Decree. Does this statement not show that the Trent Fathers established a real exception concerning Mary? Otherwise, how could they have said that they did not intend to include her in the Decree on Original Sin? What else does this phrase —"she is not included"— mean other than she is excluded? Therefore, following the spirit and the letter of the quoted text, one must conclude that the Fathers of Trent had in mind that Mary was free and preserved from the original sin from her conception. Proof of this is their declaration granting the Blessed Virgin Mary the title of Immaculate since the meaning they sought to give this word under that title refers to the nature of the stain mentioned in the Decree. It was a question of the original sin and not of actual sin; therefore, by calling Mary Immaculate, they intended to say that "She was not conceived in the original sin." — (*Card. Lambruschini, Immac. Concep.,* p. 34., Paris Ed.)

2. The Declaration received the unanimous vote of the Fathers; the opponents of the doctrine of the Immaculate Conception themselves voting for it with eagerness. The only dissentient was Cardinal Pachecco; a warm advocate of this doctrine, who thought, that as it had been in a previous assembly resolved that the statement should be stronger: namely, *"etsi credat pie, eam sine originali labe esse conceptam"* due deference was not paid to what appeared to be the wishes of so large a majority, both of the Fathers of the Council, and of the entire Catholic world.

3. The question was not a new one. It was as old as the Church itself. It was favored by all the Academies and Universities, and by all the regular orders except one. It was the general belief of the Church; which had celebrated it in its Festivals, and otherwise honored it. And finally, the solemn definition of it as a doctrine was overruled not on account of its merits, but for reasons relating to the peace and harmony of the Church.[4]

4. Those two of the Constitutions of Sixtus IV renewed by the Council of Trent, which restricted the discussion of the Immaculate Conception, afford no evidence against the Doctrine. This is proved by another of these same Constitutions, which enlarged the privileges conferred upon all who should celebrate the Festival of the Immaculate Conception and those other Offices which had been instituted by the Church in honor of it. Any other conclusion would necessarily involve a contradiction; since the Constitutions could not be supposed to forbid what they expressly open the spiritual treasures of the Church to bless its children for doing. The two Constitutions in question were, like the middle course pursued by the Fathers of Trent, restrictive from prudential motives, but struck no blow against a universal, pious belief and practice. Of the correctness of this, we shall have occasion incidentally to adduce some evidence in the ensuing chapter.

---

4. Those who wish to pursue the history of this Declaration still further may consult *Controverse sur la Concéption de la B.V.M.*, by Strozzi; and *Immaculatae Conceptionis Matris Dei Mariae*, by Piazza.

CHAPTER XV

The Sovereign Pontiffs Favor the Doctrine of the Immaculate Conception

THE DECISION OF THE SOVEREIGN PONTIFF in all controversies respecting articles of Faith is final. To him, also, pertains the undoubted right of deciding. Hence Tertullian exclaims, "I hear the Edict, and, indeed, the final decree; the Sovereign Pontiff, the Bishop of bishops, hath spoken."[1] It is true that, as the learned Archbishop Kenrick says,

> "Nothing can be added to the faith originally delivered to the saints; but points contained in the deposit of revelation may be expressly declared and defined when the obscurity which may have existed as to the fact of their revelation has been dissipated. The assembling of a General Council is always attended with immense difficulty, and is oftentimes utterly impracticable. The Chief Bishop is, as Frederick William Faber remarks, 'the natural organ of the Church,' as Peter is styled, by St. Chrysostom, 'the mouth of the Apostles.' In pronouncing judgment, he does not give expression to a private opinion, or follow his own conjectures; but he takes for his rule the public and general faith and tradition of the Church, as gathered from Scriptures, the Fathers, the Liturgies, and other documents; and he implores the guidance of the Divine Spirit, and uses all human means for ascertaining the fact of the revelation."[2]

Let us, then, entering upon this inquiry, listen to the declarations of the Sovereign Pontiffs in regard to the doctrine of the Immaculate Conception; certain that whatever they may have decreed respecting it can be no other than the voice of God, speaking to us through His vicegerent and representative, the visible head of the Church.

There is no instance of a Roman Pontiff, who has opposed the doctrine of the Immaculate Conception; while on the other hand, all of them, from Sixtus IV, to Pius IX, have advocated and favored it. Three, Pius III, Marcellus II, and Urban

---

1. "Audio edictum, et quidem peremptorium; Pontifex Maximus, Episcopus episcoporum dixit."
   — *De Pudicitia, cap. 1.* This was sarcastically spoken; and is on that account so much the more forcible, as a testimony of the power and authority claimed and exercised by the Sovereign Pontiffs at that early date, as well as now.
2. Primacy, chap. xxi, page 356.

VII, are of course excepted, as they occupied the Papal throne but one month. All the others have in various ways sealed the doctrine with their approbation, by granting concessions, favors and privileges, to those participating in the solemn celebration of the Festival of the Immaculate Conception, and the other offices especially appointed to be said, then, and during its Octave.

1. Sixtus IV, long before he had risen to the Pontifical throne, and when he was yet in Minor Orders, had written a treatise in favor of the Immaculate Conception. It was but the forerunner of his future acts, when he was elevated to the chief dignity of the Christian Church. He ascended the throne the 9th of August 1471, and in 1476 he issued those Constitutions, *Cum præexcelsa*, to which allusion has already been made. In these he concedes the same indulgences and favors to all who worthily celebrate this festival of the Immaculate Conception, as are granted to those celebrating the Festival of Corpus Christi.[3]

   Sixtus IV, in these Constitutions, not only accords indulgences and favors to those who celebrate this Festival, but in the Mass and Office, which he prescribes for the occasion, has inserted the following prayer: *"Deus, qui per Immaculatam,"* "O God, who by *the Immaculate Conception of the Virgin* hast prepared a worthy habitation for thy Son, grant, we beseech thee, that as by the death of the same thy Son, thou hast preserved her from every stain, so thou mayest also grant us purity to approach Thee by her intercession." This prayer was used in the Festival of the Conception for nearly one hundred years; namely, from the Pontificate of Sixtus IV, to that of Pius V; when, in the year 1568, the latter suppressed the Office of the Conception; conceding to the Order of St. Francis alone, the faculty of reciting it. This was not done because the Office contained anything worthy of censure; but there were in use at that time, several different offices of the Conception of the Blessed Virgin; namely, that of Leonard de Bussis, of Francis Quignonez, of Robert Gaguin, of the Abbot Helsin, and others. And the Pontiff wishing to establish uniformity throughout the Church, selected that of the latter, the Abbot Helsin, which henceforward was ordered to be used in place of those which had previously obtained in various parts of the Church. Moreover, a

---

3. "Auctoritate apostolica, hac in perpetuum valitura Constitutione statuimus, et ordinamus, quod omnes et singuli Christi fideles, utriusque sexus, qui Missam et Officium *Conceptionis ejusdem Virginis gloriosae* — in die Festivitatis Conceptionis ejusdem Virginis Mariæ, et per octavas ejus, devote celebraverint et dixerint, aut illis Horis canonicis interfuerint; quoties id fecerint, eamdem prorsus indulgentiam, et peccatorem remissionem consequantur, quam juxta felicis re-cordationis Urbani IV, in Concilio Viennensi approbatam, ac Martini V, et aliorum R. Pontificum prædecessorum nostrorum Constitutiones consequuntur illi, qui Missam et horas canonicas, in festo Corporis et Sanguinis D.N.J. Christi a primis Vesperis, et per illius Octavas, juxta Romanæ Ecclesiæ Constitutionem, celebrant, dicunt, aut Missæ, Officio, et Horis hujusmodi intersunt." — *Constitut. cum praeexcelsa, 1476 A.D.*

slight change was made in this Office, evidently in favor of the Immaculate Conception. The word *Nativitatis* gave place to that of *Conceptionis*. From this date, the Festival of the Immaculate Conception, which heretofore had been generally, though not universally observed, as a pious and wholesome practice, was established throughout the Church. For it was St. Pius V, who in the Roman Breviary, and in the Ecclesiastical Calendar, established as a precept for the whole Church, the Festival of the Conception.

2. Innocent VIII (1484 A.D.), affords us another example in his approbation of a Community of Nuns, under the invocation of the Immaculate Conception; in which approbation he, as also did Alexander VI, Julius II, Leo X, Adrian VI, and Pius IV, had praised the Festival of the Immaculate Conception, and conceded to it the usual indulgences; and also augmented it with many privileges. The third rule of this Community affirms "the soul of the Blessed Virgin to have been holy from the first instant of its creation."[4]

3. Clement VII (1523 A.D.), appointed a Breviary, to be used, which contained a great part of the Office of Sixtus IV, and in which, among others, these words are read: "Let us celebrate the Immaculate Conception of the Virgin Mary; let us adore Christ the Lord, her preserver."[5]

4. Paul III (1542 A.D.), occupied the chair of Peter during that portion of the sitting of the Council of Trent, when the Decree of that Council in regard to the Immaculate Conception was being considered. It has been already sufficiently noted; and nothing need be added, except, perhaps, to say, that this Pontiff was a most zealous advocate of the privileges of Mary. Although such weighty cares oppressed the Church at that time, he not only approved the doctrine of the Immaculate Conception, but he hailed with joy the efforts of the Fathers to obtain a solemn definition of it.

5. Paul V (1617 A.D.), has also exercised his authority in favor of this prerogative of the Blessed Virgin. He confirmed all the acts concerning it, which had been passed by his predecessors, Sixtus IV and Pius V. New contests and dissensions having arisen, in consequence of some maintaining, in public assemblies, the opinion contrary to the Immaculate Conception, his Holiness, in order to suppress these scandals, issued a decree, in which he forbade that anyone, except whom the Apostolic See permitted, should venture, either in public disputes, lectures, theses, or in any other manner whatsoever, to affirm that the Blessed Virgin was conceived in original sin. He also added the following declaration to this decree: "that he did not

---

4. "Animam Beatæ Virginis a primo creationis instanti fuisse sanctam."
5. "Immaculatam Conceptionem Virginis Mariæ celebremus; Christum eius præservatorem adoremus Dominum."

intend to reprobate the contrary opinion, nor to cast any direct prejudice upon it, but left it in the same condition and within the same bounds, in which it was at present found." — *Constit. 105.*

6. Gregory XV (1622 A.D.) four years afterwards, went further, and extended this prohibition to writings and private colloquies. In this decree, the Pontiff commands and prescribes that no one whatsoever should dare to assert "that this same most Blessed Virgin was conceived with original sin, nor in any manner emit or write (anything) concerning the affirmative of this question, with the exception, however, of those who shall otherwise be specially indulged in these particulars by the Holy Apostolic See."[6] This exception was made in favor of the Dominican Order, which, by his Indult of the 28th of July of the same year, was permitted, in their private colloquies and conferences among the members of their own Order, to discuss the question of the Conception without incurring any of the penalties contained in this decree. Gregory XV, at the same time, ordered and prescribed that no Ecclesiastic should make use of any other word in reciting the divine Office and in celebrating Mass, but that of Conception. This was done because some had ventured to substitute for the word *Conceptionis* that of *Sanctificationis*; by which they meant to show that they did not venerate the *animation or vivification* of the Blessed Virgin, but her *purification* from original sin through sanctifying grace.

    This decree of Gregory XV was well nigh the *coup de grace* of the controversy. Discord ceased, as the material upon which it fed was withdrawn from its reach: and harmony and peace reigned where before excited passions ruled the hour. To deny the Immaculate Conception of the Blessed Virgin was to run counter to the teaching of all antiquity, to the pious belief of the Church, and the growing want of an actual solemn definition of it as a doctrine. And nothing but the great and well-known clemency of the Popes would have suffered the confusion and discord so long to prevail. But clemency seemed only to add fuel to the flames; and the voice of authority was rigorously demanded finally to extinguish them. The controversy, however, did not expire without some final throes, as may be learned by the acts of a succeeding Pontiff, nearly half a century later.

7. Alexander VII (1661 A.D.), thirty-nine years after the decree of Gregory XV, was required to renew the decisions of his predecessors. The previous decrees had been universally hailed with joy by the Catholic world. Whatever dissent arose respecting them came chiefly from Spain. In the reign of the

---

6. "Quod Eadem Beatissima Virgo fuerit concepta cum peccato originali, nec de hac opinione affirmativa aliquo modo agere, seu tractare, exceptis tamen, quibus a Sancta Sede Apostolica fuerit aliter super his specialiter indultum."

two previous pontiffs, legations had arrived at Rome, from that country, in regard to it; but they could prevail in nothing against the universal voice of Christendom. Certain persons, about the year 1661, went through Spain, to the great scandal of the people, and both publicly and privately impugned the sentiment of the Immaculate Conception. A great part of the Bishops of Spain supplicated the Sovereign Pontiff that he would interpose the authority of the Apostolic See against these rising dissensions. Moved by their representations, Alexander VII renewed the former decrees, declaring that the Holy Roman Church celebrates the Festival of the Conception of the undefiled and ever Virgin Mary; that the office of Sixtus IV should be recited, and the veneration of the Conception once instituted, should be perpetually retained in the Roman Church. He also declared that this pious and devout custom of venerating and honoring the most Blessed Virgin preserved from original sin by the preventing grace of the Holy Spirit, should be defended.

Nothing more lucid or more beautiful has emanated from the Chair of Peter, than the following, which appeared in a bull of this Pontiff, published in the same year as the above. It is entitled *Solicitudo omnium Ecclesiarum*; and commences with "*Sane vetus est Christi Fidelium.*" "It is truly the ancient and pious belief of the Faithful towards the Blessed Virgin, that her soul, in the first instant of its creation and infusion into the body, was, by the special grace of God and through the merits of Christ, preserved from the stain of original sin; and in this sense the Festival of her Conception was by solemn rite observed and solemnized. And the number of these, and the veneration of the same, hath increased since the Apostolic Constitutions published in its favor by Sixtus IV: which the Sacred Council of Trent hath renewed and commanded to be observed. This pious custom, and the veneration of the Mother of God, has been further increased and propagated since religious orders and fraternities have been instituted under her invocation, the Roman Pontiffs approving it, and since indulgences have been granted by the same authority; so that, the Academies also acceding to the same opinion, almost all Catholics now embrace it."

8. Urban VII (1664 A.D.), in the bull — *In eminenti* — condemned the following proposition of Bajus, among seventy-nine others: "No one except Christ is exempt from original sin; hence the Blessed Virgin hath died on account of the sin contracted from Adam, and all her afflictions in this life, as in the lives of other just persons, were in punishment of actual or original sin."

9. Innocent XII (1693 A.D.), who was remarkable for his devotion to the Blessed Virgin, published the decree from which we make the following extract: "We command and determine by Apostolic authority, and in virtue of these letters, that the Office and Mass of the Immaculate Conception of

the Blessed Virgin Mary, shall in future, by precept, be recited throughout the world, by all and singular of the Faithful of Christ of both sexes, both seculars and regulars."[7]

10. Clement XI (1708 A.D.), has, in similar terms, ordained the solemn celebration of the Festival of the Immaculate Conception. In his decree of December 6th, of the same year, he says: "Our sincere devotion being incited towards the August Queen of heaven, our patroness and advocate, we determine, prescribe, and command, by Apostolic authority, that the Festival of the Immaculate Conception of the Blessed Virgin Mary, be in future throughout the world, by all and singular the Faithful of Christ of both sexes, included among the other Festivals of precept."[8] This same Pontiff, in the year 1710, approved of the rite of blessing and imposing the Scapular of the Immaculate Conception of the Blessed Virgin; and he also enriched it with indulgences.

11. Benedict XIII (1721 A.D.), permitted the Office of the Immaculate Conception to be recited every Saturday in the Austrian Empire. Two of the prayers contained in this Office announce the Conception of the Blessed Virgin Mary as Immaculate.

12. Benedict XIV (1750 A.D.), in concluding a sermon — which may be found in his *Tractatu de Festis B. Mariæ Virginis, cap. xv* — uses the following words: "In conclusion, we with all our mind adopt the opinion of the Immaculate Conception of the Blessed Mary. The inclination of the Church and of the Apostolic See towards this opinion, is deeply to be venerated; and the Constitutions of the Roman Pontiffs firmly observed."

13. Pius VI (1793 A.D.), granted an indulgence of one hundred days to the Faithful who should say: "In thy Conception, O Virgin Mary, thou hast been Immaculate; pray for us to the Father, whose son Jesus, conceived by the Holy Spirit, thou hast brought forth."[9]

---

7. "Ut Officium, et Missa Conceptionis Beatæ Mariæ Virginis Immaculatæ, cum octava — *ubique terrarum in posterum* ab omnibus, et singulis utriusque sexus Christi fidelibus tam sæcularibus quam regularibus, qui ad horas canonicas teneantur, de præcepto recitetur, Apostolica auctoritate tenore præsentium mandamus, et decernimus."

8. "Sincera nostra erga Augustissimam Coeli Reginam, patronam, advocatam nostram devotione incitati, festum Conceptions B. Mariæ Virginis Immaculatæ ubique terrarum in posterum ab omnibus, et singulis utriusque sexus Christi fidelibus, sicut alia festa de præcepto observationis festorum comprehendi, auctoritate Apostolica tenore præsentium decernimus, præcipimus, et mandamus."

9. "In Conceptione tua, Virgo Maria, Immaculata fuisti; ora pro nobis Patrem cujus Filium Jesum de Spiritu Sancto conceptum peperisti."

14. Gregory XVI (1840 A.D.), through the Congregation of Rites, granted to the Churches of France, America, Great Britain, Germany, and Italy, at their own request, the privilege of adding to the Preface, in the Office for the 8th of December, the following words: "*Et Te in Immaculata Conceptione.*" "And Thee, in the Immaculate Conception." And to the Dominicans, who had been permitted by Gregory XV to discuss this question with each other, permission was granted to say in the public prayers: "*Regina sine labe originali concepta,*" "Queen conceived without original stain," they themselves having requested the privilege through the General of their Order. In 1844 this same Pontiff conceded to Philip, Bishop of Asti, the faculty of adding the same words; "*Et Te in Immaculata Conceptione,*" to the Preface of the Mass; and to the Litany of Loreto the words; "*Regina sine labe originali concepta,*" as above. The letter of the holy Pontiff conceding these privileges, contains the following beautiful passage: —

"Venerable Brother, greeting and Apostolic benediction. We approve thy laudable devotion to the Most Holy Virgin Mary, Mother of God, moved by which, thou dost ardently long, that all should venerate and honor Her, conceived without original sin. Thou knowest, indeed, Venerable Brother, that We, in our great love and veneration towards the Virgin Mother of God, and the Most loving Mother of us all, which of late years is most freely practiced, the Immaculate Conception of the Most Blessed Virgin, is sung in the Preface of the solemn Mass, in our Pontifical Chapel, upon the day of her Conception. With not less alacrity We are accustomed to accede to the pious requests of all those who desire to exhibit their devotion to the Most Holy Virgin Mary, conceived without any stain, in their public ceremonies and prayers. Finally, venerable Brother, accept as the most certain pledge of our special benevolence towards thee, the Apostolic Benediction, &c.

"Given at St. Peter's, Rome, February 24, 1844.

"Gregory, PP. XVI."

Hand painted bust portrait of Pope Pius IX. Currier & Ives
(American, 1834-1907)

CHAPTER XVI

Pius IX, The Illustrious Friend of Mary

PIUS IX (1848 A.D.), THE PRESENT PONTIFF, has illustrated his glorious reign, by affixing the seal of His approbation to that act, whereby the Immaculate Conception of the Blessed Mary has been defined a Dogma of the Catholic Church. Previous to the decision, he had already assembled around his throne, the venerable Prelates of various nations, to consider this momentous subject, and complete the triumph of the Blessed Mary. Faithful Christians throughout the world awaited with eager and fond anticipation, the happy result. Their expectation, and the desire of their hearts, have not been disappointed. The present epoch will ever be an interesting one in the history of the Church; and it will be well to examine some of those indications, which the Sovereign Pontiff had previously given of his devotion and piety towards the ever Blessed and Venerable Virgin, in regard to the definition of the Immaculate Conception.

On the second of September, 1848, Pius IX permitted the African Churches to add to the Liturgy of Loreto the following versicle: *"Regina sine labe concepta;"* and also in the Preface of the Mass, the words: *"In Immaculata Conceptione;"* as the preceding Pontiff had likewise done to other Churches, and Prelates, as above noted. These acts were but the prelude to that noble and illustrious Encyclical Letter, which, in honor of the august Queen of heaven, he addressed to the Patriarchs, Primates, Archbishops, and Bishops, throughout the entire world. This renowned letter bears date from Gaeta, February 2, 1849, being the third year of the venerable Pontiff's reign. It is as follows:

"Venerable Brethren, Patriarchs, Primates, Archbishops, and Bishops, throughout the whole Catholic world.

"When without any merit of Ours, but in the secret councils of Divine Providence, we attained to the Sublime Chair of the Prince of the Apostles, to guide the helm of the whole Church, we felt the greatest consolation when we reflected how, during the Pontificate of our predecessor Gregory XVI, the most ardent desire wonderfully prevailed throughout the Catholic world, that a solemn judgment should be given by the Apostolic See, that the Most Holy Mother of God and the most loving Mother of us all, the Immaculate Virgin Mary, was conceived without original sin. Which most pious desire, the entreaties continually made to our Predecessor and to us, clearly and openly testify, and demonstrate, with what ardor and earnestness the most eminent Bishops, the illustrious Colleges of Canons and religious Communities, (among which is the renowned Order of Preachers,) requested that it might be lawful, openly and publicly to enunciate, and add, the word *Immaculate* in the Sacred Liturgy, and especially in the Preface of the Mass of the Conception of the Most Blessed Virgin. These entreaties were freely conceded by our Predecessor and by Us. It also happens, venerable Brethren, that many of your order have sent our Predecessor and Us, letters, by which, with repeated solicitations and earnest desires, you have besought that We should define as a doctrine of the Catholic Church, that the Conception of the Most Blessed Virgin Mary was Immaculate, and wholly exempt from every stain of original sin. Neither, in this our age, have there been wanting men, pre-eminent in talent, virtue, piety and doctrine, who by their learned and laborious writings have so illustrated this question and most pious opinion, that not a few wonder, that this honor has not yet been decreed to the Most Holy Virgin, by the Church and by the Apostolic See; and which the piety also of the faithful, greatly desires should be attributed to the Virgin by the judgment of the same Church and See. And indeed, this request has been very agreeable and pleasing to Us, who, from our earliest years have esteemed nothing more suitable, nothing more ancient, than with special piety and devotion, and sincere affection of heart, to honor the Most Blessed Virgin Mary, and to perform those acts which are conducive to her greater glory, and for the increase of praise and devotion towards her. Therefore, from the very commencement of our Pontificate, We have sedulously, and with the greatest anxiety, turned our attention to this momentous question; and we have not omitted to offer humble and fervent prayers to the Supreme Being, that He would deign to illumine our mind with the light of His heavenly grace, that We may be guided aright in our decision. For We confidently hope, that the Most Blessed Virgin whom the perfection of merit hath exalted above the choirs of the Angels even to the throne of the Deity, (*St. Greg. Pap. de Exposit. in libros Regum,*) and who hath crushed under her foot the head of the old serpent, and who stands between Christ and His Church, (*St. Bernard, Serm. in cap. xii, Apocalypse,*) and full of sweetness and grace, hath saved the Christian people from the greatest calamities and snares of the enemy; and rescued them from destruction, would, pitying our most sad and sorrowful vicissitudes, and grievous difficulties, labors, and necessities, interpose her ever present and most powerful intercession with God, and avert the scourges of Divine anger, with which, on account of our sins, we are afflicted; and calm, and dissipate, the turbulent storms of evil, which, with incredible sorrow to our mind, the Church is now afflicted; and convert our sorrow into joy. For well you know, Venerable Brethren, that the full extent of our reliance is reposed in the Most Holy Virgin; since, indeed,

God hath endowed her with the plenitude of all wisdom; so that if there be in us any hope, any grace, or any safety, it must redound to, as it came through, her; since such is His will, who hath wished that we should have all things through her. (*St. Bernard in Nativitate S. Mariæ de Aquæductu*.)

"Hence, we have selected certain Ecclesiastics, eminent for piety and deeply learned in theology; and certain venerable Brethren, Cardinals of the Holy Roman Church, illustrious for virtue, religion, counsel, prudence, and for their knowledge of divine things; and we have committed to them this most weighty question, that through their prudence and learning, they may most accurately and carefully examine it in all its parts, and diligently submit their opinion to Us. In the meantime, we have determined to follow the footsteps and to emulate the example of our illustrious Predecessors.

"However, We write these letters to you, Venerable Brethren, by which We may the more intensely excite your eminent piety and episcopal solicitude; and We urge it upon you, moreover, that every one of you, each in his own diocese, and according to his own prudence, shall order public prayers, by which the most clement Father of Lights may deign to pour out upon Us the celestial light of His Divine Spirit, to enlighten us by His presence and inspire Our heart, that we may receive such counsel in so momentous a question as may redound to the greater glory of His holy name, the praise of the most holy Virgin, and the benefit of the Church militant. But We also especially desire, that with all due speed you may communicate to us, with what devotion your Clergy and the Faithful people may be animated towards the Immaculate Conception of the Virgin, and with what ardor they may be inflamed, that the Holy See may define it. And especially do We desire to know, what you yourselves, Venerable Brethren, in your excellent wisdom, think concerning it, and what you desire. And since we have already conceded to the Roman Clergy the faculty of reciting the special canonical hours of the Conception, recently composed and published in place of those contained in the common Breviary, therefore We grant you the same faculty by these letters; that, if it so please you, all the clergy of your Dioceses may freely and lawfully recite the same canonical hours of the Conception of the most Holy Virgin, as the Roman Clergy now use, without further permission from Us, or from our Congregation of Sacred Rights.

"We doubt not, Venerable Brethren, but that, on account of your special devotion towards the most Holy Virgin Mary, you will be pleased with all care and diligence, to observe these our requests; and that you will hasten to return to us those opportune replies which we have earnestly demanded of you. And in the meantime, as the auspice of every heavenly gift, and the especial testimony of our benevolence towards you, accept the Apostolic Benediction, which to you, Venerable Brethren, and all the Clergy and faithful people committed to your care, We, from the bottom of our heart, most lovingly impart.

"Given at Gaeta, February 2nd, 1849, and in the third year of our Pontificate.

"Pius PP. IX."

In a subsequent Encyclical Letter of this Pontiff, bearing date from St. Peter's, Rome, August 1st, 1854, proclaiming a Jubilee, occurs the following passage: "We earnestly desire, Venerable Brethren, that whilst fervent prayers are addressed to the Father of Mercies for the causes announced above, you do not cease, according to the wish of our Encyclical Letter of February 2nd, 1849, dated from Gaeta, to implore, in concert with all the faithful, by supplications and vows more ardent than ever, the bounty of the same Father, that He may deign to enlighten our soul with the light of His Holy Spirit, and that we may, on the question of the Conception of the most Holy Mother of God, the Immaculate Virgin Mary, soon give a decision which may be to the glory of God and of that same Virgin, our well beloved Mother."

Since, therefore, the illustrious Pontiff, Pius IX, has thus raised his voice, and evinced his ardent desire to have defined as an article of Faith, that *the most Blessed Mary, Mother of God, has been, by prevenient grace, preserved exempt in the first moment of her Conception, from the least stain of original sin*, the Bishops of Spain, France, Germany, Italy, England, and America, and of other parts of the world, have with joy returned their replies to the effect, that the Immaculate Conception of the most Blessed Virgin Mary, Mother of God, should be defined as a dogma of the Catholic Church.

These letters of themselves form a mass of evidence in favor of the Immaculate Conception; and show with sufficient clearness the mind of the Church respecting it. It will be not uninteresting to note a few of them, by way of illustrating the spirit which pervades them.

1. Augustine Pavy, Bishop of Algiers, which See was anciently governed by that great light of the Church, St. Augustine, wrote, June, 1849, in reply to the Sovereign Pontiff, a letter, from which the following is an extract: "I have received, most Blessed Father, thy letters, and have sedulously examined the question of the Immaculate Conception of the Blessed Virgin Mary, exempt from the stain of original sin, and I have further inquired of the inhabitants of the Eastern nations, as well as the Catholics of France, Spain, Italy, Greece, Germany, Poland, and others dwelling in the remote States of Europe, Asia, Africa, and America, who all, with one voice, exclaim that they firmly believe '*that the Blessed Virgin Mary was exempt in her conception from every stain of original sin.*' Such being the case, it is also my opinion, most Holy Father, that you might define *this to be a Dogma of Faith.*"

2. Aloysius Fransoni, Archbishop of Turin, after having read the Encyclical letters of the Pontiff, issued a Pastoral letter, expressing his favorable consideration of the definition of the Immaculate Conception, and enjoining upon every parish in his jurisdiction, to offer solemn prayers to Almighty God; and, in honor of the Blessed Virgin, appoints the 13th, 14th, and 15th of January ensuing, as a solemnity; and directs that in the Litany of Loreto shall be added the words *"Regina sine labe concepta"* and in the proper place, the following versicle:

V. *In Conceptione tua Virgo Immaculata fuisti.*

R. *Ora pro nobis Patrem, cujus Filium peperisti.*

And after the prayer, *de Spiritu Sancto,* that the prayer *de Conceptione,* from the new office, shall be said, thus: —

"Deus, qui per Immaculatam, et cetera." This arrangement, being translated, is as follows: —

V. In thy Conception, O Virgin, thou hast been Immaculate.

R. Pray the Father for us, whose Son thou hast brought forth.

Then the prayer — O God, who, by the Immaculate Conception of the Virgin, hast prepared a worthy habitation for thy Son, grant us, by her intercession, that we may keep our heart and body immaculate towards Thee, who hast preserved her from every stain. Amen.

This venerable Archbishop then exhorts his Clergy and people to the fervent exercise of prayer, that it may please Almighty God to pour out upon the Supreme Pontiff the light of His celestial grace, that he who holds the keys of the heavenly kingdom equally as did St. Peter, may be enlightened and guided in his definition, for the greater glory of God, the praise of the most Blessed Virgin, and the benefit and edification of the Church militant. And finally, he issues the decree, authorized by the Pontiff, instituting, throughout his jurisdiction, those prayers and the Canonical Hours, and such other changes in the common Breviary as have obtained, and are now used at Rome in reference to the Immaculate Conception of the Blessed Virgin.

3. Not less interesting and momentous is the action which the Prelates of the United States of America have taken upon this important question. The Encyclical letter of the Supreme Pontiff, Pius IX, in regard to the definition of the doctrine of the Immaculate Conception of the Most Blessed Virgin, drew

from the venerable Prelates of the United States, in the Seventh Provincial Council, assembled at Baltimore, the last at which the venerable and most Rev. Archbishop Eccleston presided, the following admirable Pastoral Letter. We quote only that part which relates to the present question.

"Venerable brethren of the Clergy, and beloved Brethren of the Laity.

"The repeated solicitations of Bishops from various parts of the Church, presented to the Apostolic See, have moved his Holiness to address all his colleagues, for counsel in regard to the definition of the doctrine, that the Mother of our Lord was preserved by divine grace from all stain of original sin. This has hitherto been considered as a pious belief, which derived strength and sanction from the solemnity in honor of her Conception, celebrated during several ages throughout the whole Church. In the East, it was celebrated as early as the fifth century, under the title of the Conception of St. Anne, the Mother of the Holy Virgin; although it is not known to have been introduced into the West before the ninth century. Everywhere throughout the whole Church, from the earliest period, Mary was styled Holy and Immaculate, as is evident from the Liturgical books, and from the writings of the Fathers. St. Ephrem of Syria, in the fourth century, proclaimed her purity and sanctity to be far greater than that of the most sublime Spirits that surround the throne of God, since it is her singular privilege to be the Mother of the Word Incarnate. "She is," he says, "an Immaculate and undefiled Virgin, incorrupt and chaste, and altogether free from all defilement and stain of sin, the Spouse of God — the Virgin Mother of God, inviolate, holy, and entirely pure and chaste; holier than the Seraphs, and incomparably more glorious than all the celestial hosts."[1] Although the attention of the Church in the early ages was specially fixed on the mystery of the Incarnation, and her authority was employed chiefly against the destructive heresies that directly assailed it, yet the honor of the Virgin Mother was vindicated whenever it came in question.

"When Nestorius endeavored to divide Christ, ascribing to His human nature a distinct personality, the great Council of Ephesus, in proscribing the novelty, proclaimed Mary the Mother of God, in conformity with the constant doctrine of all antiquity. Her perpetual virginity was subsequently declared, when denied by innovators. Her exemption from actual sin was stated by the holy Council of Trent, in a definition of faith; and the same venerable authority designated her Immaculate, in a declaration annexed to the Canons, regarding original sin. These Fathers declare that it is not their intention to include the Blessed and Immaculate Virgin Mary in these decrees, but that the Constitutions of Pope Sixtus IV, on this point, are to be observed. This Pontiff, in consequence of disputes raised concerning

---

1. Orat. in SS. Dei Genitricem.

her Conception, had found it necessary to forbid, under heavy penalties, the branding as heresy either the pious sentiment, or the contradictory opinion. It happened in regard to this point, as on many others, that in progress of time doubts were excited as to the tradition and faith of the Church. The disputes which arose on this subject were tolerated by her with that consideration and patience with which the conflict of sentiment in regard to the necessity of the ceremonial observances was suffered in the first Council of Jerusalem, until the voice of Peter terminated the discussion. She abstained from pronouncing judgment whilst the excitement prevailed, content with the protestations of the contending parties, of unreserved submission to her authority, and leaving every proof and every difficulty to be maturely canvassed, and to be weighed in the scales of the sanctuary. Whilst the Pontiffs allowed to theologians the right of private investigation, they were careful to maintain the usage of celebrating the Festival, and forbade, under heavy penalties, any public expression of sentiment derogatory to the belief which the faithful piously cherished.

"Since the divine Scriptures teach that all men sinned in Adam, and that we are by nature children of wrath, the Virgin Mary, as his natural descendant, would have incurred the common penalty, had not she been preserved from it by divine grace. The Angel Gabriel assured her that she had found grace with God, and saluted her as full of grace. She was declared blessed among women, both by the heavenly messenger, and by her cousin Elizabeth speaking under the inspiration of the Holy Ghost. St. Irenaeus represents her as repairing by her obedience the evils brought on mankind by the disobedience of the mother of the human family. Her exemption from the general malediction may be inferred from the fact, that she was chosen to be the Mother of our Redeemer, whose body was formed of her substance. St. Augustine, speaking of actual sin, which, in the strongest terms, he ascribed to every child of Adam, observed that he must not be understood to include the Virgin Mother, concerning whom he would suffer no thought to be entertained when sin was in question, for the honor of our Lord; 'for we know,' he says; 'that grace was bestowed on her to overcome sin in every respect, since she was chosen to conceive and bring forth Him, who was utterly free from sin.' [2] Guided by this most just principle, we can interpret the general assertions of the Fathers without prejudice to the Blessed One, whose womb as a most hallowed shrine bore our Redeemer; whose breasts gave Him suck.

"The living faith and oral tradition of the Church must be deemed the echo of ancient apostolic tradition, and the genuine expression of revealed truth. The Holy Ghost is always with the successors of the Apostles, to guide them in all truth; and to impress on their minds those doctrines which were originally delivered by Christ, and which must always remain, although

---

2. Lib. de Natura et Gratia.

heaven and earth shall pass away. He watches over them that the revealed doctrine may be preserved free from all admixture of error.

"We do not mean to anticipate the solemn judgment of the Chief Bishop; but in the mean time we exhort you, Brethren, to continue to cherish a tender devotion to the Mother of our Lord, since the honor given to her is founded on the relation which she bears to Him, and is a homage rendered to the mystery of His incarnation. The more highly you venerate her, as the purest and holiest of creatures, the deeper sense you manifest of His divinity; wherefore her devout clients in ancient and later times have always been distinguished by zeal to maintain the great mysteries of faith. From St. Ephrem of Syria to St. Bernard of Clairvaux and St. Thomas of Aquinas, or even to St. Alphonsus de Liguori, all have glowed with the love of Jesus Christ, and have been distinguished by the purity of their lives, and by their zeal for the attainment of Christian perfection. On the contrary, those who have assailed the veneration of the Virgin have easily fallen into the denial of the divinity of her Son. Devotion to her is an outwork of the Church, protecting the belief of the divine mystery.

"We doubt not, Brethren, that the powerful intercession of Mary will obtain, through the merits of Jesus Christ our Lord and Redeemer, from the Father of lights, and giver of all good gifts, the necessary light and aid for the Chief Pastor of the Church, and graces and blessings for the Christian people. When we survey the Christian world, and see thrones overturned, monarchs fleeing in fear, society convulsed, destructive errors spread abroad by the untiring efforts of impious men, and confusion and disorder widely prevailing, we are afflicted almost to despondency; but when we raise our thoughts on high to the kingdom of light and love, where Mary stands near to the throne of her divine Son, we are inspired with confidence that she who at the foot of the cross received us all as her children in the person of the beloved Disciple, will effectually plead our cause. Through her we have received all grace, since she has brought forth Him who has redeemed us by His blood, and through Him she has crushed the head of the infernal serpent. Let us then go with confidence to the throne of mercy, relying on the infinite merits of Christ, our only Savior, and commending ourselves to the prayers of His Holy Mother, who is always heard on account of her intimate relation to Him, and her tender love for Him. Let us ask that the hydra head of heresy may be crushed forever, and that revealed truth in all its fullness may be acknowledged by all mankind; so that the prayer of the Psalmist may be accomplished: 'Let the people confess to Thee, O God; let all people give praise to Thee.' Let us pray that all division and strife may be brought to an end, and that all the professors of the Christian name may be united in religious communion, earnestly cherishing the unity of the spirit in the bond of peace. At the same time we must, with increased fervor, ask that scandals may be rooted out of the fold of Christ, and that the purity of morals and the beauty of holiness may everywhere flourish.

"Take unto you, Brethren, the helmet of salvation, and the sword of the spirit (which is the Word of God.) By all prayer and supplication, praying at all times in the spirit; and in the same watching with all instance and supplication for all the Saints; and for us, that speech may be given us, and that we may open our mouths with confidence, to make known the mystery of the Gospel. Peace be to you, brethren, and charity, with faith from God the Father and the Lord Jesus Christ.

"Given under our hand in Provincial Council at Baltimore, on the fifth Sunday after Easter, in the year of Our Lord 1849.

"Samuel, Archbishop of Baltimore, &c. &c"

In consequence of the last Encyclical Letter of the present Pontiff, dated from St. Peter's, Rome, August 1st, 1854, the Most Reverend Archbishop of Baltimore, Francis Patrick Kenrick, has issued a Pastoral announcing the Jubilee as proclaimed by His Holiness, Pius IX. In this letter the Most Reverend Archbishop says,

"The Sovereign Pontiff desires, brethren, your prayers for light to direct him in the discharge of the most solemn function of his high office: namely, the definition of a doctrine which, although cherished and professed in the Church, has not hitherto been maintained as a necessary article of Catholic faith. All the truths of revelation were taught by the Apostles, under the guidance of the Holy Spirit, and preserved always in the Church as a sacred deposit, from which nothing should be taken, and where to nothing should be added. Nevertheless, even the great mysteries of the Trinity and Incarnation, which were always most prominent among these doctrines, were not propounded from the beginning, in all their details and consequences, with that precision with which they were subsequently defined; when the subtleties of innovators compelled the pastors of the Church to guard them against the adulterations of human error. The divine maternity of the ever Blessed Virgin was declared in conjunction with the dogma of one person in two natures of our Lord Jesus Christ; when the blasphemy of Nestorius was exploded, and every believer in the Incarnation was required to acknowledge Mary as the Mother of God. Holy, pure, immaculate she was always styled, not only in the writings of the Fathers, but in the Liturgy, whilst the holy sacrifice was offered up, and the application of the blood of our Victim was sought for sinners; yet no solemn and formal declaration was made of her exemption from that stain of sin which infects all the posterity of Adam. When attention was particularly directed to this point, the devout mind easily recognized a privilege which is so immediately connected with the honor of our Lord, although some hesitated to admit such an exemption from the want of an explicit and formal declaration of it in the divine Scriptures, or in the writings of the ancient fathers. With great wisdom, the rulers of the Church suffered the discussion to proceed; forbidding either party to anticipate the judgment of the supreme tribunal, but giving their favor to what appeared most consonant to Christian piety, without venturing on the premature decision of a controversy so important in its bearings. This liberty of sentiment thus tolerated and allowed did not imply a pledge that no definition of the doctrine in question should ever emanate; much less, an avowal that no such revelation existed which would authorize such a definition. The Pontiffs, on the contrary, expressly limited these provisional measures to such time as they should issue a final decision, which they manifested no eagerness to pronounce. Ages have thus been permitted to roll by. In the meantime, the pious sentiment has sunk deeper and deeper into the minds of the faithful, and the feeling of the whole Church is now so manifest in reference to this privilege of the Mother of our Lord, that dissent is no longer perceptible. This is no doubtful indication of the teaching of the Holy Ghost, who abides in the Church to lead her into all truth. Our present venerable Pontiff, during his exile at Gaeta, called the attention of all the Bishops throughout the world to this subject, and invited them to communicate to him the tradition and sentiments of their respective churches, and to express their judgment as to the propriety of issuing a solemn definition of faith, in order to eliminate forever all doubt and hesitation. The matter has since engaged the attention of several councils — especially of the Seventh Provincial Council of Baltimore — and has been thoroughly canvassed by learned divines in treatises written expressly on this subject, and in assemblies held at Rome. As the time approaches for final action, the Holy Father again solicits the prayers of the Christian world that the light of the Holy Ghost may be vouchsafed to him, that he may determine and decree as may be expedient for the divine glory and the welfare of the Church. After the mature investigations that have been made, and the multiplied evidences that have been furnished of the general sentiment and judgment of the body of Bishops, the belief of this prerogative may well be regarded as flowing from the mystery of the Incarnation; but its formal proposition, as an article of faith, still depends on that secret impulse which the Divine Spirit may vouchsafe to the Vicegerent of Jesus Christ. His definition, if issued, will not create this article, but will give form and sanction to that sentiment which has hitherto been cherished by the spontaneous piety of the faithful, under the guidance of ancient tradition, and the influence of the Spirit of God.

"Given under our hand, at our residence at Baltimore, on the Feast of the Dolors of the Blessed Virgin, in the year of our Lord 1854.

"Francis Patrick, Archbishop of Baltimore"

In the same spirit of love and veneration, towards the Most Blessed Virgin, is the Pastoral Letter of the Bishop of Philadelphia indicted. That portion of it relating to the Immaculate Conception, is as follows:

"And since one of the principal intentions of the reigning Pontiff in proclaiming this Jubilee, has been, by means of your united suffrages, to obtain the grace of the Holy Spirit in giving a decision on the subject of the Immaculate Conception of the ever venerable Virgin Mother of Jesus Christ, shall we not confidently believe that abundant light will be imparted to him and to the Prelates now convened around his throne in the Eternal City? As the long-wished-for day approaches, let us pray still more fervently, attentive to the invitation of the Church we so often hear, 'Sursum Corda!' Let us lift up our hearts in frequent earnest prayer that the decision may be such as will redound to the praise of the adorable Trinity, the salvation of man, and to the honor of her, who, next to God, is indeed the Æterna Coeli Gloria, Beata Spes Mortalium. — "The eternal joy and glory of the heavens; the ever blessed hope of fallen man." If such be the will of God and your piety deserves it, before the close of this year we may hear again the voice of Peter, as when the days of the Pentecost were accomplished, making known by the lips of Pius IX, to the assembled representatives of every nation under heaven, that from henceforth and forever, all generations of true believers shall invoke Mary, Mother of God, as the Ever Immaculate Virgin: Conceived without Stain of Original Sin.

"Such appears to be the expectation of the whole Catholic world. The looking forward for the 'coming of the Messiah' her Divine Son, Christ Jesus, was not more general in the times before His advent, than is this universal expectation that the Vicegerent of that same Divine Son, our Holy Father, will decide that the Blessed Virgin was never stained by Original Sin: — that by a special privilege, which the Almighty could certainly grant, Mary was always exempt from that law to which all the other children of Adam are subject — that from the first moment of her existence Mary was perfect purity itself in the sight of God. And that therefore the words of Holy Writ and of Christian antiquity are to be understood in their literal sense, when it is said 'Thou art all beautiful, O Virgin Mary! And there is not a spot in thee. In thee no spot of sin either is, or ever was, or ever will be,' 'Tota pulchra es, Virgo Maria! Et macula non est in Te; macula peccati non est in Te, neque unquam fuit nec erit.'

"Although the Church has not yet declared the Immaculate Conception to be an article of faith, nevertheless it is evident she cherishes this most just and pious belief with a loving constancy, second only to that infallible certainty with which she maintains the truth of all those doctrines the acceptance of which is necessary for salvation. With a zeal probably never surpassed in former ages, the subject has been investigated by many of the most gifted and holy men now living; and with such a munificent outlay of ancient and modern learning, of profound argument, and soul-stirring eloquence, have they treated it, as to leave not only the more devout clients of Mary, but every unbiassed mind convinced beyond the possibility of doubting, that if there be anything certainly true, next to the defined doctrines of faith, it is this apostolic, and therefore ancient and beautiful belief.

"Hence, is it not surprising, that wherever the most enlightened piety exists, there also, hardly a moment's hesitation on this subject will be entertained. '*Caro Jesu! Caro Mariæ!*' 'The flesh of Jesus is the flesh of Mary!' they will at once exclaim with the great St. Augustine. How can it be that the God of all purity, to whom even the least shadow of sin is an object of eternal abhorrence, should have suffered His Virgin Mother to be, even for an instant, such an object in His sight! From her, He received that flesh and blood — that human nature in which, made one with the Divinity, He redeemed the world, and can we believe that the same in Mary's person, in any possible degree was ever sullied by the demon's breath; dishonored by the taint of guilt. Or again, with St. Cyril, the pious Catholic will ask, 'Who hath ever heard that an architect built a glorious dwelling for himself, and at once gave it over to be possessed by his most cruel and hated enemy?'

"If there were no other words of Holy Writ on this topic than these — 'Mary, of whom was born Jesus who is called Christ' (*St. Matt. i, 16*) — they would be amply sufficient. Behold the divine fact, that overthrows every difficulty; the inspired oracle that sweeps away every objection.

"Never, Christian Brethren, never can we admit that She was for one moment the slave of the devil; — the Virgin, who was destined to be the Mother of God, the Spouse of the Holy Spirit, the Ark of the New Covenant, the Mediatrix of Mankind, the Terror of the Powers of Darkness, the Queen of all the Heavenly Hosts.

"Purer than heaven's purest Angel; brighter than its brightest Seraph; Mary, after her Creator, God — who made and gave Her all, is the most perfect of beings; the Masterpiece of Infinite Wisdom, Almighty Power and Eternal Love.

"To such a being we cannot reasonably suppose that a perfection was denied, which had been already gratuitously bestowed on inferior creatures, on the Angelic Spirits, for example, some of whom afterwards fell away from God and are lost forever. And again — the first man and the first woman were created sinless — pure as the virgin world on which the Almighty had just looked down with infinite delight and declared it to be '*valde bona!*' exceeding good! How just and natural, therefore, may we not add — how unavoidable is the conclusion, that this sublime privilege was not withheld from Mary, set apart, as she was, from all eternity, for office and honors in the kingdom of God, to which no other created being ever will or can be exalted. The more so, since profound divines do not hesitate to assert, that rather than be without the grace, conferred upon her in her Immaculate Conception, and thus, though only for an instant, an object of God's displeasure, Mary would have preferred to forfeit forever the infinite dignity of being Mother of Jesus Christ.

"Gladly would we dwell more at length on the subject, but you observe yourselves, the occasion does not allow it. The few thoughts we have uttered are but the echo of Christian antiquity; of the faith, the filial love, the confidence in Mary, when apostles and evangelists were still on earth, and revered Her name.

"How profound should be our gratitude, in being able to say, that name we also reverence; their confidence in Mary we cherish; their filial love we share; their faith is ours. Could the Martyrs and Virgins, the heroic confessors of the faith, the renowned Fathers and Doctors of the Church, 'beloved of God and men, and whose memory is in benediction,' (*Eccles. xlv,*) could these arise and unite their voices to those of their successors now around the Chair of Peter, what would be their testimony? They would point to their immortal writings, and in the language of St. Augustine, so worthy a representative of the genius, wisdom and piety of the primitive Church, they would remind us, that when they speak of the law by which all the children of Adam are born children of wrath, '*they speak not of Mary,*' with regard to whom, on account of the honor due to our Lord, when they discourse of sin, they wish to raise no question whatsoever. (*Lib. de nat. et grat.*) Nay, with an Amen, loud as that which St. Jerome tells us rolled through the magnificent Churches of Rome, like the thunder of Heaven, they would respond to the following declaration of the Council of Trent, *Sess. V.* — 'This Holy Synod declares that it is not its intention to include in this decree, where original sin is spoken of, the Blessed and Immaculate Mother of God.'

"May the day soon dawn upon the world — whether it be in our unhappy times or not — when, with one mind and one heart, Christendom will acknowledge and proclaim this her most honorable privilege. Meanwhile, submitting every thought, word, and wish to the judgment of the Church, we will continue to confess her power; regarding Mary as that '*great sign*' which St. John saw in heaven — a woman, so resplendent with light, grace, and dignity, that he describes her as 'A woman clothed with the sun; with the moon beneath her feet, and on her head a crown of twelve stars; whose Son shall rule the nations with an iron rod: and her Son was taken up to God, and to his throne.' (*Apoc., xii.*)

"And should the Dragon of Impiety, spoken of in the same mysterious vision, whose power to seduce the nations is but too evident, still continue to make war on God and His Church; should the fearful days of wide-spread unbelief, foretold by the Apostles, prove to be *our own*, when men will no longer endure sound doctrine, but, according to their own desires, will heap up to themselves teachers having lying lips; turning away their hearing from the truth to give heed to fables; speaking proud words of vain philosophy; despising government and all majesty; audacious, self-willed — fearing not to bring in sects; promising their followers *liberty*, whereas they themselves are the slaves of corruption — days of calamity, in which the same inspired teachers warn us, men will blaspheme whatever things they know not; that is, the unsearchable ways of God and mysteries of religion, and what things soever they naturally do know, in these they will be corrupted mockers, murmurers, full of complaints, inventors of evil things, disobedient to parents, without affection, without fidelity, walking according to their own desires in ungodliness; filled with avarice and envy, counting for a pleasure the delights of a day; sporting themselves to excess; rioting in their feasts with you, having their eyes full of adultery and never-ceasing sin; alluring unstable souls who have lost their faith, and, leaving the right way, will, in the end, discover that they have been following 'wandering stars, to whom the storm of darkness is reserved forever.' Christian Brethren, if these be the times in store for the already afflicted Church of Jesus Christ, in the midst of which, with fear and trembling, we, her children, are to work out our salvation, to whom can we turn with more confidence than to His divine Mother, whom the Church has never invoked in vain.

"Hail! Holy Queen, Mother of Mercy! Guard the kingdom of the Christ-loving Pius, our chief bishop. Pray for the people. Intercede for the Clergy. Protect the consecrated Virgins. Unto us all give strength against our enemies and thine; courage to the fearful, joy to those that mourn, peace to the contrite of heart, perseverance to the just. Let all experience thy protection, Virgin and Mother! Through whom the nations are brought to penitence, the demons are put to flight, and they that sat in darkness and the shadow of death are filled with the knowledge and the love of thy only-begotten Son.

"Given under our hand, at our residence in Philadelphia, on the Feast of St. Charles Borromeo, in the year of our Lord eighteen hundred and fifty-four.

"John Nepomucen, Bishop of Philadelphia."

These letters clearly exhibit the mind of the Church in regard to the Immaculate Conception, and form no doubtful evidence of the continuance of the presence of the Holy Ghost in the Church of God to lead it now, as ever, in the way of truth. The Sovereign Pontiff, the Prelates, and Catholic people throughout the world, are on this point, as on all others, one: one in heart, one in faith, one in their profound love and veneration of the Immaculate Mother of God. And now, as the result of a universal desire, the resounding echo of the sovereign voice of the Supreme Pontiff salutes our ears in that joyful and soul-inspiring declaration that Mary, the Mother of God, was Immaculate from the first instant of her Conception. The Christian world has now for ages expected this solemn definition, and sighed to behold it; but died without the joyous fruition of their wish. Happier are we, whose eyes behold, and whose ears hear, the complete triumph of our loving Mother. With reverence and humility, may we not, with holy Simeon, exclaim, "Now thou dost dismiss thy servant, O Lord, according to thy word, in peace. Because my eyes have seen thy salvation, which thou hast prepared before the face of all peoples." (*St. Luke, chap. ii, 29-31.*)

"Coronation of the Virgin" by Diego Velázquez (1599–1660)

CHAPTER XVII

"He that heareth the Church, heareth Me."

THE CHURCH DOES NOT ASSUME TO HERSELF THE POWER to make new articles of Faith. Its Pastors, whether scattered throughout the world, or convened in general council, have power to teach, order, arrange, define, and command those things which have been handed down as the sacred deposit originally committed to the Apostles; but they do not assume a power to originate or construct. Hence St. Augustine has said, "Those things which we observe — things not written, but transmitted, which are, indeed, observed throughout the whole world — it is to be understood that they are to be retained, as commanded and decreed, either by the Apostles themselves, or by general Councils, the authority of which is most wholesome in the Church." (*Tom. II, Epist. 54, n. 1, Janu. col. 185.*) St. Vincent of Lerins also exclaims, "This I say: the Catholic Church hath never done anything else by the decrees of her Councils; nothing but what she previously had received from her forefathers by tradition alone: that same, she consigned thenceforward to posterity by writing also; by comprising a great sum of things in a few words; and oftentimes, for a more luminous understanding, *by marking with the propriety of a new appellation an old article of faith.*" (*Adver. Hæres., num. xxiii.*) Speaking of the Council of Nicæa, St. Cyril of Alexandria asks: "How can it be doubted that Christ hath invisibly presided at the holy and great Synod?" (*Tom. VI, Epis. in S. Symbol.*)

Innumerable are the passages to be found in the early writers of the Christian Church which testify to their powers; to the unerring character of their decisions; to the necessity of hearing the Church, through their voice; to the never-failing presence of Christ and the Holy Ghost to lead and keep the Church in the way of all truth. "It hath seemed good to the Holy Ghost and to us," is the familiar language which, derived from the first Council of Jerusalem, (*Acts xv, 28,*) is applicable to every decision of every Council, in every age. And to what purpose has our Divine Lord established His Church, if this were not so? To what purpose has He said, "Behold I am with you all days, even to the consummation of the world?" (*St. Matt. xxviii, 20.*) Why hath He said, "He that heareth you heareth me?" (*St. Luke x, 16.*) Why did He promise the Paraclete, the Spirit of Truth, to abide with His Church forever? (*St. John xiv, 16.*) Why, I ask, hath Christ, to whom all power is given in Heaven and on earth, thus fortified His Church, provided it with safeguards from error, surrounded it, imbued it, and inspired it with His protecting presence, and that of the Spirit of all Truth, if it were not to render it the living, credible, trustworthy witness of the Gospel of Truth, which He came to establish; that there might be no age, no period, no moment of time when anyone should be able to say the Church of Christ has gone wrong; it is no more worthy of trust?

If then the Church is, as reason demands she must be, and revelation declares she is, inerrant, infallible, let us, in summing up the lesson she hath taught us by her Councils and Supreme Pontiffs, listen as though it were the audible voice of the Son of God, teaching, He that heareth the Church, heareth Me. (*St. Luke x, 16.*) We have then heard His voice in the Council of Nicæa, pronouncing "the Blessed Mary altogether holy, pure, and chaste;" the Council of Ephesus, "exalted above all the choirs of angels, created without any stain, and in whom there is no spot;" the Council of Toledo, "that she hath been exempt from original sin, immaculate;" that of Trullo, that "she is holy, immaculate, and without the universal taint;" the second Nicene Council, "always holy, more sublime than any visible or invisible creature; holy, immaculate, purer than any intelligence;" that of Oxford, "that her Conception was holy, immaculate." In the Council of London, the Festival of her Immaculate Conception is solemnly and formally instituted; in that of Constantinople, her Conception is proclaimed "pure and immaculate;" and finally, we have heard the general voice of the Council of Trent favoring the proposition to solemnly define the Immaculate Conception as a Dogma. Has the Lord, who promised to be with His Church forever, failed to keep His immutable word?

Has the Divine Spirit wearied of His watch upon the battlements of Zion? And have They suffered the Church, bought with the blood of the Lamb, to err and mislead the Christian world? "Knowest thou not, or hast thou not heard, that the Lord is the everlasting God, who hath created the ends of the earth? He shall not faint nor grow weary." (*Isa., chap. xl.*) A thousand years are in His sight but as yesterday. (*Psalm xc.*) It was but yesterday, then, that He promised His perpetual presence to His Church; it was but yesterday he endowed it with the Holy Spirit; it was but yesterday He fulfilled His promise in the descent of the Holy Ghost, and in the Councils of Jerusalem, Nicæa, and Ephesus. Shall He not be present today at Rome? If not, then is the final chapter of the history of the Church of God written. It is no more; and the infinite sacrifice of Calvary is an abomination and a mockery. But, if His word is truth itself, if His promise never faileth, then is He there; then doth His Holy Spirit preside, and we, in humility and faith, hear its voice re-echoing the words of its predecessors: "Mary was conceived without the contamination of original sin; pure, immaculate;" holy in her conception; worthy to have been the second Eve; worthy to have crushed the serpent's head; worthy to have been exalted above all the choirs of angels; worthy to be the daughter of God the Father, Mother of God the Son, and Spouse of God the Holy Ghost.

The representative of Christ on earth, and the visible head of His Church, is the Bishop of Rome. He is its vocal organ, its mouth-piece, the divinely established medium of communication with the Christian world. Hence St. Ignatius says: "The Bishop holds the Presidency in the place of God." "Be ye made one with the Bishop and with those who preside."[1] Again: "It is plain, then, that we ought to look to the Bishop as to the Lord Himself."[2] "For inasmuch as you are subject to the Bishop, as to Jesus Christ, you seem to me to be living not according to man, but according to Jesus Christ."[3] "It is good to regard God and the Bishop."[4]

We have listened to the Bishop. We have heard the edict; the peremptory decree. The Supreme Pontiff, the Bishop of bishops, hath spoken — not one merely, but many. They have said, that the soul of Mary was holy from the first instant of its creation; that her Conception was Immaculate; that she was conceived without original sin; and that therefore she is exalted above all creatures, the choirs of Angels and Archangels, even to the throne of the Deity. But may they not have erred? The concurrent testimony of the world for eighteen centuries answers no; and confirms the decree. The vocal organ of the Church, they but utter its perpetual belief; its universal voice. It is their undoubted right to interpret, pronounce judgment upon, and define articles of faith; and the Lord Himself deigns to speak by their mouth. Their faith, their love, their solicitude and zeal, when the integrity of the truth of Christ's Church is in question, form the unfailing characteristics of the Pontiffs; and their solemn definitions of doctrine have never yet been wrong. The Lord Christ speaks by their mouth, and the celestial Spirit of truth and grace inspires their heart. The Popes do not originate or create an article of faith: They have never attempted it. They teach and define what is the faith; and none have yet so taught, or so defined, anything but that which the Church from its foundation hath believed. "What can restrain the Pope?" de Maistre asks, and beautifully answers: "Everything — canons, laws, national usages, sovereigns, tribunals, national assemblies, councils, prescription, representations, negotiations, duty, fear, prudence, and especially public opinion, the queen of the world."[5]

May we not add, the Spirit of God, the Paraclete, divine grace, restrains him? And the assenting voice, the universal Amen of Christendom confirms the inerrancy of their decrees. The faith of the Church of Rome was celebrated throughout the whole world in the very infancy of Christianity. (*Romans, chap. i, 8*.) And the authoritative decisions of its Bishops over its own and the affairs of the entire Christian Church, form one of the earliest as well as most notorious passages of Church history. When, in the first century, violent commotions broke out in Corinth, Clement, Bishop of Rome, interposed his authority to

1. *Ep. ad Magnes*, n. 6.
2. *Ep. ad Ephes.*
3. *Ep. ad Mag.*
4. *Ep. ad Smyrn.*
5. *Du Pape, chap. xviii.*

calm the elements of discord. Victor, in the second century, decided the Pascal controversy. Cornelius, in the following century, overcame the Novatian schism. St. Stephen shortly afterwards authoritatively interposed in the African controversy concerning Baptism. Melchiades judged and condemned the Donatists. The decisions of Damasus and Innocent, of Celestine and Leo, were received by the Bishops as the unerring expositions of the faith in regard to the doctrines of the Trinity and the Incarnation. None disputed the pre-eminence of the Bishops of Rome; even though the disaffected may have stubbornly refused to submit to their decisions. Their prerogative to settle controversies and define articles of faith, has ever been acknowledged; and its exercise often evoked.

We have seen that such is the case at present, in respect to the doctrine of the Immaculate Conception of the Blessed Virgin. That definition has long been sought, and ardently wished for. Petitions have been sent to this end to the Supreme Pontiff from every part of the Church, from Prelates, Priests, and People; and if those appeals had been at once and immediately answered, the Pontiff's decision would have been hailed with universal acclaim. But, behold the wisdom and prudence of our venerable and illustrious Chief! He does nothing impetuously or rashly, as if from his own private views, feelings, or interests. Though He has from his earliest years cherished a special devotion and profound affection towards the Most Blessed Virgin; though He has all his life long devoutly believed her Immaculate Conception, and thinks that there is no point of faith more certain or more ancient; and though confident in his faith, He has permitted the Office of the Immaculate Conception to be recited throughout the world; yet, He calmly pauses, not in doubt, but with sedulous care; pauses before he solemnly and publicly decides so momentous a question.

He addresses anew letters to the Patriarchs, Primates, Archbishops, and Bishops throughout the world, and asks anew the assistance of their prayers and their advice; He seeks anew the light of the Holy Ghost; He commits anew the whole subject to the deep and earnest attention of profound theologians, and to men illustrious for their virtue, piety, council, prudence, and knowledge of divine things. And after all is finished, and the subject has been again and again examined, still, though satisfied, He makes no decision; but invites His Venerable Brethren, the Prelates of the various Churches, to assemble around Him, that He, like Peter at Jerusalem, may hear their voice; and, invoking the illumination of the Holy Ghost, discuss the subject over again, calmly and deliberately, and commune with each other in the charity of the Gospel of Christ. How consoling is all this! What heavenly confidence it inspires! How different from the rashness and hastiness of proud innovators; and how sure the evidence, that it is not as man He speaks and acts, but, according to St. Ignatius, as one "holding the Presidency in the place of God!"

It is plain, then, as the same saint says, that "we ought to look to the Bishop, as to the Lord himself;" and receive his decision with gratitude and love. Thus is it that the Church is knit together in the bonds of charity, compact and firm;

thus is it that its unity is preserved, steadfast and sure. Thus preserving the truth in charity, we in all things growing up in Him who is the head, even Christ; "from whom the whole body, being compacted and fitly joined together, by what every joint supplieth — maketh increase of the body unto the edifying of itself in Charity." (*Eph. iv, 16.*) One in body, one in faith, even as we are called in one hope of our calling. (*Eph. iv, 4.*) Thus, too, is the sublime prayer of the Redeemer fulfilled. "Holy Father, keep them in thy name, whom thou hast given me; that they may be one, as we also are. And not for them only do I pray, but for them also who through their word shall believe in me; that they all may be one, as thou, Father, in me, and I in Thee; that they also may be one in us; that the world may believe that thou hast sent me. And the glory which thou hast given me, I have given to them; that they may be one, as we also are one. I in them, and thou in me, that they may be made perfect in one; and the world may know that thou hast sent me, and hast loved them, as thou hast loved me." (*St. John, chap. xvii.*)

The Column of the Immaculate Conception depicting the Virgin Mary, located in the Piazza Mignanelli in Rome, Italy.

CHAPTER XVIII

The Festival of the Immaculate Conception of the Most Blessed Virgin Mary, and the Ceremonies Incident to the Publication of the Dogmatic Decree—Given at Rome, December 8th, 1854

A GREAT EVENT, WHICH ALL FUTURE AGES WILL BLESS, was accomplished on the morning of the 8th of December, 1854, in the basilica of the Vatican. The Sovereign Pontiff of the Catholic Church, Pius IX, has at length defined as a dogma of faith, in pursuance of the ardent desire of the Bishops, and of the Faithful confided to their care, that which has been for ages past the pious and universal belief relative to the Immaculate Conception of the Most Holy Mary.

The dawn of that day, although on the previous evening rain fell in abundance, broke pure and serene as a beautiful morning in spring. And Rome, which, in consequence of her unbounded devotion to Mary, awaited with more of anxiety than any other city the oracle of the Vatican, was in motion from the first streaks of day, and manifested so early her joyfulness. The citizens of all classes, joined by an immense concourse of strangers who had hastened to Rome from all parts, proceeded towards the Vatican. All wished to be present at the solemn ceremony, and to hear what they must firmly believe upon the Immaculate Conception of the Mother of God, whom the Fathers of the Church call a prodigy of innocence, of purity, of perfectitude, full of grace and glory, and whom the pious Faithful invoke, employing for that purpose the proper prayers of the Church, as full of grace, Queen of Angels and of men, Dispensatrix of heavenly blessings, the Hope and the Help of all in the midst of the tempests and the agitations of life.

Rome, upon this day, has manifested in the most striking manner what is her devotion for the Most Holy Virgin; and the Bishops, on returning to their dioceses, and in announcing to their people what they have heard from the oracle of the Vatican, can also tell them what honors people render to the Virgin in the capital of the Catholic world, and if Rome on this occasion was beneath Ephesus. The history of the Church will mark amongst the most memorable this day, on which the august Mother of the Savior of the world has received from the Chair of Truth a new triumph.

On June 21st, in the year 431, the whole city of Ephesus was in activity and feverish with anxiety. Upwards of two hundred Bishops, presided over by the great St. Cyril of Alexandria, Legate of the Sovereign Roman Pontiff, were assembled in the Church of St. Mary. The object of that solemn assembly was to examine and to condemn the errors taught by Nestorius, and in particular his heresy on the subject of the maternity of the Holy Virgin, to whom he refused the title of true Mother of God. That error wounded the hearts of the Christian people, to whom the title denied was particularly dear, and therefore the inhabitants of Ephesus collected around that Episcopal assembly, impatiently awaiting the result of its deliberations. The session lasted from the morning until sunset; but nothing could weary the pious anxiety of the Faithful. Some in the sanctuary of their families prayed with fervor that the heresiarch Nestorius might be condemned, and that Mary might be preserved in the title of Mother of God; others, surrounding the church in which the Bishops were assembled, awaited the rising of the assembly to know the sooner what they should have pronounced.

At last the meeting concluded, and when the people knew that the council had decided that Mary must be called Mother of God, and pronounced anathema against whoever would think otherwise, all the people sent forth an immense acclamation of joy. That was a spectacle full of emotion; sadness gave place immediately to the most lively joy. The whole city was spontaneously illuminated and embellished with its holiday ornaments; fires were kindled in the public squares, and the Bishops were re-conducted to their residences by a multitude intoxicated with happiness, who carried lighted torches and scattered perfumes and flowers in the steps of the Fathers of the council. This was the prodigy which the faith of the Christian people and their love for Mary produced in a great city in the fifth century.

Rome has just witnessed a spectacle which yields in nothing to that which we have just recalled. The nineteenth century has produced a festival which does no less honor to the faith of its children and their devotion for the Queen of Heaven. The number of Bishops assembled in Rome on the 8th of December, 1854, was the same as at Ephesus. The object of their meeting was also the proclamation of one of the most glorious privileges of Mary, of that which is the foundation of all the others, and without which the title even of Mother of God would not, without doubt, have been conferred on her by the Most High. How could God have chosen for His Mother a creature who might have been for a single instant the subject of Satan and a daughter of sin? Not less dear to the Christian people is the title, the possession of which has just been assured to the Queen of Virgins, and which has been from the cradle of the Church the object of universal belief, and every age had sighed for the oracle which would proclaim it the irrefragable truth.

As at Ephesus, all the Christian people were in expectation and anxiety, demanding of God that its wishes might be heard, and that Mary might be proclaimed without spot or stain, and immaculate in her conception. But, more happy than the Pope St. Celestine, Pius IX could preside himself over the assembly of his brethren the Cardinals, Patriarchs, Archbishops, and Bishops of all the earth. He had not to strike one of his brethren in the Episcopacy; and the haughty Nestorius had no emulator in the august assembly of Rome. The glory of Mary had not to be defended against any person, and in this brilliant victory gained by the Queen of Heaven impiety only has been vanquished; Hell alone has trembled; the entire Church has applauded; and the dogma defined on the 8th of December, in the Basilica of the Prince of the Apostles, by the Vicar of Jesus Christ, was proclaimed beforehand by the voice of all the Bishops, and by the ardent prayers and supplications of all the faithful children of the universal Church.

Let us describe, then, as far as it may be possible, a festival that so many saints have desired, that so many ages have called for with their vows, that so many Pontiffs have wished to give to the Church, and that the Lord in His infinite mercy had willed to reserve to our unhappy times as their hope and their resource. The festival of Rome is the festival of the entire world; it is presided over by the august Head of the Church. Two hundred Bishops come from all corners of the world, from the far-off regions of China, the deserts of America, of the most distant islands of the ocean, to the court of the Vicar of Jesus Christ, and encircle him as by a brilliant crown; two or three hundred Prelates of all ranks, of all titles, of all costumes, serve as his retinue of honor.

Oh, but it is beautiful to see that magnificent, that incomparable procession descending the grand stairs of Constantine. In the first rank walked the Apostolic Preacher and the Confessor of the Pontifical household, followed by the Purveyors-General of the Religious Orders, by the Papal Messengers, the Chaplains in Ordinary, the Pontifical Couriers and Assistant Chamberlains. Next came the Private Clerks, and the Honorary Private Chaplains, the Consistorial Advocates, the State Chamberlains, and the Pontifical Precentors. After them the Abbreviators of the Briefs, the Votants of the Signature, the Clerks of the Chamber, the Auditors of Rota, and the Master of the Holy Hospital. Then followed the Cross, borne by an Auditor of Rota, in the midst of seven Prelates, bearing candlesticks with lighted wax tapers; following the Cross walked the Latin Sub-Deacon, the Greek Deacon and Sub-Deacon, the Penitentiaries of St. Peter's, the Bishops, the Archbishops, and the Cardinals. Lastly, under the canopy came the Sovereign Pontiff, immediately following whom, before the Roman magistracy, came the *Vice-Camerlengo* of the Holy Church, the two Assistant Cardinal Deacons, and the Cardinal Deacon, whose duty it is to assist the Pontiff in the celebration of the Solemn Mass; then followed the Dean of the Rota, the Auditor of the Chamber, the Major Domo, the Master of the Chamber, the Regent of the Chancellery, and the Apostolical Purveyors.

Contemplate the magnificence of that consecrated throng. What variety, what richness in the sacred ornaments! Six Cardinal Bishops, thirty-seven Cardinal Priests, eleven Cardinal Deacons, a Patriarch of the East, forty-two Archbishops, a hundred Bishops, of all rites, of every country in the world, marching in two majestic files, invested in cope, and the mitre on their heads. The Vicar of Jesus Christ followed them in all the splendor of his Pontifical ornaments! The chant of the Litany, commenced in the Sistine Chapel, was continued through the royal hall, the stairs of Constantine, the peristyle, and the grand nave of the basilica. An immense concourse crowded to see the procession of the Pastors of the Church, and to receive the benediction of its Supreme Chief, who advanced, praying with pious recollection, a holy joy playing on his lips and in his eyes.

Having arrived in front of the Chapel of the Holy Sacrament, the procession halted, and, after adoring God concealed in the tabernacle, the Pope finished the chanting of the Litany by the consecrated prayer; then the retinue recommenced its procession towards the altar of the Confession, all resplendent with tiaras and precious mitres, with the cross and candlesticks of gold, with reliquaries, with flowers and lights. It passed before the ancient statue of the first Pope, of him who received from Jesus Christ himself the government of the holy Church, of Peter, the fisherman of Galilee, become the Sovereign Pontiff, the Vicar of Jesus Christ, the head of the Universal Church; Pope Pius IX, being his 259th successor, gloriously reigning, the heir of his authority and of his virtues. The College of the Holy Apostles found itself again, and recognized itself in the two hundred Bishops who followed their Supreme Pastor; and the Clergy, and the Faithful, who filled the immense basilica, are the faithful type of the primitive Church. It was thus that in Jerusalem the Apostles assembled together, under the presidency of Peter, and the Holy Ghost was in the midst of them.

When the Sovereign Pontiff was seated upon his throne, the Cardinals, the Archbishops, the Bishops, and the Prelates went in turn to render obedience to him and venerate their august Chief; he from whom flows all spiritual jurisdiction and authority, he who sits in the Chair of Peter, and who feeds both Pastors and sheep. China sent him one of her Vicars-Apostolic; America several of her Archbishops and Bishops; the isles lost in farthermost ocean had their representatives there. Europe deputed thither the greatest part of her Pastors. Rome counted there sixty Bishops, of whom thirty are Princes of the Church; the Pontifical States, France, Austria, Spain, the Two Sicilies, Piedmont, Belgium, Bavaria, all the Catholic powers were there blended in the same respect and in the same love; Lutheran England, Evangelical Prussia, Calvinistic Holland, sent the chiefs of their young Hierarchies thither. Empires, kingdoms, republics gave each other the hand in unity there; and when these two hundred Bishops had taken place on their seats, having behind them an infinite number of inferior Prelates, of Generals of Orders, of Priests, of Religious and Faithful, and at their head the Sovereign Roman Pontiff, could we not say that the Universal Church was present?

The chanting of the Tierce is terminated; the Obedience is finished; and, if we may presume to employ this term, the assembly has assumed that aspect that we admire in the old paintings and engravings, in which the Council of Trent and the other great assizes of the Holy Catholic Church are represented, but with that additional majesty and that grander character that the presence of the august and Supreme Pastor imprints upon it. The Holy Sacrifice is about to commence, and the High Priest of the Universal Law advances towards the altar to immolate the Adorable Victim. We do not wish to describe the beauty of the ceremonies, the harmonious melody of the chants consecrated by ages, and the rites so grand, so splendid, which invest the holy function celebrated by the Supreme Pontiff: this picture would carry us too far, and we must hasten to arrive at the solemn moment, to the reading of the Decree, in honor of which all this pomp is displayed, all these Bishops have come from afar, and which must assure to Mary the most glorious of her privileges, and the purest of her Mysteries.

The Gospel has been chanted in the Latin and Greek — the two languages consecrated by the Holy Liturgy, and in the two rites prescribed for the Papal Mass. It is the moment so impatiently expected, the hour marked from all eternity in the decrees of the mercy of the Most High: all eyes are turned towards the throne of the Supreme Pontiff; a solemn silence reigns in the immense assembly; every heart is elevated towards Heaven. The Universal Church deputes to the throne of the Vicar of Jesus Christ five of her Pastors to beg of him to satisfy at last the devotion of the Christian people, and to define that the belief in the Immaculate Conception of Mary is an article of Catholic faith. His Eminence the Cardinal Macchi, in his capacity of Dean of the Sacred College, accompanied by the Deans, the Archbishops, and the Bishops present at the august ceremony, and also by the Archbishop of the Greek rite and the Archbishop of the Armenian rite, presented himself at the foot of the throne and addressed in Latin these words to the Sovereign Pontiff: —

"That which the Catholic Church, Most Holy Father, ardently desires and calls for with all her heart for a long time past is, that your supreme and infallible judgment should pronounce on the Immaculate Conception of the Most Holy Virgin Mary, Mother of God, a decision which may be for her an increase of praise, of glory, and veneration. In the name of the Sacred College of the Cardinals, of the Bishops of the Catholic world, and of all the Faithful, we demand humbly and urgently that the universal wishes of the Church may be accomplished in this solemnity of the Conception of the Blessed Virgin.

"At the time, then, when the August Sacrifice of the Altar will be offered in this temple consecrated to the Prince of the Apostles, and in the midst of this solemn assembly of the Sacred College, the Bishops and the people, deign, Most Holy Father, to raise your Apostolical voice, and to pronounce that dogmatic decree of the Immaculate Conception of Mary, which will be a subject of joy for Heaven, and of the most lively gladness for the earth."

The Pontiff replied to these words that he received willingly the prayer of the Sacred College, of the Episcopacy, and of the Faithful, but that in order to grant it it was necessary to invoke first the assistance of the Holy Ghost. Immediately the "Veni Creator" was intoned, and the improvised chant of that hymn was executed not only by the singers of the Papal Chapel, but by all the people assembled. Animated with the most ardent faith and love towards her whom all the nations called Blessed, each invoked the light of Heaven upon the Sovereign Pontiff, who was ready to give from the height of the Chair of Peter a decision which would cause immediately to bend with respect the forehead of every faithful Catholic, spread abroad throughout the whole earth, and notwithstanding all diversities of language, of legislation, of manners, and of climates.

After the singing of the hymn, the Vicar of Christ arose and chanted the prayers; then, in presence of all the Catholic Church, represented by fifty-four Cardinals, by one Patriarch, by forty-two Archbishops, and by one hundred Bishops, by two or three hundred inferior Prelates, by many thousands of Priests and of Religious of all rites, from all countries, of all Orders, and of all costumes, and at least fifty thousand Faithful of all conditions and of all countries; with the mitre on his head and in the attitude of the Supreme Doctor, charged with interpreting the sentences and the traditions, and with pronouncing the oracles of the Faith, he commenced the reading of the Decree in that voice, grave and sonorous, sweet and majestic, which gives to his words an indefinable charm.

After the invocation of the Most Holy Trinity, of the Apostles Peter and Paul, to the moment in which he reached the passage concerning the Immaculate Conception, his voice softened, tears mounted to his eyes, and when he pronounced the sacramental words *definimus, decretamus et confirmamus* (*define, decree and confirm*), his emotion interrupts him, and he is obliged to stop to wipe away the tears which stream from his eyes, yet we see that he makes a powerful effort to control his emotion, and he then resumes the reading with that voice, firm and full of authority, which becomes the judge of the Faith. His heart mounts to his lips, and we know not whether he preaches or reads, so animated is his voice, so full of emotion, and we feel that the Father of Christendom, the devoted Son of Mary, the Supreme Pastor of the Church, and the infallible Judge of the Faith, speak together; or, rather, that it is the Divine Spirit which speaks by his mouth, and which mingles with the oracles of the doctor of the truth the sentiments of a heart tenderly devoted to Mary.

His emotion recommenced when, after having declared that the belief in the Immaculate Conception has been from all time the belief of the Catholic Church, that consequently it must be professed by all her children, and, after establishing the penalties they incur who will be sufficiently rash to contradict it, he came again to speak of the graces for which he acknowledged himself indebted to the Most Holy Mother of God, of the hopes that he founds upon her protection for the assuaging of the evils of society and of the Church, and of the happiness that he experiences in advancing the glory of Her whom he has always loved so much, and from whom emanates all the gifts and graces from on High.

But to what purpose prolong an analysis made upon recollections which cannot be perfect or faithful; yet we cannot but admire the manner, strong and sweet at the same time, with which the Vicar of Jesus Christ has proclaimed the infallible oracle, which places securely upon the forehead of our great Queen and Mistress the glorious diadem of an Immaculate Conception! Oh! But it was beautiful to see Pius IX shedding tears of tenderness in crowning his beloved Mother! O precious tears, which the Angels have gathered, and which will sparkle like diamonds upon the crown that the Queen of Angels reserves for the Pontiff who has given her a glory so magnificent! But they were beautiful, those Cardinals, those Archbishops, and those Bishops, listening with love to the Decree which proclaimed the greatness of Mary, gathering with respect the words which fell from the lips of the Supreme Pontiff, and which they will go to repeat throughout the universe, to infidels of China, to the savages of America, and to the far distant isles of Polynesia, in every language, in all the empires, in all the quarters of the habitable world! O august senate of the Catholic Church, may you be blessed for assisting at so beautiful a festival! May the fatigues of your long voyages, of your long travels, be superabundantly recompensed by the splendor added on this day to the diadem of the Queen of the Church! May they be happy, your faithful people, when they gather from your lips the words which you have gathered yourselves from the infallible lips of the Sovereign Pastor, and that you say to them: — "We were there, we have seen, we have heard! That crown which glitters on the brow of our Mother and thine we have helped to place there!"

But it was beautiful, all those Clergy of the inferior ranks of the Hierarchy, uniting themselves with the Bishops to hail the decree, and prepare themselves to go to proclaim it in the most remote places, in the most distant missions, in the pulpits of the greatest cities and the most humble hamlets! And you, Faithful of all ranks, of every sex and condition, who filled the immense church of the Prince of Apostles, have you ever seen a higher expression of Catholic unity? Oh! But it was beautiful! But it was agreeable to the Lord that innumerable assembly, in which all hearts throbbed like one for love of Mary, in which only one mouth was opened as it were, although all spoke, first to beg light from the Holy Ghost in unison with the Holy Father, the Bishops, and the Clergy, afterwards to thank God and salute Mary crowned with the diadem of the Immaculate Conception; for in that consists one of the characteristics, the most touching and the most Catholic, of this admirable fête! Scarcely issued from the lips of the Vicar of Christ, the invocation to the spirit of light and of love is found upon all lips, and one might have said that only a single voice, a voice composed of fifty thousand voices, mounted to Heaven. So the "Te Deum" was no sooner intoned by the Supreme Pontiff than it rose throughout the entire basilica, and it was a hymn boundless in thanks and gratitude, an immense, a universal acclamation of the glorious privilege of Mary. A prayer, ardent and unanimous, which the salvos of the artillery and the pealings of the bells of the city carried to Heaven, and deposited at the feet of the Immaculate Virgin.

But that brilliant crown, which the word of the Vicar of Jesus Christ had just placed upon the blessed head of our Queen and our mistress, shall it not have a material sign which will symbolize it and transmit the memory of it to future generations? Pius IX thinks so. A crown of the finest gold, enriched with the most precious stones, is prepared to decorate the head of the Immaculate Virgin, which the mosaic art has represented, *in æternum*, above the high altar of the Chapel of the Canons. After the "Te Deum" this splendid diadem is blessed by the Pope on the same altar of the Confession, and the Sovereign Pontiff, preceded by his magnificent and imposing train, goes processionally to carry to the venerated Madonna the diadem prepared by the signal piety of the Chapter of St. Peter's. With his sacred hands he deposited the precious crown upon the brow of the august Sovereign of Heaven and earth, of the glorious Queen of the Church, in presence of the whole court of the Church Militant, in presence, too, of the whole court of the Church Triumphant; for it is not permitted to doubt that the Angels assisted at that fête in which she whom they had eighteen centuries and a half since saluted with these words: *Ave Maria, gratia plena*, is today saluted with these other words: *Ave Maria, sine labe originali concepta!* A double salutation which is only one, for the last is the development, the completion of the first. Reign, then, forever, O glorious Princess! Oh! Most beloved Mother, crowned doubly in Heaven by thy Son, who is God, on the earth by the Vicar of thy Son, who is the Pope Pius IX, by the Universal Church, and by all the Christian people.

But there is not, in the Catholic Church, any feast which is truly beautiful if the people do not make the principal ornament of it. We have spoken of the Princes of the Church, of all the Orders of the Clergy; we have seen all the holy Hierarchy rival each other in eagerness and love; but the Faithful, but the people, what part did they take in this festival? To them it appertained to impress its true character upon it. Have their hearts been moved? Is it really and truly a popular and universal belief that has been defined, and are the children of the Church really desirous to see decreed to Mary the title of Immaculate in her Conception? Ah! The reply to that question has been made; it is there all living. See that multitude from seven o'clock in the morning direct itself towards the ancient basilica of the Prince of the Apostles, and which fills its vast nave and even the chapels, which eagerly presses forward and is incessantly renewed. There is a continual flowing and reflowing of the human tide. The vast entrances of the basilica cannot suffice for these thousands of Faithful who besiege and encumber them. Thirty thousand persons are together in the Church, and as the crowd entered and flowed away without cessation from seven o'clock in the morning until an hour after midday, at least sixty thousand persons must have assisted at the *fête*. And what pious recollection in that multitude! What an air of satisfaction! How heartily they prayed! How the "Veni Creator" and the "Te Deum" moved and agitated it, and how it chanted with love and with faith those prayers of invocation and praise! And the rest of the population, as it filled the churches of the Holy City, as it gave itself to the movement to prepare the illumination which changed the night of this beautiful day into a heaven all strewed with stars! How, at the sound of the bells which announced the consummation of that great act, it prostrated itself, and hailed the Virgin without spot or blemish! What holy canticles were addressed to her in the convents, in the bosom of families, in the secret hearts!

The evening came on, and it was then that the faith, that the joy of the people again shone and burst out, and the entire city became a temple raised to Mary. From the previous evening, notwithstanding the rain, and despite the tempest, thousands of lights saluted the dawning of the day which was about to break; but the evening of the fête the city was literally a city of fire; not a balcony, not a window, not a skylight which had not its illumination lamps. The great thoroughfares of the city, the Corso, the Papal way, Ripetta, are luminous streams; the public squares, the monuments, the churches, bear piles of fire. The Capitol gleams and flashes with light, and the orchestras in the open air hail in the name of the Roman people the triumph of the Queen of Heaven, who is also the Queen of the Church and of Rome. Everywhere are transparencies and images of Mary, inscriptions in her honor, above all the device — *Maria sine labe originali concepta.* An immense multitude urged their way through the city; the whole population is in the streets, on the squares, but especially at St. Peter's, whose dome bore high in the air a sparkling diadem. One might say that a special providence had wished to give to that illumination, of which everyone acknowledged the greatness and the beauty, an unaccustomed splendor. A dark cloud, the only one there was in the sky, which was there as if to keep us in mind of the rain and tempest of the preceding night, formed behind the cupola a sombre and dark background, which admirably set off that crown of fire which the Eternal City offered to the Queen of the Universe. O night more beautiful than the day! O pavilions of light, kindled to illuminate the festival of Our Mother! O Queen of the Heavens! What crown more beautiful can the earth offer to you?[1]

---

1. *Giornale di Roma* and *L'Univers.*

Portrait of Pope Pius IX, engraved by Joseph Swain. Published in the magazine "Once a Week" in 1860.

CHAPTER XIX

Letters Apostolic of Our Most Holy Lord Pius IX, by Divine Providence Pope, Concerning the Dogmatic Definition of the Immaculate Conception of the Virgin Mother of God

Pius, Bishop, Servant of the Servants of God.

FOR THE PERPETUAL REMEMBRANCE OF THE THING.

The Ineffable God, whose ways are mercy and truth, whose will is omnipotence, and whose wisdom reaches powerfully from end to end, and sweetly disposes everything, when He foresaw from all eternity the most sorrowful ruin of the entire human race to follow from the transgression of Adam, and in a mystery hidden from ages determined to complete, through the incarnation of the Word in a more hidden sacrament, the first work of his goodness, so that man, led into sin by the craft of diabolical iniquity, should not perish contrary to His merciful design, and that what was about to befall in the first Adam should be restored more happily in the second; from the beginning and before ages chose and ordained a Mother for His only-begotten Son, of whom made flesh, He should be born in the blessed plenitude of time, and followed her with so great love before all creatures that in her alone He pleased Himself with a most benign complacency. Wherefore, far before all the angelic spirits and all the Saints, He so wonderfully endowed her with the abundance of all the heavenly gifts drawn from the treasure of divinity, that she might be ever free from every stain of sin, and all fair and perfect, would bear before her that plenitude of innocence and holiness than which, under God, none greater is understood, and which, except God, no one can reach even in thought. And indeed it was most becoming that she would shine always adorned with the splendor of the most perfect holiness, and free even from the stain of original sin, would gain a most complete triumph over the ancient serpent; she the Mother so venerable, to whom God the Father, disposed to give His only Son, whom begotten and equal to Himself from His heart He loves as Himself, in such a manner that He would be by nature one and the same common Son of God the Father, and of the Virgin, and whom the Son himself chose to make substantially His Mother, and from whom the Holy Ghost willed and operated that He would be conceived and born from whom He himself proceeds.

Which original innocence of the august Virgin agreeing completely with her admirable holiness, and with the most excellent dignity of the Mother of

God, the Catholic Church, which, ever taught by the Holy Spirit, is the pillar and ground of truth, as possessing a doctrine divinely received, and comprehended in the deposit of heavenly revelation, has never ceased to lay down, to cherish, and to illustrate continually by numerous proofs, and more and more daily by splendid facts. For this doctrine, flourishing from the most ancient times, and implanted in the minds of the Faithful, and by the care and zeal of the Holy Pontiffs wonderfully propagated, the Church herself has most clearly pointed out when she did not hesitate to propose the conception of the same Virgin for the public devotion and veneration of the Faithful. By which illustrious act she pointed out the conception of the Virgin as singular, wonderful, and very far removed from the origins of the rest of mankind, and to be venerated as entirely holy, since the Church celebrates festival days only of the Saints. And, therefore, the very words in which the Sacred Scriptures speak of uncreated Wisdom and represent His eternal origins, she has been accustomed to use not only in the offices of the Church, but also in the holy liturgy, and to transfer to the origin of that Virgin, which was pre-ordained by one and the same decree with the incarnation of Divine Wisdom.

But though all those things, everywhere justly received amongst the Faithful, show with what zeal the Roman Church, the mother and mistress of all Churches, has supported the doctrine of the Immaculate Conception of the Virgin, yet the illustrious acts of this Church are evidently worthy that they should be reviewed by name; since so great is the dignity and authority of the same Church, so much is due to her who is the center of Catholic truth and unity, in whom alone religion has been inviolably guarded, and from whom it is right that all the Churches should receive the tradition of Faith. Thus the same Roman Church had nothing more at heart than to assert, to protect, to promote, and to vindicate in the most eloquent manner the Immaculate Conception of the Virgin, its devotion, and doctrine, which fact so many illustrious acts of the Roman Pontiffs, Our predecessors, most evidently and fully testify and declare, to whom in the person of the Prince of the Apostles was divinely committed by Christ Our Lord the supreme care and power of feeding the lambs and the sheep, of confirming the brethren, and of ruling and governing the universal Church.

Indeed, Our predecessors vehemently gloried to institute in the Roman Church, by their own Apostolic authority, the Feast of the Conception, and to augment, ennoble, and promote with all their power the devotion thus instituted, by a proper Office and a proper Mass, by which the prerogative of immunity from hereditary stain was most manifestly asserted; to increase it either by indulgences granted or by leave given to states, provinces, and kingdoms that they might choose as their patron the Mother of God, under the title of the Immaculate Conception, or by approved Sodalities, Congregations, and Religious Families instituted to the honor of the Immaculate Conception; or by praises given to the piety of those who have erected monasteries, hospitals, altars, or churches under the title of the Immaculate Conception, or who have bound themselves by a religious vow to defend strenuously the Immaculate Conception of the Mother of God. Above all, they were happy to ordain that the Feast of the Conception should be celebrated through the whole Church as that of the Nativity; and, in fine, that it should be celebrated with an Octave in the universal Church as it was placed in the rank of the festivals which are commanded to be kept holy; also that a Pontifical service in Our Patriarchal Liberian Basilica should be performed yearly on the day sacred to the Conception of the Virgin; and desiring to cherish daily more and more in the minds of the Faithful this doctrine of the Immaculate Conception of the Mother of God, and to excite their piety to worshipping and venerating the Virgin conceived without original sin, they have rejoiced most freely to give leave that in the Litany of Loreto and in the Preface of the Mass itself, the Immaculate Conception of the same Virgin should be proclaimed, and that thus the rule of faith would be established by the rule itself of supplication. We ourselves, treading in the footsteps of so many predecessors, have not only received and approved what had been most wisely and piously established and appointed by them, but also mindful of the institution of Sixtus IV, We have appointed by Our authority a proper Office for the Immaculate Conception, and with a most joyful mind have granted the use of it to the universal Church.

But since those things which pertain to worship are evidently bound by an intimate chord to its object, and cannot remain fixed and determined, if it be doubtful, and placed in uncertainty, therefore Our predecessors the Roman Pontiffs, increasing with all their care the devotion of the Conception, studied most especially to declare and inculcate its object and doctrine; for they taught clearly and openly that the festival was celebrated for the Conception of the Virgin, and they proscribed as false and most foreign to the intention of the Church the opinion of those who considered and affirmed that it was not the Conception itself, but the sanctification to which devotion was paid by the Church. Nor did they think of treating more indulgently those who, in order to weaken the doctrine of the Immaculate Conception, drawing a distinction between the first and second instant and moment of the Conception, asserted that the Conception was indeed celebrated, but not for the first instant and moment; for Our predecessors themselves thought it their duty to protect and defend with all zeal both the feast of the Conception of the Most Blessed Virgin, and the Conception from the first instant as the true object of devotion. Hence the words, evidently decretive, in which Alexander VII declared the true intention of the Church, saying: "Certainly, it is the ancient piety of the Faithful of Christ towards His Most Blessed Mother the Virgin Mary, believing that her soul, in the first instant of creation, and of infusion into the body, was, by a special grace and privilege of God, in virtue of the merits of Jesus Christ her Son, the Redeemer of mankind, preserved free from the stain of original sin, and in this sense they keep and celebrate with solemn rite the Festival of her Conception."

And to the same, Our predecessors, this also was most especially a duty, sedulously to guard and preserve the doctrine of the Immaculate Conception of the Mother of God. For not only have they never suffered that this doctrine should ever be censured or traduced in any way or by anyone, but they have gone much farther, and in clear declarations on repeated occasions they have proclaimed that the doctrine in which we profess the Immaculate Conception of the Virgin is, and by its own merit, held evidently consistent with Ecclesiastical worship, that it is ancient and nearly universal, and the same which the Roman Church has undertaken to cherish and protect, and, wholly worthy to be placed in its sacred liturgy and its solemn prayers. Nor content with this, in order that the doctrine of the Immaculate Conception of the Virgin should remain inviolate, they have most severely prohibited the opinion adverse to this doctrine to be defended either in public or in private, and they have wished to crush it as it were by repeated blows. To which reiterated and most clear declarations, lest they might appear empty, they added a sanction; all which things Our illustrious predecessor Alexander VII embraced in these words: —

"Considering that the Holy Roman Church solemnly celebrates the festival of the Conception of the Immaculate and Ever-Blessed Virgin, and has appointed for this a special and proper office according to the pious, devout, and laudable institution which emanated from Our predecessor Sixtus IV, and wishing, after the example of the Roman Pontiffs, Our predecessors, to favor this laudable piety, devotion, and festival, and the worship according thereto, never changed in the Roman Church since the institution of the worship itself; also in order to protect this piety and devotion of venerating and celebrating the Most Blessed Virgin, preserved from original sin by the preventing grace of the Holy Ghost, and desiring to preserve in the flock of Christ unity of spirit in the bond of peace, removing offences, and brawls, and scandals; at the instance and prayers of the said Bishops, with the Chapters of their Churches, and of King Philip and his kingdoms, We renew the constitutions and decrees issued by the Roman Pontiffs, Our predecessors, and especially by Sixtus IV, Paul V, and Gregory XV, in favor of the sentiment asserting that the soul of the Blessed Virgin, in its creation and infusion into the body, was endowed with the grace of the Holy Ghost, and preserved from original sin; likewise, also, in favor of the festival of the same Virgin Mother of God, celebrated according to that pious belief which is recited above, and We command that it shall be observed under the censures and punishments contained in the same Constitutions.

"And against all and each of those who try to interpret the aforesaid constitutions or decrees so that they may frustrate the favor shown through these to the said belief and to the festival or worship celebrated according to it, or who try to recall into dispute the same belief, festival, or worship, or against these in any manner, either directly or indirectly, and on any pretext, even that of examining the grounds of defining it, or of explaining or interpreting the Sacred Scriptures or the Holy Fathers or Doctors; in fine, who should dare, under any pretext or on any occasion whatsoever, to say either in writing or in speech, to preach, to treat, to dispute, by determining or asserting anything against these, or by bringing arguments against them and leaving these arguments unanswered, or by expressing dissent in any other possible manner; besides the punishments and censures contained in the constitutions of Sixtus IV, to which we desire to add, and by these presents do add, those: We will that they should be deprived *ipso facto*, and without other declaration, of the faculty of preaching, of reading in public, or of teaching and interpreting, and also of their voice, whether active or passive, in elections; from which censures they cannot be absolved, nor obtain dispensation, unless from Us, or Our Successors, the Roman Pontiffs; likewise We wish to subject, and We hereby do subject, the same persons to other penalties to be inflicted at Our will, and at that of the same Roman Pontiffs, Our Successors, renewing the constitutions or decrees of Paul V and Gregory XV, above referred to.

"And We prohibit, under the penalties and censures contained in the Index of Prohibited Books, and We will and declare that they should be esteemed prohibited *ipso facto*, and without other declaration, books in which the aforesaid belief, and the festival or devotion celebrated according to it, is recalled into dispute, or in which anything whatever is written or read against these, or lectures, sermons, treatises, and disputations against the same, published after the decree above mentioned of Paul V, or to be published at any future time."

All are aware with how much zeal this doctrine of the Immaculate Conception of the Mother of God has been handed down, asserted and propagated by the most distinguished Religious Orders, the most celebrated theological Academies, and the most eminent Doctors of the science of Divinity. All know likewise how anxious have been the Bishops openly and publicly to profess, even in the Ecclesiastical assemblies themselves, that the Most Holy Mother of God, the Virgin Mary, by virtue of the merits of Christ our Lord, the Savior of mankind, never lay under original sin, but was preserved free from the stain of origin, and thus was redeemed in a more sublime manner. To which, lastly, is added this fact, most grave and, in an especial manner, most important of all, that the Council of Trent itself, when it promulgated the dogmatic decree concerning original sin, in which, according to the testimonies of the Sacred Scriptures, of the Holy Fathers, and of the most approved councils, it determined and defined that all mankind are born under original sin; solemnly declared, however, that it was not its intention to include in the decree itself, and in the amplitude of its definition, the Blessed and Immaculate Virgin Mary, Mother of God. Indeed, by this declaration, the Tridentine Fathers have assented, according to the times and the circumstances of affairs, that the Blessed Virgin Mary was free from the original stain; and thus clearly signified that nothing could be justly adduced from the sacred writings, nor from the authority of the Fathers, which would in any way gainsay so great a prerogative of the Virgin.

And, in real truth, illustrious monuments of the venerated antiquity of the Eastern and of the Western Church most powerfully testify, that this doctrine of the Immaculate Conception of the Most Blessed Virgin, every day more and more so splendidly explained and confirmed by the highest authority, teaching, zeal, science, and wisdom of the Church, and so wonderfully propagated amongst all the nations and peoples of the Catholic world, always existed in the Church as received from Our ancestors, and stamped with the character of a Divine revelation. For the Church of Christ, careful guardian and defender of the dogmas deposited with her, changes nothing in them, diminishes nothing, adds nothing; but, with all industry, by faithfully and wisely treating ancient things, if they are handed down from antiquity, so studies to eliminate, to clear them up, that these ancient dogmas of heavenly faith may receive evidence, light, distinction, but still may retain their fullness, integrity, propriety, and may increase only in their own kind, that is, in the same dogma, the same sense, and the same belief.

The Fathers and writers of the Church, taught by the heavenly writings, had nothing more at heart, in the books written to explain the Scriptures, to vindicate the dogmas, and to instruct the Faithful, than emulously to declare and exhibit in many and wonderful ways the Virgin's most high sanctity, dignity, and freedom from all stain of original sin, and her renowned victory over the most foul enemy of the human race. Wherefore, repeating the words in which, at the beginning of the world, the Almighty, announcing the remedies of His mercy, prepared for regenerating mankind, crushed the audacity of the lying serpent, and wonderfully raised up the hope of our race, saying — "I will place enmities between thee and the woman, thy seed and her seed," they taught that in this Divine oracle was clearly and openly pointed out the merciful Redeemer of the human race — to wit, the only-begotten Son of God, Christ Jesus, and that His Most Blessed Mother, the Virgin Mary, was designated, and at the same time that the enmities of both against the serpent were signally expressed. Wherefore, as Christ, the mediator of God and men, having assumed human nature, blotting out the handwriting of the decree which stood against us, fastened it triumphantly to the cross, so the Most Holy Virgin, bound by a most close and indissoluble chain with Him, exercising with Him and through Him eternal enmity against the malignant serpent, and triumphing most amply over the same, has crushed his head with her immaculate foot.

This illustrious and singular triumph of the Virgin, and her most exalted innocence, purity, and holiness, her freedom from all stain of sin, and ineffable abundance and greatness of all heavenly graces, virtues, and privileges, the same fathers beheld in that ark of Noah, which, divinely appointed, escaped, safe and sound, from the common shipwreck of the whole world; also in that ladder which Jacob beheld to reach from earth to Heaven, by whose steps the Angels of God ascended and descended, on whose top leaned God Himself; also in that bush which, in the holy place, Moses beheld blaze on every side, and amidst the crackling flames, neither to be consumed nor to suffer the least injury, but to grow green and to blossom fairly; also, in that tower unassailable in the face of an enemy, from which depend a thousand bucklers and all the armor of the brave; also, in that garden fenced round about, which cannot be violated nor corrupted by any schemes of fraud; also in that brilliant city of God whose foundations are in the holy mounts; also in that most august temple of God, which, shining with divine splendor, is filled with the glory of God; likewise in many other things of this kind in which the Fathers have handed down, that the exalted dignity of the Mother of God and her spotless innocence, and her holiness, obnoxious to no blemish, have been signally pre-announced.

To describe the same totality, as it were, of Divine gifts, and the original integrity of the Virgin of whom Jesus was born, the same Fathers, using the eloquence of the Prophets, celebrate the august Virgin as the spotless dove, the holy Jerusalem, the exalted throne of God, the ark and house of sanctification, which Eternal Wisdom built for itself; and as that Queen who, abounding in delights and leaning on her beloved, came forth entirely perfect from the mouth of the Most High, fair and most dear to God, and never stained with the least spot. But when the same Fathers and the writers of the Church revolved in their hearts and minds that the Most Blessed Virgin, in the name and by the order of God himself, was proclaimed full of grace by the Angel Gabriel, when announcing her most sublime dignity of Mother of God, they taught that, by this singular and solemn salutation, never heard on any other occasion, is shown that the Mother of God is the seat of all Divine graces, and adorned with all the gifts of the Holy Ghost — yea, the infinite storehouse and inexhaustible abyss of the same gifts; so that, never obnoxious to an evil word, and alone with her Son partaker of perpetual benediction, she deserved to hear from Elizabeth, inspired by the Holy Ghost, "Blessed art thou amongst women, and blessed is the fruit of thy womb.'"

Hence it is the clear and unanimous opinion of the same that the Most Glorious Virgin, for whom He who is powerful has done great things, has shone with such a brilliancy of all heavenly gifts, such fullness of grace, and such innocence, that she has been an ineffable miracle of the Almighty, yea, the crown of all miracles, and worthy Mother of God; that she approaches as nearly to God as created nature can do, and is more exalted than all human and angelic encomiums.

And, therefore, to vindicate the original innocence and justice of the Mother of God, they not only compared her to Eve as yet virgin, as yet innocent, as yet uncorrupted, and not yet deceived by the most deadly snares of the most treacherous serpent, but they have preferred her with a wonderful variety of thought and expression. For Eve, miserably obeying the serpent, fell from original innocence, and became his slave, but the Most Blessed Virgin, ever increasing her original gift, not only never lent an ear to the serpent, but by a virtue divinely received utterly broke his power.

Wherefore they have never ceased to call the Mother of God the lily amongst the thorns, earth entirely untouched, virginal, undefiled, immaculate, ever blessed, and free from all contagion of sin, from which was formed the new Adam; irreproachable, most sweet paradise of innocence, immortality, and delights, planted by God himself, and fenced from all snares of the malignant serpent; incorruptible branch that the worm of sin has never injured; fountain ever clear, and marked by the virtue of the Holy Ghost; a most divine temple, or treasure of immortality, or the sole and only daughter, not of death but of life; the seed, not of enmity but of grace, which by the singular providence of God has always flourished, reviving from a corrupt and imperfect root, contrary to the settled and common laws. But as if these encomiums, though most splendid, were not sufficient, they proclaimed in proper and defined sentences, that when sin should be treated of, no question should be entertained concerning the Holy Virgin Mary, to whom an abundance of grace was given to conquer sin completely. They also declared that the Most Glorious Virgin was the reparatrix of her parents, the vivifier of posterity, chosen from the ages, prepared for himself by the Most High, predicted by God when He said to the serpent, "I will place enmities between thee and the woman," who undoubtedly has crushed the poisonous head of the same serpent; and therefore they affirm that the same Blessed Virgin was through grace perfectly free from every stain of sin, and from all contagion of body and soul, and mind, and always conversant with God and united with him in an eternal covenant, never was in darkness but always in light, and therefore was plainly a fit habitation for Christ, not on account of her bodily state, but on account of her original grace.

To these things are added the noble words in which, speaking of the Conception of the Virgin, they have testified that nature yielded to grace and stood trembling, not being able to proceed further; for it was to be that the Virgin Mother of God should not be conceived by Anne before grace should bear fruit. For she ought thus to be conceived as the first-born, from whom should be conceived the firstborn of every creature. They have testified that the flesh of the Virgin, taken from Adam, did not admit the stains of Adam, and on this account that the Most Blessed Virgin was the tabernacle created by God Himself, formed by the Holy Spirit, truly enriched with purple which that new Beseleel made, adorned and woven with gold; and that this same Virgin is, and deservedly is, celebrated as she who was the first and the peculiar work of God, escaped from the fiery weapons of evil, and fair by nature, and entirely free from all stain, came into the world all shining like the morn in her Immaculate Conception;

nor, truly, was it right that this vessel of election should be assailed by common injuries, since, differing very much from others, she had community with them only in their nature, not in their fault.

Far more, it was right that, as the Only Begotten had a Father in Heaven whom the Seraphim extol three times holy, so He should have a Mother on the earth, who never should want the splendor of holiness. And this doctrine, indeed, so filled the minds and souls of our forefathers, that a marvelous and singular form of speech prevailed with them, in which they very frequently called the Mother of God immaculate and entirely immaculate, innocent and most innocent, spotless, holy, and most distant from every stain of sin, all pure, all perfect, the type and model of purity and innocence, more beautiful than beauty, more gracious than grace, more holy than holiness, and alone holy, and most pure in soul and body, who has surpassed all perfectitude and all virginity, and has become the dwelling-place of all the graces of the Most Holy Spirit, and who, God alone excepted, is superior to all, and by nature fairer, more beautiful, and more holy than the Cherubim and Seraphim; she whom all the tongues of Heaven and earth do not suffice to extol. No one is ignorant that these forms of speech have passed, as it were, spontaneously into the monuments of the most holy Liturgy, and the Offices of the Church, and that they occur often in them and abound amply; since the Mother of God is invoked and named in them as a spotless dove of beauty, as a rose ever blooming and perfectly pure, and ever spotless and ever blessed, and is celebrated as innocence which was never wounded, and a second Eve who brought forth Emmanuel.

It is no wonder, then, if the Pastors of the Church and the faithful people have daily more and more gloried to profess with so much piety and fervor this doctrine of the Immaculate Conception of the Virgin Mother of God, pointed out in the Sacred Scriptures, according to the judgment of the Fathers, handed down in so many mighty testimonies of the same, expressed and celebrated in so many illustrious monuments of a revered antiquity, and proposed, and with great piety confirmed by the greatest and highest judgment of the Church; so that nothing would be more dear, more pleasing to the same than everywhere to worship, venerate, invoke, and proclaim the Virgin Mother of God conceived without original stain. Wherefore from the ancient times the Princes of the Church, Ecclesiastics, Regular Orders, and even emperors and kings themselves, have earnestly entreated of this Apostolic See that the Immaculate Conception of the Most Holy Mother of God should be defined as a dogma of Catholic faith. Which entreaties were renewed also in these Our times, and especially were addressed to Gregory XVI, Our predecessor of happy memory, and to Ourselves, not only by Bishops, but by the Secular Clergy, Religious Orders, and sovereign princes and faithful peoples.

Therefore, with singular joy of mind, well knowing all these things, and seriously considering them, scarcely had We, though unworthy, been raised by a mysterious dispensation of Divine Providence to this exalted Chair of Peter, and undertaken the government of the whole Church, than, following the veneration, the piety, and love We had entertained for the Blessed Virgin from Our tender years, We had nothing at heart more than to accomplish all these things which as yet were amongst the ardent wishes of the Church, that the honor of the Most Blessed Virgin should be increased, and her prerogatives should shine with a fuller light. But wishing to bring this to full maturity, We appointed a special congregation of Cardinals, illustrious by their piety, their wisdom, and their knowledge of the sacred sciences, and We also selected Ecclesiastics, both Secular and Regular, well trained in theological discipline, that they should most carefully weigh all those things which relate to the Immaculate Conception of the Virgin, and report to Us their opinion. And, although from the entreaties lately received by Us for at length defining the Immaculate Conception of the Virgin, the sentiment of most of the Bishops of the Church was understood; however, We sent Encyclical Letters, dated at Gaeta, the 2nd day of February, in the year 1849, to all our Venerable Brethren the Bishops of all the Catholic world, in order that having offered prayers to God they would signify to Us, in writing, what was the piety and devotion of their flocks towards the Immaculate Conception of the Mother of God, and especially what the Bishops themselves thought about promulgating the definition, or what they desired, in order that we might pronounce Our supreme judgment as solemnly as possible.

Certainly We were filled with no slight consolation when the replies of our venerable brethren came to Us. For, with an incredible joyfulness, gladness, and zeal, they not only confirmed their own singular piety, and that of their Clergy and faithful people, towards the Immaculate Conception of the Most Blessed Virgin, but they even entreated of Us with a common voice that the Immaculate Conception of the Virgin should be defined by Our supreme judgment and authority. Nor, indeed, were We filled with less joy when the Cardinals of the Special Congregation aforesaid, and the consulting theologians chosen by Us, after a diligent examination, demanded from Us with equal alacrity and zeal this definition of the Immaculate Conception of the Mother of God.

Afterwards walking in the illustrious footsteps of Our predecessors, and desiring to proceed duly and properly, We proclaimed and held a Consistory, in which we addressed our Venerable Brethren, the Cardinals of the Holy Roman Church, and with the greatest consolation of mind We heard them entreat of Us that we should promulgate the dogmatic definition of the Immaculate Conception of the Virgin Mother of God.

Therefore having full trust in the Lord that the opportune time had come for defining the Immaculate Conception of the Virgin Mary Mother of God, which the Divine words, venerable tradition, the perpetual sentiment of the Church, the singular agreement of Catholic Prelates and Faithful, and the signal acts and Constitutions of our predecessors wonderfully illustrate and proclaim; having most diligently weighed all things, and poured forth to God assiduous and fervent prayers, We resolved that We should no longer delay to sanction and define, by Our supreme authority, the Immaculate Conception of the Virgin, and thus to satisfy the most pious desires of the Catholic world and Our own piety towards the Most Holy Virgin, and, at the same time, to honor in her more and more the only-begotten Son, Jesus Christ Our Lord, since whatever honor and praise is given to the Mother redounds to the Son.

Wherefore after We had unceasingly, in humility and fasting, offered Our own prayers and the public prayers of the Church to God the Father through His Son, that He would deign to direct and confirm Our mind by the power of the Holy Ghost, and having implored the aid of the entire Heavenly Host, and invoked the Paraclete with sighs, and He thus inspiring, to the Honor of the Holy and undivided Trinity, to the glory and ornament of the Virgin Mother of God, to the exaltation of the Catholic Faith and the increase of the Catholic religion, by the authority of Jesus Christ Our Lord, of the Blessed Apostles, Peter and Paul, We declare, pronounce, and define that the doctrine which holds that the Blessed Virgin Mary, at the first instant of her conception, by a singular privilege and grace of the Omnipotent God, in virtue of the merits of Jesus Christ, the Savior of mankind, was preserved free from all stain of original sin, has been revealed by God, and therefore should firmly and constantly be believed by all the Faithful. Wherefore if any shall presume — which God avert — to think otherwise than as it has been defined by Us, they should know and understand that they are condemned by their own judgment, that they have suffered shipwreck of the faith, and have revolted from the unity of the Church; and besides, by their own act they subject themselves to the penalties justly established, if what they think they should dare to signify by word, writing, or any other outward means.

Our mouth is filled with joy and Our tongue with exultation, and We return, and shall ever return, the most humble and the greatest thanks to Jesus Christ Our Lord, because through His singular beneficence He has granted to Us, though unworthy, to offer and decree this honor, glory, and praise to His Most Holy Mother; but We rely with most certain hope and confidence that this Most Blessed Virgin, who, all fair and immaculate, has bruised the poisonous head of the most malignant serpent, and brought salvation to the world, who is the praise of the Prophets and the Apostles, the honor of the Martyrs, and the crown and joy of all the Saints — who is the safest refuge and most faithful helper of all who are in danger, and the most powerful mediatrix and conciliatrix with the only-begotten Son of the whole world, and the most illustrious glory, and ornament, and most firm guardian of the Holy Church, who has destroyed all heresies, and snatched from the greatest calamities of all kinds the faithful peoples and nations, and delivered Us from so many threatening dangers, will effect by her most powerful patronage that, all difficulties being removed, and all errors dissipated, Our Holy Mother the Catholic Church may flourish daily more and more throughout all nations and countries, and may reign from the rivers to the ends of the earth, and may enjoy all peace, tranquility, and liberty;

that the sinful may obtain pardon, the sick healing, the weak of heart strength, the afflicted consolation, and that all who are in error, their spiritual blindness being dissipated, may return to the path of truth and justice, and may become one flock and one shepherd.

Let all the children of the Catholic Church most dear to Us hear these Our words, and, with a more ardent zeal of piety, religion, and love, proceed to worship, invoke, and pray to the Most Blessed Virgin Mary Mother of God, conceived without original sin; and let them fly with entire confidence to this most sweet Mother of Mercy and Grace, in all dangers, difficulties, necessities, doubts, and fears. For nothing is to be feared, and nothing is to be despaired of under her guidance, under her auspices, under her favor, under her protection, who, bearing towards us a maternal affection, and taking up the business of our salvation, is solicitous for the whole human race, and, appointed by God the Queen of Heaven and Earth, and exalted above all the choirs of Angels, and orders of Saints, standing at the right hand of the only-begotten Son, Jesus Christ Our Lord, intercedes most powerfully, and obtains what she asks, and cannot be frustrated.

Finally, in order that this Our definition of the Immaculate Conception of the Most Blessed Virgin Mary may be brought to the knowledge of the universal Church, We will these Letters Apostolic to stand for a perpetual remembrance of the thing, commanding that to transcripts or printed copies, subscribed by the hand of some notary public, and authenticated by the seal of the proper Ecclesiastical authority, the same faith shall be paid which would be paid to those presents if they were exhibited or shown.

Let no man interfere with this Our declaration, pronunciation, and definition, or oppose and contradict it with presumptuous rashness. If any should presume to assail it, let him know that he will incur the indignation of the Omnipotent God and of His blessed Apostles Peter and Paul.

Given at Rome, at Saint Peter's, in the year of the Incarnation of our Lord, one thousand eight hundred and fifty-four, the sixth of the Ides of December, in the ninth year of our Pontificate.

Pius PP. IX.

CHAPTER XX

The Immaculate Conception: a Dogma for the Errors of our Times

THE TRIUMPH OF MARY IS COMPLETE. The Lord hath spoken by the mouth of Peter. The Edict, the final Decree, is published — Mary was conceived without the least stain of original sin. That which the Church from the beginning hath ever believed and cherished with a loving and devoted fidelity, has now taken that form which all have longed to see — a Dogma of the Catholic Church. The time for speculation has transpired, and the hour has come for sweet, confiding, humble Faith. There is no more need of words; but love influences the heart, and woos it still to linger at the shrine of her, whose supernatural story, we have humbly essayed to portray; and the heart will not cease to beat responsive to the maternal affection of the divine, the Immaculate Maid, whom we have chosen for our Mother and Protectress.

By this dogmatic definition, the Church has put her final seal upon the fourth of those special privileges which distinguish the Blessed Mary above all the daughters of Eve — namely, the perpetual virginity; the divine maternity; exemption from all actual sin; and the Immaculate Conception. Nearly four centuries of the life of the Church had transpired, when Pope Siricius (390 A.D.), assembled a Council at Rome, and condemned the impiety of Jovinian and his partisans, whose audacity went so far as to deny the perpetual Virginity of the Mother of God. The perpetual Virginity was then solemnly defined a dogma of faith. About forty-one years afterwards (431 A.D.) certain sectaries (a member of a religious or political sect) arose, who, distinguishing two persons in Jesus Christ, dared to refuse to Mary the title of Mother of God; according to her only that of Mother of Christ. An error of such gravity demanded a solemn condemnation, which was at that time pronounced in the Council of Ephesus. It was this which gave rise to the dogmatic definition of the divine maternity of Mary. The belief of the third special privilege, exemption from all actual sin, engraven upon the hearts of the Faithful in the primitive ages, and at all times professed in the Church, did not receive its final and more glorious expression until the sixteenth century, when the Council of Trent judged proper solemnly to define it, although no one thought of denying its truth. It may be seen, by these three examples, how the Church, embracing the opportunity, proposes to the belief of the Faithful as Dogmas of Faith, the truths contained in the deposit of Revelation. The perpetual Virginity of Mary was declared and defined in the fourth age; the divine Maternity in the fifth age; the privilege of exemption from all actual sin only in the sixteenth age. What Catholic would venture to declare that these truths were not before the above-named three epochs, comprised in the deposit of Revelation, and that the Church in defining them has arbitrarily created new dogmas?

That which has thus, at various epochs, taken place in regard to these three privileges of the Blessed Virgin, declared and defined as Dogmas, has now been gloriously renewed in regard to the fourth privilege, that of the Immaculate Conception; which, like them, is contained in the sanctity that the sublime dignity of Mother of God implies, and which, also, like them, is deduced as a direct consequence of that article of the Creed, "conceived by the Holy Ghost; born of the Virgin Mary;" since a union is impossible of two things so dissimilar as the supreme dignity of Mother of the only Son of God, and the abject condition, even if it be but momentary, of a creature plunged in the slavery of sin — a state which manifestly must have existed if the soul of the Virgin had not, at the moment of its creation and union with the body, been, by the special grace of God, preserved from the stain of original sin.

The evidences of the Immaculate Conception, though clear and decisive when the Angel Gabriel hailed the Mother of our Lord, *Full of grace,* and the blest one among women, as they now are when Pius IX, the successor of Peter, has defined it as a doctrine of Faith, have nevertheless increased in brilliancy with the onward movement of time. Age after age has gradually developed the mind of the Church, and contributed new accretions to the swelling flood of truth. As the melodious voice of the Apostles, Evangelists and Martyrs, commemorating in solemn Liturgical offices the Immaculate nature of the Blessed Mary, died upon the ear, the ensuing generations took up the theme, and continued their harmonious notes until the entire Christian world re-echoed with the inspired song. The humblest Christian, the most exalted Saint; Emperors, Kings, and Princes; Priests, Prelates and Popes; Confessors, Martyrs, Theologians, and holy men of every age and nation, as we have seen, conspired to evoke the solemn definition just pronounced. The doctrine is no novelty, no new thing; but old as the Church itself; and men have with amazement asked, why has this honor to the Queen of heaven been so long delayed? It is upon this point we now propose to speak.

1. The doctrine needed no such solemn authorization to increase the devotion and faith of Christians in regard to it. It was believed as devoutly and as fondly cherished before the definition as after it. There was no need therefore of haste in defining it. From the first moment the term Immaculate was applied to the Holy Virgin by the Apostles, to the time when the Vicegerent of Christ defined the doctrine, that title has been indelibly affixed to the Mother of God. As far as the Church then, was concerned, there was nothing to gain by the final act which places the Virgin's Immaculate Conception

among the other glories which deck her crown.

2. The Church of Christ never hastens to affix her seal to her solemn acts. Such a course might suit the ephemeral sects, who rush headlong into a thousand different definitions upon one and the same doctrine. But centuries had rolled by before the Catholic Church had defined some of the primary and most important doctrines of the Christian faith. She rested satisfied, as in this case, that they were believed; she knew that the Church was constituted for all days even to the consummation of the world; she knew that her power and authority would never decay, but would be as fresh, as strong, and able to define at one as at another period of her history; and, being thus conscious of her eternity, her Catholicity in point of duration, as well as in that of place, she can afford to wait, as she has done in the definition of every doctrine, until that occasion or period of time shall transpire in which it shall seem good to her to raise her divine voice in proclamation of her decrees. Not that she ever varies, or believes today what she did not believe yesterday, for she is like her divine and infallible head, with whom "there is no change, nor shadow of alteration."

3. Hence, in the order of Divine Providence, and in the secret councils of the Most High, it seemed good to the Holy Ghost and to the divinely constituted authorities of the Church, now, in the middle of the nineteenth century, rather than at any former or later period, to define this ancient belief of the Catholic Church. And without impiously seeking to pry into the invisible secrets, the mysterious councils of the Most High and His Church, yet there is so plain and so emphatic a reason why all this should have been delayed for the action of the Church at this precise period of the world, that it seems rather a duty than an assumption to record it. Three hundred years have now expired since the impetuous, turbulent, and petulant geniuses of the sixteenth century first began to play the harlot against the Church of Christ. The impure sects which then arose were confessedly conceived and born in lust. The monarch who laid the corner-stone of those synagogues of Satan, first rebelled because a just restraint was imposed upon his lustful passions. Those heresiarchs, who, in Germany, and in other countries, broached their heresies, exceeded the bounds to which even he had gone. These are they, whom St. Peter describes, as *"them who walk after the flesh in the lust of uncleanness, and despise government, audacious, self-willed, they fear not to bring in sects."* (2 Peter, chap. ii, v. 10.) St. Paul also describes them, "For of this sort are they who creep into houses, and lead captive silly women laden with sins, who are led away with divers desires; ever learning and never attaining to the knowledge of the truth." (*2 Timothy chap. iii, v. 6, 7.*) "For there shall be a time, when they will not endure sound doctrine; but according to their own lusts they will heap to themselves teachers, having

itching ears." (*Idem., chap. iv, v. 3.*) St. Peter also in another place prophesied that "In the last days there shall come deceitful scoffers, walking after their own lusts." (*2 Peter, chap. iii, v. 3.*) Such were the men who, at the period referred to, departed from the Catholic Faith; and such were the principles, upon which they founded their various systems of religion.

The result, after three hundred years of deception, cruelty and blood, stands fully before the world. The country where these prurient movements first began, Germany, has sunk into infidelity and *free love*; in France, as far as these movements prevailed, they took the form of infidelity and *Socialism*; in England it is a mongrel Christianity and *Communism*; America has had the misfortune to receive some of all these Sodomitic Sects, but has added to them by swift and sure degrees, until it holds the unenviable distinction of having given open and public sanction to sexual license without benefit of the sacrament of marriage. These crimes are not only not condemned, but they are supported by law and encouraged by public proclamation. There is no limit to its extent, but the endurance of the fiery passion which feeds the unholy desire. Luther began by allowing the Landgrave of Hesse to have two wives at one and the same time; Joseph Smith, founder of Mormonism, his lineal and legitimate descendant, finished, by permitting each man to have an unlimited number of them.

The three Angelical Virtues, Obedience, Poverty and Chastity, are annihilated; the mention of them is laughed to scorn, and the very possibility of their existence, denied, especially that of the latter. Among these sects all the unruly passions are allowed free and unrestricted sway. The opposites of the three virtues just named are the uppermost and most prominent evils of the present age. The spirit of disobedience is nourished in the child, and allowed to grow and strengthen itself as he grows. It is first marked by disrespect to parents and superiors, and ends in setting all law and all authority at defiance. Avarice, or the thirst and struggle after wealth, drags millions down to perdition. And, finally, chambering, wantonness, impurities, and every kind of lasciviousness is not merely a prevalent feature of the times, but it is publicly systematized, colonized, and legalized. Not only does it take the form of Communism, Socialism, Fourierism, and Spiritualism, but, springing up like these in the very heart of Protestantism, it takes a religious form.[1]

These crimes, with the frightful sequences that follow in their train, devastate society. Outside of the Church there is no restraining influence.

---

1. Mormonism sprang directly out of a religious revival among some Methodists, Baptists and Presbyterians in the State of Pennsylvania. Joe Smith was one of the first fruits of this affair. And when each sect besought him to join each their particular Zion, he concluded that they all could not be the true Church. It was then he got up his particular revelation. These facts were related to the author by one of the parties immediately concerned.

Within the Church there is. Our holy Mother not only defends her children by the sacramental graces; not only presents the perfect example of our divine Lord for their imitation; but she offers to their contemplation the examples of all the virtues in the Saints of God, who have already found a happy entrance into the Church triumphant. But chiefly and far above all other created intelligences, she presents for their imitation the Immaculate Virgin, the Mother of God, the celestial embodiment of all the graces, of all the virtues, especially those already named. Whatever can be imagined as an ornament or grace, she possesses in a transcendent degree. Every virtue, every trait of beauty, every merit, every honor, every perfection, that has been showered upon any being, human or angelic, Mary possessed in an infinitely superior manner. None but God alone can truly estimate her worth, her excellence, her matchless perfections. No creature can sufficiently admire, no tongue adequately praise her, whom the Holy and ever Blessed Trinity hath predestinated to repair the fault of Eve by bringing forth Him, who alone could amend the broken law. Hence it has been well said: "It is easier to err in falling short of sufficiently praising her, than there is danger of offending God by giving her too much praise; since man can never sufficiently praise her who was destined to be the Mother of God."

Whatever were the perfections of Eve when she came fresh from the hands of her Maker, still, by transgression, she obscured them all. That hideous monster, sin, veiled all her beauty in the dark pall which envelopes the eternally condemned. But Mary knew no sin; its baleful touch had never sullied her angelic soul. She was all beautiful, and there was no spot in her. She was exalted above the Angels, not only in every virtue, grace, and perfection, but in position; she was exalted even to the throne of the Deity itself. How sublime then must have been the degree of those perfections which heaven in its bounty had lavished upon this favored being; how immense the sum of the celestial graces which it had poured out upon her unsullied soul! "Try me in this, saith the Lord; if I open not unto you the floodgates of heaven, and pour out a blessing even to abundance." Thus had He done to Mary; and however exalted may have been the personal graces with which He had been pleased to adorn this Vessel of Election, those spiritual blessings and favors with which she was interiorly adorned exceeded them a thousand fold.

If a single ray of divine grace illumines the soul, and fits it for the august indwelling of the Spirit of God, how luminous must be that soul into which is poured the entire sum of all the graces; and which, being created without the least stain of original sin, and never having been sullied with the faintest trace of actual sin, was never for the least moment of time an object of displeasure to Almighty God! Such was Mary; who, of all the daughters of Eve, alone preserved the perfect innocence in which she had been created; never for one instant dimming the luster of the heavenly graces which united in her. And thus it is that the Church presents her to her children in this corrupt and sensual age as the Immaculate Model of Chastity and of every perfection. Immaculate in her

Conception; Immaculate in her birth; Immaculate in her earthly life; Immaculate in her joys; Immaculate in her sorrows and sufferings; and Immaculate in every phase of her existence. Thus God looks upon her with infinite complaisance and love; thus the Angels contemplate her with wonder and admiration; and thus the Church regards her with confidence and veneration.

Happy, yes, thrice happy, are those who, while the tempestuous waives and the storms of life shall buffet them, learn thus to regard her; learn thus to imitate her, and conform their lives to the example of hers. Never was there a period of the world when the virtues which adorned her life were more needed to be held up, extolled, illustrated and enforced, than in the present age. And a most happy contemplation it is for the sincere Christian that he belongs to a Church which understands its mission and fears not to fulfil it. Everywhere, at home and abroad, now, as in the primitive times, the finger of scorn is pointed at the Church, the Spouse of Christ. Everywhere she is assailed with ribald abuse, with false accusations, with secret, and with open and avowed persecutions.

It is well: well for her, because she will pass through the fire, as she has often done before, and reappear again bright as the gold which has been heated seven times. "Behold, saith the Lord, I will refine them as silver is refined; and I will try them as gold is tried. They shall call on my name and I will hear them. I will say; Thou art my people; and they shall say; The Lord is my God." (*Zach., chap. xiii, 9.*) It is well therefore for the Church; well for all those who stand steadfast; for they that persevere to the end shall be saved. (*St. Mat., chap. x, 22.*) But woe to the ungodly whose hand is raised against His Church. It were better for him that a millstone should be hanged about his neck, and that he should be drowned in the depths of the sea. (*St. Mat., chap. xviii, 6.*) "Seeing it is a just thing with God, to repay tribulation to them that trouble you — who shall suffer eternal punishment in destruction, from the face of the Lord and from the glory of his power." (*2 Thess., chap. i, 6, 9.*) Resort then with confidence to her whose intercession is more powerful than that of all the Saints — the Immaculate Mother of Him, who feels His own heart pierced by every wound inflicted upon His Church.

CHAPTER XXI

Conclusion — Motives for Venerating the Most Blessed and Immaculate Virgin Mary — and Certain Duties and Obligations Arising Out of the Recent Dogmatic Decree

IT IS AN ARTICLE OF CATHOLIC FAITH that the Angels and glorified Saints are deeply and intimately interested in our salvation; that they watch over us; pray for us; rejoice at our conversion and well-doing; and weep over our fall and alienation from good — in a word; that they concern themselves about us. No article of faith is more clearly defined in the Sacred Scriptures than this. When Agar, becoming perverse, fled from the house of her mistress, her Angel appeared to her in the wilderness, and reproving her, said, "Return to thy mistress and humble thyself under her hand." (*Gen., chap. xvi, 9.*) Here the Angel was not only present, but reproved her in her wrong doing. "The angel of the Lord shall encamp round about them that fear him, and shall deliver them." (*Psalm xxxiii, 8.*) In like manner the Angels are present in order to protect us from evil. "He hath given his Angels charge over thee to keep thee in all thy ways; and in their hands they shall bear thee up, lest thou dash thy foot against a stone." (*Psalm xc. 11.*) They are present at our death to dispose of our souls according to the justice of God. Thus our Lord tells us that when Lazarus "died, he was carried by angels into Abraham's bosom." (*St. Luke, chap. xvi, 22.*) The Angels also are "all ministering spirits, sent to minister for them who shall receive the inheritance of salvation." (*Heb., chap. i, 14.*) And the glorified Saints display in like manner their interest in our welfare.

St. Paul informs us that they surround us as a great cloud of witnesses. (*Heb., chap. xii., 1.*) He further tells us that we have not come, as did Moses, to the mount of terror, "but to Mount Sion, and to the city of the living God, the heavenly Jerusalem, and to the company of many thousands of angels, and to the church of the first born, who are written in the heavens, and to God the Judge of all, and to the spirits of the just made perfect." (*Heb., chap. xii, 22, 23.*) Such is the grand assemblage of Saints which surround, watch over, and interest themselves about the Church militant. "I believe in the communion of Saints," is that article of the Apostles' Creed which expresses this close relationship of the Church militant with the Church triumphant; and we no more dishonor God or detract from the merits of Christ as our Redeemer and Intercessor in asking their prayers and such spiritual offices as they are permitted to exercise in our behalf, than we do in asking the prayers and friendly offices of our brethren who are still in the flesh.

And if such be the power and interest the humblest Saint or Angel may take in our regard, how much more powerful with God, and how infinitely greater the degree of interest with Him, must she have who is Queen of all the Angels and Saints; who is the Mother of God; and who, by the greater love He bore her, has been exempted from every stain of sin. Such being the sublime dignity to which the Most Blessed Virgin is raised above all other creatures, it affords the strongest motive for especially resorting to the assistance of her prayers in all our necessities. The Holy Ghost, speaking by the mouth of Job, tells us that "they that serve God were not steadfast, and in his angels he found wickedness." (*Job, chap. iv, 18.*) But not so with Mary. She was ever an object of God's eternal complaisance and love. She was never for an instant sullied by the breath of the venomous serpent, and hence worthy to have been elevated to the most intimate relations with the Holy Trinity — Daughter of God the Father, Mother of God the Son, and Spouse of God the Holy Ghost. What a sublime view this gives us of the infinite dignity of Mary! Would God refuse her anything to whom He gave His only-begotten Son? It is this reflection which has caused the Saints to say that it is impossible that anyone who obtains the favor of Mary's prayers should be finally lost.

1. It is for this reason that the Church resorts with confidence to her intercession, and with fervor implores, "O Mary, conceived without the stain of sin, pray for us sinners who have recourse to thee." From these, among many other considerations, it is that the Catholic Christian has such frequent and ardent recourse to the Virgin Mother of God.

2. Another motive for resorting to her above all the other Saints is, because she loves us more than they. Next to the love of God for the Church is that of Mary. Her love for us exceeds the love of all others by as much as the dignity of Mother of God exceeds all other dignities. Besides, she is also our Mother; for when Jesus hung upon the cross, seeing his Mother and the disciple whom he loved standing, he saith to His Mother: "Woman, behold thy Son;" after he saith to the disciple, "Behold thy Mother." (*St. John xix. 26.*) We are represented in the person of St. John, and Mary is our spiritual Mother. Christ, having become man for us, is called our elder Brother; in this sense, also, Mary becomes our spiritual Mother. Can a mother forget her child? How much less then can such a Mother as the Blessed Virgin forget us her spiritual children? Again, the love of souls in anyone is always proportionate to their love of God. Now who could possibly have such love for God as she whose relations are so near to Him as are those of the Blessed Virgin? She is His Mother; He deigned to take flesh of her flesh, bone of her bone, and the blood of each flows in the other's veins. She felt every drop of blood which her divine Son shed for our redemption, as if it had flowed from her own body; her flesh quivered in view of His every wound; and when He expired,

the sword pierced her heart. Next to our Redeemer, then, Mary longs for and desires our salvation. We are told that God "wills not the death of a sinner, but rather that he should return and live," "He wills not that any should perish, but that all should return to penance" and "He wills that all men should be saved." We are further assured that there is joy in heaven over every sinner who returns from sin to holiness of life. Now if the Angels and Saints thus rejoice in the salvation of souls, how much more must the Immaculate Virgin rejoice, who is so much nearer to God, so much more assimilated to Him in every divine perfection, whose soul has been created so much more capacious for love, and who has been so much more richly endowed with every celestial grace. Here, then, is abundant motive for resorting to the aid of the Most Holy Virgin's prayers above those of all other creatures. To her with confidence may we go, believing with St. Bernard, that it was never heard of that any who has had recourse to her protection, and implored the succor of her prayers, has ever been abandoned.

3. We find a further powerful motive for special devotion to, and veneration of, the Most Blessed Virgin, in her matchless perfections. All the graces of the Christian life were showered upon her in a superabundant and special degree. Humility, which St. Bernard calls the foundation and guardian of all the virtues, shone conspicuous in her holy life. "My soul doth magnify the Lord, and my spirit hath rejoiced in God my Savior, because He hath regarded the humility of His handmaid; for behold from henceforth all generations shall call me blessed:" is the divine canticle which attuned her grateful heart in view of the wonderful work which the Most High had wrought in her. Charity, the queen of the celestial graces, fired her soul with infinite desire. This so penetrated and pervaded the soul of Mary, says St. Bernard, that no part was left untouched by it; she loved with her whole heart, her whole soul, and her whole strength. The King of love descended from heaven that He might enkindle this divine flame in every heart; and how deeply must it have penetrated Hers, who bore Him. Hence, St. Jerome, alluding to the Canticles, has said: "The heart of Mary became all fire and flames." (*Cant. viii. 6.*) Fire burning within through love, as says St. Anselm, and flames shining forth upon all, by the practice of virtue. "Well might even the seraphim," says the holy Abbot, Richard, "descend from heaven to learn from the heart of the Virgin how to love God." "This command we have from God, that he who loveth God, loveth also his neighbor." (*1 John iv. 21.*) If Mary was so inflamed with love towards God, how intensely must have glowed her love for mankind, and especially for those who by faith in her divine Son become her spiritual children. This it is which also greatly increases our confidence in the Queen of love, and inspires us with a desire for an interest in her prayers with God.

4. Besides all the virtues and graces which adorned the soul of the Blessed Virgin, besides the unblemished innocence of her holy life, and the inconceivable dignity of being Mother of God, we find a further motive for venerating her, and asking the favor of her prayers, in view of her unequalled sorrows. We are all children of sorrow; our path through life is watered with our tears; trials, and griefs, and disappointments, afflict us at every turn. But what mother's heart has ever been lacerated like that of Mary; whose trials have equaled hers; what griefs have so pierced the heart of any other of the daughters of Eve? The life of her divine Son was sought after while yet He was an infant in her arms, and she fled with Him in terror by night into a strange country. Numberless were the times during which she thought Him lost to her and slain. His own people again and again sought to take His life; and though He daily went about seeking the salvation of the spiritually blinded Jews, yet they would now have stoned Him, and then have cast Him down headlong from some eminence. He was at other times driven from the haunts of men; He had not a place to lay His sacred head; He was buffeted, bruised, betrayed, spit upon, scourged, derided, mocked, imprisoned, crowned with thorns, and finally crucified as a malefactor. "He was despised, and the most abject of men; a man of sorrows, and acquainted with infirmity; and His look was as it were hidden and despised. Surely He hath borne our infirmities, and carried our sorrows." (*Isa. liii.*)

Whose heart does not bleed, and whose eye can refrain from tears, at the recital of the story of redeeming woe? How much more, then, hers, from whom He derived His sacred flesh and blood, — His Mother. Holy Simeon had already prophetically told her: "*Thine own soul a sword shall pierce*" (*St. Luke ii. 35.*) Alas! Had it been a material sword, how slight would have been the wound, how trifling the pain. But no, that sword was the sorrows of her Son, — which daily transfixed her soul, and slew without destroying life. Who could feel the pangs like His own Mother — and such a Mother, like Him, Immaculate, sinless, and pure. If such, then, were the sorrows of Mary, whom the Lord has given, in the person of the beloved disciple, to be the Mother of His Church, how deeply must she sympathize with us in all our troubles, trials, and crosses; how tenderly must she feel all our griefs; and how earnestly must she beseech her Son for the Church Militant and the Church Suffering. "And when he had opened the fifth seal, I saw under the altar the souls of them that were slain for the word of God, and for the testimony which they held. And they cried with a loud voice, saying: How long, O Lord, holy and true, dost thou not judge and revenge our blood on them that dwell on the earth?" (*Rev. vi. 9, 10.*) Whose heart could so tenderly feel for, whose voice would more earnestly cry in behalf of, and who stands so near to the throne of the Redeemer to aid, the suffering children of Faith, as Mary, the spotless Mother of that Lord, holy and true?

If Esther could successfully prevail with the powerful King of the East for the salvation of her people, how much more Mary, the Mother of the King of kings, and supreme Lord of lords? Touched with the sorrows of her people then, and remembering her own, what a powerful advocate have we in the holy Virgin, who cannot with indifference regard the afflictions of her children, especially since so many of them originate in the same cause as did her own, faith and devotion to her Son, the Redeemer of mankind. It is not, therefore, only the virtues and graces of the Mother of God that incite the devotion of the Church, and cause Mary to be so powerful an advocate with God for us. Her very sorrows endear her the more to us, and us to her.

The dogmatic definition of the Immaculate Conception imposes several duties and obligations upon every sincere Christian.

1. The first of these is to make an act of divine faith upon the truth of this doctrine; since all are bound to believe it with a divine faith, from the Sovereign Pontiff, who issued the decree, even to the humblest lay person, who shall learn the tidings of it. This is evident not only from the very nature of defined dogmas, but also from the following considerations. In order to know that God has spoken by the mouth of the Church, it is sufficient to know that the Church has really spoken in the name of God, which it does every time it makes a dogmatic definition. The Church, in its dogmatic definitions, is ever assisted by the Holy Spirit, in such a manner as that, however the individuals who compose it, acting simply as individuals, may deceive themselves in other things, all error becomes impossible when the Church defines what they ought to believe, since it then acts (not as it were in a human capacity), but as the pillar and ground of truth, as the depository and infallible interpreter of Revelation. This cannot be doubted, unless we doubt the divinity of the Church, the divinity of the Christian religion.

How consoling therefore must it be to the Catholic heart that God still speaks to us through His Church, and enlightens us also with a new light, to the confusion of the wisdom of this world, the pride of whose pretended lights renders it an enemy to faith, and which, moreover, proudly heaps question upon question only to sink still more deeply into the darkness of the most cruel uncertainty upon those very points which it imports the most to know.

2. The second duty will be openly to profess this interior faith. This duty is inherent in the Christian profession; for, saith the Apostle: "The heart believeth unto justice, but with the mouth confession is made unto salvation." Interior faith is the foundation of our justification before God; but, in order to be saved, there is still the necessity to confess this faith

before men. It is necessary that the Christian should exhibit this courage, without which he could not please God, of whom he would blush; and man even would overwhelm his pusillanimity with contempt.

This recommendation is not inappropriate, because, although the present question is not one of an incomprehensible truth, but simply of a privilege of the holy Virgin; the impious, ignorant, or pretending to be ignorant, of the infallibility of the Church, and the correct ideas which it may give, whether upon the Immaculate Conception, upon original sin, or upon other truths, will not fail, upon the publication of the definition which has now been given, to make it the object of their sophistical reasoning, satires and derision. If the question was of a worldly matter, "the world," to use the words of our Lord, "would love its own;" it would then acknowledge that the Church had done a thing worthy of itself and of its mission. Praises, plaudits and gratulations would salute it on all sides. But the world (that is to say, the friends of the things of the world), finds nothing appertaining to itself in that which is done in honor of the holy Virgin; on the contrary, it has much to lament, inasmuch as whatever tends to increase the religion and to revive the faith which condemns it, is a thorn in its side, and it will not be long before it will exert all its strength against the decision of the Church. But this warfare will only serve to prove that the Holy See accomplished a truly glorious mission. The cries and groans of the enemy are a sufficient indication of the blow he has received.

A beautiful occasion of merit before God is then offered to the Christian, that in the very face of the enemies of religion he may manifest a docility and submission, refusing to lend an ear to the seductions of the wicked, who cause themselves easily to be recognized by their conduct in the present affair. Among the wicked, on such occasions, it is proper to reckon those doubtful characters, who, imbued with a worldly spirit, think they display their wisdom by adding their impious laughter and mockery against the Catholic faith. Let none of the Faithful be astonished at this old trick of bad men railing at the good and at holy things. Of the foolishness of their hearts their mouths speak. Rather let the Christian feel grateful to God for the grace He hath conferred upon him in uniting him to His Church whose empire is so great, so extended, so full of glory, even in the eyes of the world, that worldlings themselves would be ambitious of the honor of belonging to it could they do so without renouncing their vices and passions.

3. The third duty will be to rejoice from the bottom of the heart in view of the renewed glories of the holy Virgin and of the luster which will be reflected upon the Church. Every Christian is supposed to be filled with respect, with gratitude, and with love for the Virgin Mother of God. Every son is naturally

led to rejoice at the exaltation of his mother, and the Mother of God is also the Mother of all Christians. Their joy will therefore be no less great to see a fourth and more precious jewel added to the crown of glory which encircles the head of the Virgin, by the act which declares her conceived without the stain of original sin. And since the Church will also acquire new glory by the sincere submission of so many millions of Catholics of every age, sex and condition, and of every country, respectfully bowing their heads before her shrine, in the face of a corrupt world, which ceases not to repeat that its final hour has been sounded, every Christian, revering the Church as his Mother, will rejoice also at this new honor.

Let us, then, in conclusion, ascertain how her exalted merits may be most efficaciously applied to our souls. Is it by offering her a degree of devotion which exceeds what justly belongs to the creature, and from which she would shrink with displeasure and horror? Perish, the impious thought; it dwells in no Christian breast. No, it is by imitating her holy example; in cherishing all the virtues of her consecrated life; it is by following her through the valley of Humility, and imitating her there, and after her example exercising the virtues which shone so conspicuously in her; her purity, her chastity, her patience, her meekness, her ardent love for the Lord Jesus Christ, her strict conformity to the will of God in all her afflictions, and in her tender love and compassion for others. It is by frequently meditating upon her sublime virtues, and the reward she has obtained for them; and thus encouraging ourselves with the hope that, by patience and perseverance, we may, through the merits of Christ, and by the influence of her prayers, one day attain to the blessedness of joining her in the kingdom of her dear Son. And finally, it is by frequently asking the assistance of her prayers, with a firm confidence in God that He will be graciously pleased, through the merits of the Redeemer, to "accept her face," as He did that of Job for his three friends, (*Job xlii. 8,*) and thus by her intercession grant us those spiritual favors and blessings which, from our unworthiness, we cannot hope to receive.

Such a result the eye of Faith can now clearly realize from the public and solemn act which has just authoritatively pronounced the Immaculate Conception of the Most Blessed Virgin. Already have innumerable offerings of devotion, love, and gratitude been placed upon her shrine, which rise as hallowed incense to the Queen of heaven, and which return, through her intercession, in rich blessings from the hand of her divine Son, comforting the Church, assuaging its griefs, smoothing its rugged and thorny path through this vale of tears, and adding to its mystic unity thousands of such as are to be saved. With renewed accents of thanksgiving, therefore, and with fresh ardor, may it again be said: "Behold, from henceforth, all generations shall call me Blessed."

THE END.